HOLDING GROUND

*one passionate adventure
toward discovery of self
and what even matters*

by

Melanie Hallstein

*to Tesse—
in honor of the good,
the radiant, the healthy,
+ the beautiful moments that life
offers us. Thanks for being here!!
♡ Melanie
10/26/2022*

ISBN-13 9798626674859

I would like to thank Laura Marland for her guidance on editing the beginning stages of this book.

Printed in the United States of America.

All the experiences and inter-personal exchanges have been documented as accurately as possible with a memory as bad as mine.

Don't use this for anything without asking me real quick first.

Dedications

my sister Khaiti
(who taught me that you can live your dreams)
my mother Heather
(who gave me life and taught me how to love)
all the dedicated farmers
(who shared their lives and spaces with me)

Contents

Part 2

Introduction
Seeking Something

I was tan and tank topped. My scraggly leg hair had turned golden from the sun. My purple backpack and I were perched on the curb outside the O'Hare airport in Chicago. It was gaudy and tremendous and futuristic, the epitome of what had driven me away from America in the first place.

I'd rushed through the crowd, past the flurry of travelers holding papers and anxiously scanning the departure list. I'd heard babies crying, strangers getting into arguments about whose bag was whose, and the generic intercom announcing flights that were delayed. My passport had been stamped by a blasé character in a glass box who hadn't even asked where I was coming from. Whatever, I'd thought, *he* didn't need to know my story. My friend and sister were driving down from Minneapolis to pick me up. Surely, *they* would be eager to hear it all.

Cars filed into the arrivals area to pick up members of the mass surrounding me. Each time I heard a honk or a yell, my head flipped around to assess the arrival of excited people. The Midwestern accents caught me off guard. I had despised the inflection before, but now a wave of nostalgia rushed through me. After one solid year of traveling around the world, I was home.

I pulled my flip phone out of its hibernation in the bottom of my backpack. It still had a charge, somehow. I turned it on, eagerly awaiting a message from them.

Then there was a series of phone calls, assuring them that I was, in fact at the arrivals area. Have you guys ever been to an airport before? After what felt like an entire afternoon, my sister's familiar beige Nissan pulled up. I stood up and squinted my eyes to be sure. Then I ran to them, flailing my arms and yelling their names. We hugged for a while.

"You guys, I wait here for a long time!" I said excitedly, kissing their cheeks.

They exchanged a glance. My sister Leah laughed and said, "Why are you kissing me? What happened to your voice? You don't sound like yourself."

"Yeah," my friend Maggie said as she leaned casually against the car. "You have a weird accent. Did you forget English?"

She was right, I almost had. When I'd called my father from France many months before, he was delighted to find that my pronunciation was finally clear. "You don't sound like Mel," he'd said. "I can understand you perfectly."

Within the last year I had learned to speak simply, using only words that had a purpose. "Like" and "um" and many adjectives had been extinguished from my speech, as I'd mostly been communicating with people who didn't speak my language. I'd learned to say things like, "I brush my teeth," instead of "I'm-gonna-go-brush-my-teeth." The confident and friendly "Minnesota Nice" quality in my voice had disappeared. I hadn't considered it a defining characteristic until now, feeling like an outsider in my own country.

We loaded into the car together. I cleared my throat in preparation for an eight-hour conversation on the way home to Minneapolis, though now a bit insecure about my speech. I settled into the backseat and went silent, waiting. The car stopped at a stoplight before merging onto the highway, and my sister Leah turned the radio on. My stories filled me like a heady pint of beer, ready to spill over. I waited for Leah and Maggie to ask about the people, the countries, the food, the loves I'd had and lost. Instead, we merged into traffic and they conversed casually about how tired they were after a long drive. I looked out the window as my heart sank. Who wanted to hear my story?

*　　　*　　　*

I grew up in the suburbs of Minnesota with my three older sisters, surrounded by many other families. The neighborhood kids and I would get together to drink grape juice on rainy afternoons, knocking back our glass jars and giving each other old man names: Richard, George, Michael, and Willis. We put on gruff voices and slapped each other on the back, emptying our jars and chuckling about the good ol' days. When the rain stopped, we brought our drunken selves out into the street between our houses and marveled at the purple, green, and orange cascades across the sky. The air was humid after a heavy Midwestern rainstorm. Breathing it in prevented a hangover the next day.

We'd pretend to eat burritos from the gigantic leaves of the Catalpa tree looming over the front lawn, play kickball in the yard, climb tree limbs and throw walnuts in the road to listen to them pop when clunky cars passed. We had lemonade stands and made money to buy candy to rot our teeth; we made forts to cover the anthills from the rain. In the winter, we'd put on our thick, neon gear and sled down the hill into the road, stopping traffic. Sometimes we'd get lodged under a vehicle parked in front. We were always outside.

I was happy to have friends, as long as I maintained the privilege of sleeping next to my mom every night. She convinced me to go to summer camp, sweetening the deal with a $20 canteen tab. I begrudgingly accepted, provided she came too. At the end of the first day, we all went into our dorm rooms with bunk beds. After I could hear the girls snoring, I crept out into the darkness where I found my Mom's tent at the bottom of a grassy hill. I unzipped her it. "Mom!" I fake-sobbed, wiping my face from the fake-tears. "Can I sleep with you?"

I could pee on the floor or throw a tantrum in Target about needing a new toothbrush. I could play hooky in school and she'd let me come with her to college, where she was going to get her teaching degree. I could make a mess and she would clean it up, singing a sweet song. I didn't have to appreciate or even acknowledge her love; it was just always there.

When two neighborhood girls invited me for a sleepover, I made any excuse I could muster to stay home with my mom. "I don't want to go over there. It's weird. They eat pizza rolls all the time and they have angel figurines all over the basement," I said. "They even have Santa Claus in a birdcage."

Mom tucked my hair behind my ear lovingly. I played with the gold rings on her fingers, as I did during the long sermons in church. "Oh, Melanie," she cooed in her gentle lullaby-of-a-voice. "If you turn down opportunities, they won't be offered anymore."

My two oldest sisters, Khaiti and Liz, dyed their hair different colors, made provocative feminist art, went vegan, and explored their personalities. I can't say my conservative father was proud. He would come home from work and slam the door behind him, yelling at my mother for letting Khaiti paint red spirals on her ceiling. Yelling at my mother for being too accepting of Liz's girlfriend. Yelling at my mother for things that were nobody's fault, differences in personal explorations that should be embraced and not inspire anger or frustration.

My sister Leah and I, being the youngest of the family, were a second chance for him. He never let us skip church or a piano lesson, no matter how Jesus-ed out we were or how appealing the green grass outside the window was, when a piano just looked boring and lifeless. "Do I *have* to?" I would whine to Mom, as she held my hand tightly, pulling me toward the piano.

5

"Come on, Mel-a-nie," she would sing, relentlessly cheerful. "If you stop playing now, you'll forget when you're older. And I promise," she would sit me up on the bench and tap my nose, "you'll regret it!"

One month before my fourteenth birthday, Mom died. The breast cancer she had been struggling with for eight years had finally come back with a vengeance. It took over her brain. Even after chemo and radiation, her body just gave up.

Khaiti decided amidst the pain to live her dream, so she started a small organic farm. Liz decided she didn't want to live at all and got into hard drugs. Leah closed her emotions out from the world and hid behind marijuana. And I opened up to every single older woman I met, trying to replace my mom.

Before she died, our mother had enrolled me in a small Christian school in Wisconsin, where I would live in a dormitory with other girls and learn about religion in an isolated environment.

The first day I arrived, the girls in my class surrounded me cross-legged in someone's room in a circle to talk about our lives. When the progression led to me, I said bluntly, "My mom died three weeks ago."

The room of a dozen fourteen-year-old girls went silent. One of them stood up from where she had been cross-legged and gave me a tight hug. The other girls followed suit, perhaps not knowing how to respond in such a serious situation. All these strangers wanted to offer love. The first who had hugged me, Mikel, whispered gently in my ear, "I am so sorry."

My dad would come pick me up occasionally, before holidays or just for a long weekend to hang out with friends in my hometown. His car would pull up, blasting classical music, and I'd giggle and hug my new classmates goodbye. "There's my Dad," I'd say. "See you guys Sunday!" I'd run up to the driver's side of the car.

"Hey Dad!"

"Hey, Mel," he'd say as he got out of the car and stood up to kiss me on the cheek. "You look like you need some exercise. You gain weight?"

I'd look down at my body and shrug my shoulders. "No," I'd say. "I'm in volleyball."

And I'd get in the car with him and hunker down for two hours of father-daughter time. He'd blast the concertos, turn up the heat, and tell me I could lean my seat back if I wanted to take a nap. I'd turn the music down and ask him about my mom. I'd question every bit of their relationship, going over details again and again. I wanted to learn who she was, and he was forced to sit through it. After all, we were stuck in a car together for two hours. She'd passed away during my coming-of-age time, and I'd only known her as a mother, not as a human.

During my senior year, I started saw a flyer on the wall of my high school. There was a picture of an American girl I knew, a few classes above me, surrounded by smiling dark-skinned children with ragged clothing and crosses on the building behind them. The flyer promised travel throughout the country of Nepal, teaching Bible stories and singing with the children. I was completely intrigued.

I finally applied to the "Mission Helper Program" after the poster had been up for a few months, writing my application letter about losing my mother and how it had propelled me into independence and individuality. Who was I without my Mom? I was trying to discover that, and travel was what I wanted to pursue.

Within a few weeks I got an email back from the pastor who was organizing the trip, telling me the quota for young travelers was already filled. I told my friends and they hugged me in sympathy. That's fine, I told them. I don't have the money for it anyway.

A month later, I received an email back from the pastor. He told me another person had also applied. With a very faithful heart, he took it as a sign from God to expand, he wrote. The mission group would now be twelve instead of ten. He told me I was accepted, and I would be hearing from him soon with more details.

My church pooled extra offerings for me so that I was able to get out of the country in a group of people who would tour Nepal and visit churches. For free.

And so began a lifelong passion for leaving my comfort zone behind, creating challenges to work through. All my travel stories are told as truthfully as I can remember. All the emotions are as embarrassing and wonderful and passionate as they can be for a young woman exploring a world of beauties and beasts beyond the front door.

Part 1

"Tell me and I forget.
Teach me and I remember.
Involve me and I learn."

—Benjamin Franklin

Australia

Love on a Plane

I spent Christmas in Canada with my mom's extended family. Her death had brought us very close and seeing them made me feel like she was still alive. I scored big with a cheap flight from Vancouver to New Zealand for $775 with two layovers, in Los Angeles and Fiji. As a teenage missionary helper, I'd made two trips to India and Nepal. But this was my first international trip without a group, all on my own.

I took the ferry from Vancouver Island to Vancouver. I was huddled in a group of strangers waiting for the airport shuttle, which was behind schedule. Everyone was shifting their weight, bouncing on their feet trying to keep warm. We were growing increasingly frustrated as we waited, our breath materializing into a cloud above us. A bus finally came around the corner, and we all collected our things, eager to get into a warm, enclosed space. We started moving as a mass towards the approaching bus. It pulled up slowly enough for us to read the destination panel. The first line read, "SORRY" and the second read, "OUT OF SERVICE."

The crowd let out a collective groan. After what felt like an hour, our shuttle bus finally pulled up and we loaded quickly. I sat in front, wanting to get off first. I had a plane to catch.

The last person to board the bus was a wild-looking woman with a huge red coat, red scarf, and red boots. She paid her fare and gave a long, meaningful look at the bus driver. "Thank you," she said, as she smiled, "so very much for your service." She shuttled her way through the suitcases strewn about the bus and sat next to me. She tucked her coat across her mid-section and folded her hands on her thigh, like a lady. She smiled at me and complimented me on my green sweater. She noticed my Christian fish tattoo on my wrist and we started talking about religion.

The woman gave me a detailed account of a miracle she had performed years before. She had used Diatomaceous earth to bring a dead man back to life. She had been given healing powers by God. She also swore by this gray powder's miraculous properties to revive her husband's balding head. She told me that she saw God in me, and wanted me to utilize my powers to the fullest extent. I discretely glanced down at my wart-covered hands. I'd struggled with this affliction for the past year and found myself wondering if that powder could help me.

I smiled when I should have and commented when necessary. I nodded my head up and down enthusiastically but I was also wondering how strange this conversation was for the other passengers to overhear. We got off the bus. She gave me a tight hug. I thanked her and ran to get ahead of the crowd. I travel with nothing but a backpack. Huge advantage.

The plane delivered me to Los Angeles. I had a four-hour layover and time to kill. I opened my computer near the gate and started typing a blog post. Next to me, a young girl in tight black pants did yoga.

I was nervous. This twelve-hour journey would not only be my first overseas journey alone; it would be the longest flight I'd ever taken. I concluded my blog post and tucked my computer back into my bag. I got in the line at the gate a half-hour before boarding time. A tall, young guy with a mustache and a flannel walked past me. He smiled. Ten minutes later he went past me again, smiling, walking the other direction. A minute later he was next to me.

A few moments passed awkwardly, as we were within one foot of each other. I tried to think of something to say to break the tension. Instead, he did.

"What are you going to Fiji for?"

"Uh, actually I'm just flying to Fiji to catch my flight to New Zealand."

He nodded with familiarity as he gazed toward the huddled mass of people before us. "Oh cool. What are you doing in New Zealand?"

"I'm going to work on a farm there. I'm a volunteer." I turned my head to look at him confidently. "I stay for free and help with whatever projects they have. What about you?"

13

"Oh, I'm an Aussie. I mean, I'm American, but I moved to Australia."

He proceeded to explain that he'd travelled a bunch on his own already, was 24, had fallen in love with Australia and decided to settle there. He'd put his wandering ways behind him and had established a bit of a community. He asked me where I was going on my big trip. I laughed and began to list the countries I had planned to visit and what I was hoping they would be like. I explained Czech Republic's promising religious commune, "I'm excited to see how they mix conservativism with the organic farm, liberal mentality of today's world. I think it might be like an Amish community—"

"Are you Christian?" He interjected, motioning to the fish tattoo he'd seen on my wrist.

"Yeah," I responded, "But not like that."

"Nice. Me too, but not like that."

I slowly looked up into his eyes and we smiled at each other, suddenly aware of another huge thing we had in common. Not only were we both passionate about travel, but perhaps we shared the same view of a defiance of tradition and a more personal connection to God. The gate opened and our flight began boarding. He reached out for a handshake as I made my way toward the line. "I'm Taylor," he said gently.

We got in line and he bent down to whisper in my ear, "I usually never get in line until the last minute. I travel with such a small bag I don't have to worry about making it fit."

"Well, then, why are you in line now?"

"Because I want to keep talking to you," he responded, oh-so-casually.

Flattery flushed my face and I fixed my gaze at the employees collecting boarding passes. He asked me more questions and we shifted up the line as boarding progressed. Once we finally got into the aircraft, we were directed down different aisles toward our seats. We maintained eye contact, although a row of seats separated us. He made a funny face. I giggled.

As we made our ways down our respective aisles, Taylor got stopped from someone holding up the line, trying to frantically shove their bag into the cubby above the seat. He shrugged his shoulders at me with a wide smile. I kept making my way down the aisle and pretended I was running. As if we were competing and I was winning.

Then I got far ahead and looked over to see Taylor, but he wasn't there. He was already settling into his seat a few rows back, and he wasn't looking at me. I guess he hadn't noticed my jest. I glanced down at my ticket, found my seat, and kept nervously checking behind me to see if he noticed we weren't going to be near each other. Then I saw him start chatting with someone next to him.

I put my backpack in the overhead compartment and smiled at the lady sitting next to me. I sat down and angled my gaze through the seats ahead of me to Taylor. I could see the side of his face, and he looked like he was laughing. Flirting even? *Damn it*, I thought to myself. He probably already met a new, more interesting girl. He's just a nice guy.

I began speaking to the woman next to me as a distraction. She was kind of interesting, a retired Brit looking to enjoy her life again. Look at me, Taylor, I can make friends, too.

The flight began and the food arrived. I had a brownie and a snickers bar as a part of my vegetarian meal, but I usually stay away from dairy-based (and processed) foods. I offered them to the woman next to me. She smiled politely and declined. "It's not good for my figure," she said. But I hated wasting food.

I put the sweets into a napkin and tucked the bundle into the pocket of the seat in front of me. I finished my meal, got another complimentary glass of wine and took out my journal.

Dear Taylor, I began on a blank sheet. I concluded the note of random thoughts and ripped it out, finished my wine, and folded up the tray in front of me. I grabbed the note and the napkin of sweets and walked to the back of the plane so I could cross to the other aisle. I approached his seat and saw, to my delight, the person sitting next to him was a man. After a second of hesitation, I tapped him on the shoulder, knelt beside him on one knee, and looked him in the eyes. "This is for you," I said, "because you're sweet."

His eyes widened and his expression was shock. "Thank you," he managed to muster, as he reached his hand out to accept the gift.

What followed was a series of chicken-scratch notes on our turbulent, lengthy flight. We shared stories about our childhood on these tiny scraps of paper, our goals in life, our best friends, our favorite albums.

One time during the night I drifted off into an hour of sleep, listening to Fleet Foxes. I woke up to a glass of red wine on my tray and a letter in the pocket of the back of the seat in front of me. "I love long flights," he wrote, "and I love when the flight attendants recognize me after all the free wine."

He wrote about the man in the seat next to him, the person I had been jealous of when I saw him talking earlier. "I was hoping if I got to know him and had an opportunity to share my story about you with him, he would offer to switch seats with you," he wrote. "After you gave me the brownie and the note, he said, 'who's that babe?'"

In my last note I asked if we could please meet up in Fiji, our only destination together, where he would catch his flight to Australia and me to New Zealand. He ran out of time to write me a response.

Exiting the plane was a flurry of drunk and sleep-deprived passengers, and my nervous scanning of the crowd, trying to find Taylor. Our group of passengers made it to the baggage claim area. Taylor appeared from behind me and gave me a big hug.

"This is crazy, huh? We're in Fiji together!" He invited me for a coffee, and I accepted without hesitation. We approached customs together.

The border patrol agent was very hesitant to let me through into the country, as I had only a four-hour lay-over. Taylor, however, had twelve. Confident young man that he was, he told the agent our little romance story, how we just wanted to have a coffee to get to know each other better, "outside the airport in Fiji! It would complete our romantic love saga."

He promised the agent he would personally make sure I got back in time for my flight. The agent smiled at that and stamped my passport. "You know, you're much more beautiful in real life than in your picture," he said, as he handed my passport back to me. I must have had a flush of color, just standing next to Taylor.

We helped some locals carry their bags outside, and I asked them to take a picture of us.

Over the next two hours, we got to know each other even better. We had coffee after coffee, and Taylor paid for all of them (which made me feel valuable). We talked easily about our family lives, our friends, our religion. Both Christians and travelers, we could relate to experiencing the beauty the world has to offer but limiting our indulgence in it.

I was sweating from the caffeine, the humidity in the air, and the idea of the man sitting in front of me soon to be out of my life forever. I was so comfortable with him, but I knew it was going to end in a few minutes, and I knew it would be hard to say goodbye to him. He already, suddenly, had my heart.

I grabbed my backpack from the ground and he grabbed his. He said his idea of the perfect layover in Fiji was take a random bus, buy a cigar and find a beach to smoke it on. He walked me to the ticketing area and politely waited for me to check in for my flight to Auckland. I turned around and he engulfed me in a big sweaty flannel embrace.

"Thank you so much for spending time with me," he said. "It was really amazing to meet you." As we said goodbye and I turned to walk away, he grabbed my elbow and slipped me a slip of paper with his email address on it.

I got in line for security and bounced on my toes anxiously. I couldn't resist, I glanced back. He was wiping his eyes. He was crying? From meeting me?

I pulled out my laptop and sent him an email immediately. I wanted to explain how I felt. I didn't want to leave him, but I had to.

I caught my flight to Auckland, to stay on a hobby farm with Earl and Linda, an older Kiwi couple. Earl and I had arranged to meet up at the airport, yet I'd only seen one picture of him where he looked like an older man with a full head of white hair.

I exited customs and frantically read the names on the signs held by eager family and friends, standing on their tiptoes looking at every passenger. I scanned the crowd with no luck and walked back through. "Melanie Hallstein" was written on none of the signs. I walked back through the people once again, tapping any old man on the shoulder so I could evaluate his face. "Earl? Oh, no? Sorry."

I stayed in the arrivals area of the airport for quite some time. Frustration crept over me and I walked outside. I had probably approached ten old men, and my confidence was dissipating. As I walked over to the map by the bus station, a thin older man with white hair and a beard blowing in the wind was walking toward me. "Earl?" I called out to him.

19

We hugged and laughed as I explained my difficulties in asking random elderly men if they were him. He laughed at that. "Wait, how old do you think I *am*?"

We hopped into his small white truck and rolled the windows down as we exchanged a few pleasantries. The sun was shining and the vegetation was lush surrounding us, even as we pulled into the grocery store. Earl said he had to pick up a few things. He had an interesting accent.

As we walked through the vegetable section and I ogled at the passionfruit and figs and bananas, Earl explained a local dilemma. "In New Zealand we grow more food than we import. However, we import the majority of our food." He reached for some bananas and went on. "In fact, we export bananas as one of main products, and we import them from Australia for ourselves." He seemed to be disgusted by this fact, however he put a bunch of them in his shopping basket. Earl also picked out some no-name cheese and a loaf of white bread.

Arriving to the farm, we went down a winding tree-covered driveway edged with blue hydrangeas. Earl parked and carried my backpack into their tanned, wooden house. It was filled with trinkets and shelving and glassware and books and patterns, a plethora of things to catch my eye. I met Earl's wife, Linda, a short, sassy woman with gray hair and circular glasses, with a high parrot-like voice.

I was offered a seat on the couch after putting my backpack in my new bedroom. I sat down and casually glanced at their huge book collection. Linda chuckled from the kitchen, although she was unable to see me. "Trying to analyze us with our book collection, are you? Can't say it's possible. We've got a bit of everything!" Richard Dawkins and Ayn Rand made it clear religion would not be a topic of conversation for us. I was then introduced to the other WWOOFers, Tjasser ("chaw-sir") from Holland, and a young guy from Michigan with a strong Midwestern accent.

Our days usually began with weeding near to the house for an hour. Tjasser would always try to engage me in some religious discussion, which I successfully evaded. Usually I loved talking about religion, but I really preferred to zone out and mindlessly daydream about Taylor. Then we would have breakfast and a morning activity, like sorting the greenhouse, sowing seeds, or collecting cow pies from the field. Our lunches were usually fun and delicious, as we would be salivating by that time of day. After lunch, our afternoon activities were always engaging, as Earl would usually be helping us.

After work, we would spend time reading, walking in the woods, or cooking dinner. Linda was very protective about her dishwasher. Every time I helped load it, she would critique my placement of anything. I helped as much as I could with cleaning and cooking but was a bit intimidated by her abnormal anal retentiveness in the kitchen.

We were each given a glass of wine with dinner. Earl and Linda were absolute wine freaks, teaching us volunteers how to smell and taste the grapes. They were a sweet couple, often holding hands and kissing in private, calling to each other in their exotic strange accents and truly seemed to be in love. After dinner and attempting to help with the dishes, I would say goodnight and retreat to my room. I would turn on my computer and my heart would race as I loaded my email, hoping to see an email from Taylor.

He and I usually wrote emails twice daily. He said casually in one of his first few, "if you ever want to visit Australia, you are welcome here!" I took that as an invitation. I figured I was closer to Australia than I may ever be in my life. And… He obviously wanted me to visit.

I decided to cut my stay in New Zealand short, after receiving the invitation to go visit this man I felt so connected to. The last few days that were supposed to be a part of my stay here, I decided to spend in Australia with Taylor.

I booked my flight in a rush, although figuring it out was a bit complicated. I had to buy a round-trip ticket from Auckland to Melbourne and make it back in time to catch my flight from Auckland to Indonesia. I felt confident enough, and with my excited fingers I paid $400 for the flight. I immediately send Taylor an email explaining my plan to visit him for a few days.

I came out of my room to print my flight itinerary and told my hosts a bit of my whirlwind romance, which I hadn't yet disclosed before. They seemed incredibly skeptical yet found a way to be excited for me. I didn't mention that I'd only met him a week prior.

I spent the next week counting down the days till I would leave someone who felt like my soulmate.

Unfortunately, falling in love was enough of a justification for me to change my plans. I did like this farm, I did like the work, and New Zealand was beautiful. But my heart was thumping every second I allowed it to dwell on the memory of that tall, mustached man. The idea of him in Australia and maybe even thinking about me? It made my entire body tingle. I was being pulled to him by that mysterious, incredible, powerful, crazy little thing called love.

Alas, I had a few more days left to get work done on the farm. Earl had paid some man with a big digger machine to create a huge pit to collect rainwater and make a pond. We spent the better part of a day crawling down the steep slopes with tiny native plants to wedge between the sod layers that were put to hold the dirt back from eroding and filling the pond in with dirt.

Another day was spent tearing up the old fence line. It had been there nearly 100 years and the posts were rotting and divided their property into sections they didn't want. A true "outback" Australian man came over with his huge tractor and we split into two groups. Earl and the two volunteer guys went first, rolling up the old fence wire, and my job was to wear a hard hat and strap the tractor's chain around the base of the post, signal to the Aussie, and he would pull it up. We took a break for lunch and we were all sharing our projects. The Aussie, between huge mouthfuls of his chicken sandwich, chuckled. "Well, I got LEGEND over here!" That sent us all into fits of laughter, and I felt my face turn bright red, proud to get recognition from such a rugged man.

For my last evening with Earl and Linda, I decided to make them dinner: homemade raviolis filled with squash and greens and covered in fried garlic and olive oil. We sat outside during the sunset and had wine with our meal. I took a picture with them. After dinner I got my things together and collected email addresses from the other volunteers. "In case you ever need a place to stay in Holland," Tjasser had offered kindly.

The next morning Earl drove me to the airport. He wished me luck as I got on my flight. "Sorry to see you go, but we wish you luck!"

After a day of travel (I had to catch a connecting flight in Sydney to Melbourne) I arrived in the airport in Melbourne. The customs officer asked me what I was doing in Australia.

I looked down and smiled. "Uh, romance?"

He laughed. "You're looking to find it? Sure, we *do* have a lot of romantic beaches."

"No," I giggled and corrected him. "I think I kind of fell in love a few weeks ago. I'm here now to see if it's real."

"Really?" He asked, incredulously. "That's awesome. Good luck," he said, as he stamped my passport and smiled. "Go get him!"

Butterflies crept up in my stomach, but this customs officer had put a little spring into my step. This time, when I walked past the crowd of faces in the arrivals area, I knew who I was looking for. I hoped he was on time.

Right near the end of those waiting, someone pushed through the crowd and ran into me, arms open wide. I couldn't see his face; it was already buried in my neck. A big man, a head above most, with large engulfing arms, a huge grin, and a familiar warm flannel. He smelled good.

He picked me up there, in the crowd, and spun me around. He set me down gently and hugged me for another few seconds. Then he pulled away and looked me in the eyes. "Thanks for coming! Just follow me."

He grabbed my hand and pulled me through the crowd of people, who were all staring at us. At least, that's how it felt: like we had love or something, and they were all jealous.

We made our way outside of the airport and passed an ATM machine. "Oh, I should get some cash," I said, as I pulled my wallet out.

He grabbed my other hand and pulled me away from it. "We can figure it out later," he said. "I just want to show you my place!"

A motorcycle was parked a few feet away from us, between the airport and the hotel across the street. Taylor grabbed one of the two helmets sitting on top of it. "Put this on."

I looked at him, and at the motorcycle. He could see I was confused. "This is mine!"

He could see I still looked confused and went on to explain. "No one questions if you park here," he said as he latched his own helmet on and sat down on the seat. "They just think I stay at the hotel and I never get a ticket! Get on. And hold tight!"

We zipped out of the parking lot. I laughed in disbelief. What was happening? This felt like a movie! He turned his head halfway and yelled into the traffic, "Are you good?"

I nodded, although with the helmet he couldn't really see it. "Yeah, I'm great!" I said.

"Well, can you hold on tighter now?" He revved the engine. "You're going to need to." He started zipping between the cars that were all lined up. "This is why I got into motorcycles," he yelled over his shoulder. "Most of the time, you can just ignore the rules. It's *awesome*!"

As soon as we pulled into the driveway of a red brick house, a bunch of young people came outside to meet me. Another American, an Aussie, and some other guys who were all his friends. All Christian, their goal was to have some sort of free hostel to invite travelers to stay and be a part of their lifestyle. Hugs and laughs were exchanged, everyone eager to meet his girl he had talked about for the last few weeks. The Australian guy mentioned something about wanting to go around town looking for garage sales. He needed to expand his music collection.

I brought my backpack inside and Taylor showed me the cute kitchen and the chickens they had in the backyard. He brought me back out to the front and five of us piled into a tiny car to go garage-sailing. Taylor blasted some old school hip-hop. He glanced at me in the mirror as he drove us through the neighborhood. "You know who this is?"

"A Tribe Called Quest," I said as I looked out the window, casually, as if it was no big deal we happen to like the same music. Taylor looked in the mirror again to smile in approval, and his Australian friend in the passenger seat offered me a high-five. "Good on ya, mate," he said. I looked out the window at Melbourne, and tried to absorb it fully with these people.

After looking through old stuff laid out on blankets, Taylor and I went out to pick up some groceries to make dinner. He loved to cook, but I'd offered to take the lead. We picked out carrots, cabbage, peppers, onions, and garlic. On our way back to the house, we stopped to grab a beer. Taylor knew one of the bartenders and he came up to us, also excited to meet me. He said our beers were "on the house." Taylor picked an unfiltered apricot IPA for me and we sat in the sun on the patio, looking at each other's faces, giggling at how lucky we were.

We went back to the house and started cooking. The rest of his friends crowded around, as we busted out some wine and danced while we prepared rice and lentils to eat beneath our ginger-garlic stir-fried vegetables. We sat outside around a big table and everyone dug into their bowls of steaming food. One of Taylor's roommates said, between bites, "you fit right in here, Mel. You are such a good person."

The next day Taylor wanted to take me camping at his favorite beach. We grabbed a hammock, mocha pot, a blanket, some snacks, and a bottle of red wine.

We got on his motorcycle once again and headed off for a four-hour journey. He insisted on listening to music through earbuds while he drove his motorcycle. He offered me one of his pair, so we could listen to the same music. He showed me how to stick it in my ear under the helmet. Suddenly we were zipping down the highway together, once again, my arms clamped tightly around his waist.

At one point I could feel the earbud starting to slip out of my ear, and then it disappeared completely. Taylor occasionally turned his head around to look at me and yell, "I *love* this song!" I smiled and nodded my head, even though my earbud was flying in the wind behind me.

We stopped to get a beer and some fries at a little place by the beach. I remember feeling upset with him, a bit disconnected, because he was talking to other people there. I was only with him for three days. Couldn't he give his full attention?

We got back to the motorcycle and he handed my helmet back to me. I didn't look him in the eyes. The last hour of the journey was the most beautiful. I forgot about my moment of frustration with Taylor and completely fell back into the beauty of my surroundings.

The road curved back and forth between the Pacific Rainforest of eucalyptus trees and the rocky edge overlooking the sea. I gripped Taylor's waist as we tilted our bodies in unison with the swaying of the bike. The tree limbs sprawled overhead and I bent my head backward to look up at the leaves and vines, hoping to spot the native koala.

As we approached the rocky cliffs, I could feel my body tensing, apprehensive of the upcoming curve. I knew Taylor had a lot of experience riding a motorcycle, as it was his preferred mode of transportation when he travelled (especially in China, he'd told me in one of our chicken-scratch notes). He raced down the roadway. I breathed deeply and let the flush of this experience fill me. I held tight to Taylor and closed my eyes. I trusted him.

One of the times the road dipped back under the trees, we saw a car parked on the shoulder. Taylor slowed down a bit so we could see what they were pointing at and taking pictures of. A Koala! It looked like a small bear, much larger than I anticipated. It was silver and seemed to be comfortable just lounging on a branch, chewing its leaves slowly.

Eucalyptus has toxic properties, I had discovered earlier in California, when my friends at an animal sanctuary had carved gauges for their ears from the Eucalyptus wood. Within 24 hours, both of them were throwing up their dinners and their bodies were weak. It took them a few days to discover why they were both sick. The Koalas prefer this vegetation, but it makes them sluggish and slow, as they are effectively poisoning themselves. They build up a tolerance, as it's their only food source, but this explains their delayed movements and notoriously sluggish behavior.

After another hour of navigation, we spotted a small wooden sign that said, "Joanna Beach." The sky's colors switched from light blue to purple and orange as we pulled into the parking lot. It was "Australia Day" and campers were everywhere, grilling and laughing, playing games, setting up their tents. We heard car stereos blasting the "Top 100 Countdown" from Triple X, the local radio station.

As we drove slowly through the party people, the station announced the Number One Song of the year. The song was "Riptide" by Vance Joy, and we heard it chorusing between different sound systems.

We parked and grabbed our stuff and ran down to the beach and got knee-deep into the ocean. We found a secluded area behind a big rock where Taylor began to set up the hammock. I got some twigs to make a fire. We watched the rest of the sunset together, his arm around my shoulders. We talked about this, how it felt to be together. Once the last of the colors left the sky, we lit up the campfire and sat around it. Taylor opened the bottle of wine and we sipped in unison, acknowledging the natural lulls in conversation.

"I brought something for you," I said as I reached into the backpack. I pulled my journal and opened it to where I had written about him as I waited to board my plane to New Zealand. "I wanted to show you how much you affected me, even after just a few hours."

A huge, powerful grin lit up his face across the fire's orange wisps. "I actually did the same. I brought my journal too."

We exchanged them and sat there in a lull of the crackling embers, reading. A tear rolled down my face as I realized I loved this man. He was just like me, but he'd already done everything I had planned for myself. We spoke a few more hours about how lucky we were, then retreated to the hammock. We curled up together under a sky full of stars. I don't remember even a single kiss that evening.

The next morning, I woke up first and scrambled my way out of our hammock. Somehow, he continued sleeping. I walked into the ocean and let the waves cascade against my body. I felt good here, in Australia. I felt loved by Taylor, and I felt happy to be sharing these days in my life with him.

After a shared cup of coffee from the mocha pot heated over the fire, we packed up and began our ride back to Melbourne. We had today, tonight, and tomorrow during the day left together, as I'd booked a midnight flight. We arrived back to the house and hung out with his roommates. We made dinner together again and the two of us went up to sit on the balcony. Taylor smoked a pipe and offered me a puff. I declined and he offered me a cigarette instead, which I accepted. He told me he used to smoke regularly, and now just replaces his daily nicotine with a pipe or a cigar a few times a week.

We retired inside and he invited me into his room, where he showed me his greatest creation. He'd taken a retro, desk lamp and ran the cord through the wall, coming out into a little shelf that illuminated his desk. The cord was nowhere to be seen and the shelf was built into the wall. He had made his bed and his chairs. Hm, I thought to myself. A man who actually does something he *loves*.

We sat on his bed and started talking about travel ethics. Why do we like being outside ourselves, going places and meeting new people? Christianity was clearly at the heart of his travel, his main motivator. He wanted to share his passion for God with people, while being in their comfort zone. I told him I thought he was too good for me.

Taylor took my hand in his and began a long story. He told me about a woman he met when he was traveling in China. She was mesmerizingly beautiful, and she kept appearing in the background wherever he was. She would be at the bar where he was having a beer, in the road when he was picking out vegetables at the market. Eventually he got the motivation to speak to her, and they hit it off. Her name was Melissa Wilson, an American.

They'd travelled together for a few weeks, until she told him she had to leave. He was brokenhearted. Melissa had told him about her years abroad and she was much more experienced than he. Naturally, Taylor idolized her. When she wanted to split off from him, he felt so worthless. Looking back, he realized it was best for him anyway; he needed to experience things himself and learn through his own eyes that travel is beautiful, instead of following someone else's dream.

He told me I may not know it now, but I will understand later why we can't be together. He assured me he had real feelings for me, but I had a huge life of travel ahead of me. He didn't want to hold me back.

The denial of what he was trying to explain to me about myself rose up. "I'm already at a place in my life where I understand a lot," I said. "What could you hold me back from?"

He laughed gently, like a father to his all-too-eager son. "No way. You haven't peaked, Mel. You have so much left to experience. I would hate to keep you from your dreams."

We agreed to disagree. I leaned over to him, staring into his eyes. I let my lips touch his.

He smiled but put his hand out to stop me. "Is this a good idea?"

"Yes," I responded adamantly. We started making out, and it went on for hours. I could tell he wasn't experienced with kissing, and I felt proud that I could be better than he was at something. We had fun, giggling like teenagers, on top of each other. We didn't go any further than kissing, because neither of us ever had. After a few hours we fell asleep, curled up in each other's arms. During the middle of the night he whispered to me that he'd never kissed a girl before. I acted shocked.

I woke up in his sweaty embrace. I went downstairs to make some coffee and his friends slowly filtered in, enchanted by the promising aroma of a fresh brew. Taylor didn't wake up for a while, so I just talked to one of his roommates for a few hours, and eventually went upstairs to get him out of bed.

I kissed him while he slept, and he woke up. "What time is your flight today, Melanie?"

"Good morning!" I kissed him again and said, "I think around midnight. Can you give me a ride?"

"Yeah, of course. Let me get up and we can check your schedule."

We went down into the empty room where I had my bag. I pulled out my flight itinerary and looked at the dates. I thought I had booked the flight out of Melbourne for midnight that night, but I made a mistake. I had booked the flight for the following midnight, meaning if I followed the itinerary I had made, I would miss my flight from Auckland to Indonesia!

Taylor noticed the error immediately. We looked at each other briefly, a moment of consideration. Was this a sign? I knew I'd made a stupid error, and maybe it was so stupid it couldn't be resolved. In his eyes was a moment of hope, of excitement. Maybe we had to stay together for a while.

The moment passed and we realized action had to be taken. He grabbed his phone and called the airline. "Hello, I've booked a flight improperly through your airline. Can you please fix it? It was a simple mistake."

The woman he was speaking with asked if he was the passenger. He said no, and I piped up in the background. "Hi, I'm Melanie. I'm not an experienced traveler and I made a mistake."

Taylor smiled at me while she asked us for a moment of patience to validate my travel information. He gripped my hand and whispered gently, "It'll be okay."

After a minute of silence and then her *tap-tap-tap* into the computer system, she told us there was nothing she could do and recommended purchasing another flight. Taylor ended the phone call and looked at me. "Hey, it's okay, we can find you another flight."

We found one, but it was leaving in four hours. That meant we would have to catch it in two hours. Originally I thought I would be staying with him all afternoon, through the evening.

I collected my things and we had a quick lunch together. He got out his motorcycle and we rode together in silence. This ride was much less spirited. He was driving slowly, taking his time before delivering me back into my travel world. He didn't do any zipping between vehicles or pop-a-wheelies. I clutched him tightly, anyways. I was scared to let him go.

We arrived and he parked his bike in the same parking space that he'd used before when he picked me up just a few days before. He walked me inside and stood with me in line as I checked in for my flight. He sweet-talked the airlines employee and got me a seat in an exit row, with extra leg space. As we walked to security, he whispered, "You just gotta be nice to them and they'll put you wherever you want," with a wink. He was so confident and savvy, I loved that about him.

He politely walked me up to the door of security. A minute of silence passed between us, and then we turned to each other. He bent his head down and held my hands. He prayed to God in thanksgiving for bringing us together. When he concluded, I kissed him. I thanked him for everything, and I walked through the door. He yelled after me, "Don't look back!"

After I cleared security, I did look back. He was standing there watching me. He laughed and waved.

Indonesia
Mango Jam

I arrived in the airport in Medan, Indonesia, after a 48-hour stint of five consecutive flights. The only time I ate was when the airlines offered free food. Each airport was in a different country and if I'd bought food, I would have had to exchange many currencies.

It was early in the morning, maybe 5 AM, and the airport in Medan was filled with small, dark men with wide smiles and business attire. When I walked out of customs, a group of them surrounded me.

"Help? I help you?" They eagerly asked me.

"Uh, yes, thank you. I have to go to Parapat."

Confused, they looked at each other before beckoning me to come with them. I followed them, passed an ATM, and stopped to get cash. A man stood next to me the whole time. They walked me into a sectioned-off glass-walled room in a coffee shop, sat me down on a recliner, and ordered me a coffee that someone else must have paid for. The men started pulling out packs of cigarettes and smoking, right inside the airport. I asked for one.

They looked at each other, confused. "You?" One man said, as he made a smoking gesture.

"Yes," I said confidently.

At least four men pulled their packs back out. Someone set a clean ashtray in front of me. One man distinguished himself from the crowd with a lighter, flaming it in the open space between us. He started speaking to me in heavily accented English. "So, you need go where?"

I explained where I was going and they all laughed. The confident leader guy spoke up. "It take long time. Parapat very far. Very expensive." He introduced himself as Samuel, and when I said my name, he reached for my hand and kissed it.

At first, I'd thought they were concerned locals. Now, I realized they were all individual taxi drivers. I was hoping to take a cheap bus, but they were coercing me into using their services. Someone brought me another coffee.

Samuel made an offer.

I laughed in his face. All the men turned to look at each other. I supposed they expected yet another ignorant tourist. I despised the term *tourist* and I also despised how they under-estimated me. I had done my research, and I knew the exchange rate. I low-balled him with a counteroffer, about half what he had asked for, and I also asked him to bring me back at the end of my stay when I would need to be back at the airport to leave Indonesia. My offer was something like $40 USD for two four-hour trips.

The men all started laughing and speaking together in their local language. I put out my cigarette, finished my coffee, and grabbed my backpack. I would find another option.

Standing now, I reached my hand out for another smoke. A man hesitantly gave me another and lit it for me. Then I waded through the sea of men and exited the airport. I stood outside in the humid air, near a parking lot filled with nice cars. Odd. I had read there was a bus that came here a few times a day to go to Parapat. I smoked the last of the cigarette while I thought about it.

I wasn't waiting more than five minutes before Samuel came out the door. I could see him in my peripherals, watching me as he lit another smoke. He approached me. "Okay, come now. I take you now."

"How much?"

"Your price, it's okay. Today is for work."

We approached his lime-green SUV together. The inside was filled with decorations. Half the windshield was covered in tacky, brightly colored stickers of what seemed to be religious idols. How could he even drive with those clogging up his view? I got in the backseat. Off we went.

Within the first ten minutes, we stopped to pick up his brother. Why he was coming along for the ride, I never understood. He had darker skin than Samuel and his teeth were terrible. He kept asking me questions and joking with me, occasionally reaching his arm back around the passenger seat to tap my leg in jest. I moved it because I didn't get a good feeling from him.

What was supposed to be a four-hour journey turned into something like six hours. They kept stopping to buy me juice in a plastic bag with a straw, or mango covered in chili and salt, or some peanut noodles with little fish heads sticking out of them (which I didn't notice until the last bite), or a coffee at a spot overlooking the mountainous jungle surrounding us.

I was headed to a tiny village on a tiny island on a freshwater lake inside the biggest island in Indonesia. I was planning to stay on this farm for three weeks.

Finally, we arrived to Parapat. I paid Samuel the agreed-upon price including my return trip home. I took his business card and told him I would call him when I wanted to return; he could meet me in the same place. We were in a market area, where the small island producers of the region traded and sold their products. He pointed to the harbor crowded with boats. He looked at his watch and said we had an hour before my boat would leave. We had lunch and his brother joined us. They spoke together in their language, motioning to me and laughing. That was the most uncomfortable feeling. What were they saying?

Another new character approached, a young man with a bright smile. He high-fived Samuel and his creepy brother in greeting.

"This good man. Charlie. He speak English. He help you." He glanced at his watch and started walking away. "Bye!"

Charlie and I sat at the table for a few more minutes, and he told me about "jungle juice," some sort of fermented cane juice. "It's green," he said laughing, "and it's go-o-od!"

Charlie walked me over to the harbor, where boats of all different colors and shapes were lined up. Colorful stickers masked the boat exteriors. One boat was filled with a few women; he called to them. They nodded in gentle recognition; eyes fixated on me. The inside of the boat was filled with stuffed animals all over the driver's dashboard. Teddy bears and plastic toys and plushie fishes. Strange.

As I held the bar with my right hand to keep my balance, jumping from the dock onto the floating vessel, Charlie pointed to my finger. "What's this?" He asked, referring to a wart on my thumb.

I ignored him, and we settled into a bench on the boat, surrounded by women shelling peanuts and looking at the water. No one seemed rushed. No one seemed to know when the boat was leaving. I certainly had my doubts that we were even in the right boat.

He tried again. "What's on your finger?"

I rubbed my hands together and casually slid them between my thighs. My nervousness piqued the curiosity of four of the women on the boat, who stood to touch my hands.

Yes, I had warts on my hands. Thirty-seven of them, to be exact. It was my biggest insecurity. If they were noticed, there was no way to change the subject.

"I know this problem," Charlie started. "The people here, they catch fish. They take off scales and sometimes one go inside the skin and it makes *this* problem. You go here, Silimalombu, the woman here she knows. She can give help, a natural medicine."

My eyes started watering. I was so embarrassed to have people notice my warts, especially when they would try to touch them! I feared if someone touched them, they would get them too. But he promised they could help me here, perhaps with some exotic jungle treatment. I felt a flush of excitement, imagining having hands like a normal person again.

Then Charlie left, assuring me I was on the right boat. I remember watching my small battery-powered alarm clock. An hour passed. Another two hours. Before I knew it, I had been sitting there for four hours, waiting for the boat to take me to the farm I was supposed to be at hours ago. Hungry and anxious as I was, Murphy's Law taught me that if I left, the boat would have left without me.

Finally, the motor started up. The women looked completely neutral. Every available space was somehow, suddenly, filled. I was surrounded by children, men, raw fish and plastic baskets filled with fruits and veggies. The boat started across the lake. I would be subjected to another hour; my village was the last stop.

We passed rice fields and small huts on the islands around us. The people on the boat had red lips and were chewing leaves mixed with some chalky white paste. One man in particular had the reddest lips I'd ever seen, especially on a man. They were all smiling, easily fitting the Indonesian stereotype—they are happy people.

We pulled up to a huge dock. It must have been 5 or 6 in the afternoon. There were chickens and ducks running around and a few buildings. A woman came out to meet us.

"Melanie! Welcome!"

She was a tiny, dark woman with a wide face. She looked tired, but her giant smile revealed a beautiful set of straight teeth. She reached out to steady the boat as I tentatively stepped out. "I'm Ratna," she said kindly. "Happy to meet you!"

She walked ahead of me and glanced back to look me in the eyes. "We are happy to have you. I make special fish for you today!"

As we walked toward her little house and entered through the door, I tapped her on the shoulder, "I'm sorry, Ratna, I told you, I'm a vegetarian. Remember? I explained in the email I don't eat fish."

Her smile evaporated. "No. You never say that!" She sighed loudly as she motioned me through the dining area. "Well, rice for you."

The house had crumbling walls but was filled with bright colors. In the middle of the room was an off-white table surrounded by eight or ten vibrant plastic chairs. The floor was linoleum. The walls were decorated with what appeared to be a children's mural. It felt like a place that many people had contributed to.

She showed me where I could sleep, a thin mattress covered in a sheet with teddy-bear cartoons and told me to go meet the other volunteers. She waved her hand in the air as if she was already sick of me, a mother dismissing her child out of the room.

I headed out the door and walked along a path in the direction she'd pointed to, under a dense jungle canopy. It led up the mountain, behind the house, and passed under some impressive white-trunked trees with limbs growing in all directions. The floor of the jungle was covered in tropical plants and large stones. I saw people ahead of me, an older woman and a young girl with dark hair. They were speaking together in a foreign language, and when they saw me, they waved and came down the mountain towards me.

Lia was the older woman, she was Dutch. Molly ("mole-lee" in the proper French accent) was the younger girl, my age, with deeply sun-kissed skin.

"Wow, you're tan!" I said.

She giggled. "Uh, yeah not so nice sometime," she pointed to the lines on her back. "Come with us, we go for some food. You are, uhn-gry?"

Hungry? Yes I was! I nodded my head enthusiastically as another girl came down the hill to meet us.

"This is Yola," Molly introduced her.

"Melanie," I said, pointing to myself, as I'd learned that preemptive gestures can bridge the gaps in translation.

Yola was a bit taller than me, thin and poised, with dark hair and eyebrows. She smiled coolly at me, and I smiled back. I gathered she didn't speak English.

We headed back down the hill as Lia explained the situation here. "Ratna isn't a very good host," she said.

"She never gives us anything to do, so we make our own jobs. We make a garden, we cook dinner, we have fun together. She just gives us the place. You will see."

Back at the house, a meal was served. A spicy fish and white rice was on the menu for the evening, and there was a dark condiment in a plastic bottle on the table. "Kechup Manis" it said. I dished up a big plate of white rice and Molly saw me scoping out the bottle.

"Oh, yes, Melanie. So good, this one," she encouraged me. I poured it all over my rice. It tasted like soy sauce and ketchup mixed together.

After I helped with the dishes, the volunteers invited me to come sit on the patio with them. I put on some leggings and a jacket and joined them on a small wooden terrace. There was jungle on one side and freshwater Lake Toba on the other.

Molly and Yola rolled their own cigarettes as we all told our stories in a mixture of French and English. Lia was there with her husband, Pim. They were from the Netherlands (or Holland, as they referred to it affectionately) and had moved to France some years ago. They were about ten years apart, Lia late 60's and Pim mid 70's. He had a way about him--glassy blue eyes that analyzed you, while his wide smile reassured that he was kind. He immediately reminded me of Anthony Hopkins. Lia held herself confidently, but often poised her arms across her waist and made comments about how old or overweight she was, although she wasn't either of those things.

Lia and Pim had come out to Indonesia to do good for someone. They wanted to volunteer their time and skills to help local people, instead of just offering money. They disclosed to me in hushed voices that our host had great expectations for work. When they met her expectations, she rarely acknowledged or appreciated them. They didn't feel capable of helping as much as she wanted, so they offered to pay a bit for their stay. Now they just did light work in the morning and relaxed in the afternoon.

Over the course of the next few weeks, we developed a routine together. Every morning we would get up at 6 AM and have coffee, watching the sun rise over the lake. The French girls taught me how to roll a smoke from their packs of "Rasta" tobacco. They made it look so easy, but it really wasn't. Sometimes they would roll one for me instead of watching me struggle, and we'd sit there on a rock and drink coffee and smoke. Yola sighed into her cigarette. "Ohhh, the first one in the morning, so nice."

We'd then grab huge wicker baskets and head up the mountain to collect mangos. We'd come back, make breakfast and have more coffee and cigarettes. We'd find ways to occupy the rest of our day--climbing trees for fun, clearing the lake of invasive plants, caring for the chickens, harvesting cinnamon, weeding and maintaining the vegetable gardens. I never asked Ratna what she wanted help with; I just followed the do-what-you-want vibe the other volunteers had established for themselves.

We looked forward to the weekends, when we could catch the boat to go explore the market and have a day away from the farm. Our host occasionally had huge tasks for us, but as Lia had said, she didn't communicate her expectations very well. She was also hesitant to allow us to go to the market for some reason.

The kitchen looked like somebody's woodshed. It had a tiny sink and pots and pans hanging from the wall. The floor was dirt and there was no fridge. Eating vegetarian here was a big struggle. To avoid being a burden to my farm host, I would buy my own vegetables from the market so I could make things for myself. I bought fresh tempeh, carrots, and tomatoes to stir fry and eat with my white rice.

The vegetarian food I cooked would disappear if I left it alone for a minute. I think everyone assumed it was a communal plate. I didn't want to stand in the way of people eating vegetables, so I usually just kept my mouth shut and ate a lot of white rice.

It seemed like Ratna always cooked the same thing for dinner. A whole fresh fish tossed raw into a wok, covered with a few sliced tomatoes. She would also toss garlic, chilis, fresh turmeric, ginger root, and whole peppercorns into a tremendous stone mortar that permanently sat on the floor of the kitchen, and she would grind them up with a huge pestle. She'd scoop the mush out of the stone bowl and toss it in with the fish. She would let it cook all day on the stove.

Lia's husband Pim would often cook and would offer to help with my veg dishes. I resisted at first, but before long, the two of us began to cook almost every meal together. We would make pancakes together for breakfast with mango jam, lunch was a big salad and rice with Pim's delicious mango-juice salad dressing, and a curry or fried rice for dinner. One night, Yola asked if she could help me cook, so I showed her how to make homemade pasta. An American teaching cooking to a Frenchie? Yet together we impressed everyone with our handcrafted pasta and creamy white garlic sauce.

Eventually, I think Ratna got annoyed that I wasn't eating her fish. I wasn't about to go against my morals; I was cooperating and doing everything she asked of me. Did she ask anything of me? Not that I could remember, but I still did things to "earn my keep,"--digging sweet potatoes, maintaining the garden, planting corn and green beans, installed some terracing on the hillside. Yola and I even cleared out a road that was completely overtaken by weeds. From my perspective, I was a good volunteer. And I was also cooking every day, as my food seemed to get increasingly popular.

One night, Pim and I were crammed into the tiny kitchen together. He was chopping green onions and I was tending a pot of glistening carrots. I reached across him to grab a spoon and his eyes fixated on my hand.

"What's that on your thumb?" He asked.

I pulled my hand back and laughed to deflect his interest. "Oh, nothing, nothing."

"Is it a wart?"

"No, it's nothing, don't worry."

He stopped chopping and held his hands out to me. "Let me see," he said gently, intensely. His crystal eyes locked onto mine for a few seconds, just long enough to stir some emotion from me. Tears plopped down from my eyes, onto the dirt floor below. I set my shaking, ugly hands into his. He looked down and studied them. He turned them over. After a few seconds, I felt I'd made a big mistake.

Retracting my hands and turning my body away from him, I laughed to lighten the intensity I felt. "You see, I have a lot. Way too many."

I started stirring the soup I was making for dinner. I could see in my peripheral vision his stance hadn't changed since I took my hands away. He was just standing there staring at me.

"I'll buy them from you."

I stopped stirring and turned to face him. Was this some sick joke? I finally exposed my biggest insecurity to someone and now I'm being made fun of?

"Uh, no, Pim. You *cannot* buy my warts." I chuckled awkwardly, not sure how to read him. I returned to the food as he continued standing there, facing me.

I thought about it more and continued. "Even if you could buy them from me, which you can't, that is utterly ridiculous," I paused mid-sentence, exaggerating my disbelief. "I wouldn't sell them to you. I couldn't give these to anyone else. Everyone notices them and comments on them, or worse, just stares at them. I hate cooking with these hands, I hate using them for anything. I hate how they look and how disgusting they make me feel, how inadequate—"

I interrupted myself with surprising sobs. Pim reached out and held me as I sobbed into his shoulder for a minute. "I can help you," he offered kindly. "Just sell them to me and you can be rid of them forever."

I pulled back from his embrace and my tears stopped flowing. He was being serious. I snapped out of whatever trance he had put me in to even consider his offer, and I grabbed the pot of soup and brought it out to the table.

The next day I approached Ratna and asked her if she could help me with my wart problem. I held my hands out to her to inspect. I remembered what Charlie had told me when I first arrived. He said that the local people here knew how to cure warts. It was worth a shot. She nodded her head and said she had a special solution for me. "Yes, the people here have this many times. Come see me after dinner. I can fix this."

After dinner that night, I approached her. She beckoned me to follow her through the kitchen where Lia and Molly were washing dishes. She took me into a tiny back room where they cooked grain in water to feed the pigs. She reached under a tiny wooden bench and pulled out a huge red jug. It looked like the jug my dad kept gasoline in to fill up the lawn mower; it even had a long spout on my top.

"Put your hands out," she directed me, and poured it all over both of my hands. It smelled so bad. "This petrol. You know, petrol?" I nodded my head slowly as I let it drip from my hands onto the floor. "Put on your hands in the morning," she continued, "and night. You sleep with this medicine on the skin. In one week, the problem is gone."

When she said she had a "local medicine" I was romanticizing the concept I suppose, imagining her taking me into the jungle and cutting off bark from trees and pieces of roots and leaves. I thought she would muddle the exotic ingredients in the mortar and pestle, cook and stir it with a wooden spoon, and apply it three times a day.

This seemed like the worst idea ever, pouring petrol—gasoline—on my skin. Nevertheless, I went into my bedroom that night using my elbows to open the door handle. I maneuvered the bed sheet back with my right elbow and wiggled my way into my bed. I slept with my elbows tucked under the sheets, my hands poised in front of my chest. I didn't want any of this local medicine to seep into the sheets. I promised myself I would give her method a proper attempt and maintained the routine she proposed for a few days. A small part of me wondered whether Ratna just didn't like me, and this was a trick.

About a week into my stay on the farm, I learned that the mangos we were harvesting from the ground came from trees that were no longer Ratna's. They had belonged to her family, but she had sold them to some other mango farmers. There was no discussion about whose property the fallen mangos were on, though, so she assumed she could take all she wanted. The local people didn't get around to their harvest until late afternoon, so we always picked them in the morning. If they had caught us, we might have gotten into trouble.

Ratna's mother lived in the house. She was in her late 50's, but after a life of hard work, she looked about 90. She walked slowly and occasionally used a cane. One day, Yola and Molly went to a nearby school to help teach the children. When they returned, they told me a story about a funeral they happened upon. It was a huge celebration party, and in the middle of the dancing was a young man's dead body. As we spoke about it over dinner, Ratna piped up. "Yes, the people here have a party for the person when he dies. They save the water buffalo to kill for the party. They cut the buffalo into pieces and give it to guests."

Her husband, Tomas, had just returned from a trip and was sitting with us at dinner. He was German, a tall man who walked with his head lowered. He added, "That's what her water buffalo are for." His voice trailed off as he looked down at his plate. "She tends them daily in anticipation of the party for her mother's death." At that, he uttered a soft, awkward *ha-ha*.

We had a few late nights sorting coffee *luak* in the attic of a small, decorative wooden house. Luak was a special variety of coffee that was eaten by the wild cats and pooped back out. Originally it was a foraged delicacy, scouted out by locals who looked for it where they knew the cats defecated. The beans fermented in the cats' stomachs with all the other things they would eat in the wild. Foreign markets have been tapped, and demand for this strange product has surged. Now, locals catch the wild cats and keep them in cages, feeding them coffee beans and raw meat. Our host said the quality of the coffee is not what it used to be, but the European consumers don't know the difference and it's easier to produce larger quantities when the cats are confined and their feces are easier to gather.

We dried the coffee beans and packaged them as unroasted, or "green" coffee beans, in zip-top plastic bags. Sixty grams would be sold in the specialty markets for 28 Euros. Our host's German husband was able to bring the packaged coffee in his checked luggage on his trips back home as a cheaper alternative to shipping it alone. This was a huge profit for the farm, and they used volunteers to help them make the money. We had all come out to the farm to learn about traditional lives and help with farm-related things. This felt a little far from our intention.

Another late night we spent packaging dried leaves, also sold throughout Europe, claimed to cure cancer. The leaves were called *Graviola*. Ratna had hired local people to pick the leaves, paying them by the weight they brought in. But the local people cheated her by throwing heavy sticks and stones in with the leaves. That resulted in less-than-perfect products, leaves that were torn and crinkled and not dried properly. The coloring was a dull gray rather than the ideal dark green. Being cheated on threw Ratna into a bad mood. Even though we stayed up packaging some nights past midnight, feeling her stress and wanting to help, we didn't receive a single "thanks" from her.

So, things got tense between our host and our united volunteer front and I still had healthy-looking warts on my fingers. I decided to ditch my whole petrol routine and revisit Pim's offer. I needed to get his help before we all split ways.

One night when we were cooking dinner, I brought up my problem again and told him about the petrol cure. He just started laughing.

"If you let me, I will still buy them," he offered.

I thought about it for a minute as we continued chopping vegetables. "But, even if I could sell them to you, then they're your problem. Then you have to deal with them." I looked at him. "I wouldn't wish this curse on my worst enemy. I would love to just get rid of them, but I don't want someone else to have them."

He turned his head and smiled genuinely. "That's where you're wrong. I can buy them from you because they wouldn't be a problem for me. I am not vulnerable; they can't take over my life like they did yours."

He could see my confusion. "I used to be a homeopathic doctor," he said. "I understand the mind and body connection. You have issues with creativity, Melanie. For some reason you gave up on your artistic side. That's why the warts are here, taking over your hands. It's your mind trying to exemplify that your issue is with your hands and what you do with them. The warts appearing are trying to tell you something. Do you know what it is?"

"So, am I just supposed to use my hands more?"

"You have to value yourself and your accomplishments," he continued. "Things you do with your hands, like cooking and ceramics. You have to remember to believe in yourself." He paused to catch his breath and concluded. "Ratna's method of putting petroleum on your hands . . well, maybe that would help for a while. I have a hard time believing that's a medicine," he chuckled, "but perhaps it would take away the warts. I don't believe it would cure the cause, though, which is your self-confidence."

We continued to speak about it as we finished cooking. I have three older sisters, all confidently artistic in their own ways. I'd never felt I could compare to their talent. My artistic attempts disappointed me. I did well in art classes, but I never felt like I had my own style. What he said had definitely struck a chord.

We brought dinner out to the hungry people. After the meal, while Yola and Molly did dishes, Pim offered me 3,000 Indonesian *rupiah* to buy my warts. I laughed and asked for 5,000. He went into his room and returned with currency equaling something like $3 USD.

I didn't feel a magical release when I took the money, because I couldn't *give* the warts to him. I had to wait for them to leave me. But I believed what he said. It made sense in some mystical, foreign way.

The two French girls decided they wanted to leave earlier than planned. They loved hanging out with us, Molly said, but they didn't like the workload and they weren't feeling fulfilled. The next leg of their journey was Bali, where they planned to go have a relaxing time at spas and hotels before embarking to their next volunteering place, another farm in Java.

Lia and Pim looked at each other and smiled as Molly told us of her plan.

"Actually, I think we will go, too," Lia said. "It's time for this journey to conclude."

We made a plan to all reconnect in a few days, and Molly scribbled down the name of a hotel where they would be staying on the mainland. The French girls left and a few days later, Lia, Pim, and I went to the market and met up with them. We found the hotel where they were staying and had a fun night complaining as loudly as we needed to about everything we'd experienced together. Our disappointments and our frustrations, but also the highlights. We found a thatch-roofed restaurant where we got beer and banana pancakes so large, we had to pause in the middle of eating them and smoke cigarettes.

"Yes, smoke," Yola said. "It's good. After, you can to eat more." She made a downward motion with her hand and closed her eyes to illustrate her point of easing the stomach.

After our sweet two-day vacation, we all said our goodbyes. Yola and Molly gave me their email addresses and said they hoped it went well back on the farm, where I would be alone with Ratna. Lia hugged me for a while and told me she would like me to come visit them in France. "We love visitors," she said in her kind, breathy way.

Pim held me at arm's length as he said gently, "I can't wait for your future."

I took the boat back by myself to the farm, after another few hours of waiting. I was dropped off on the dock, and no one was waiting for me. I waved goodbye to the boat and wandered back up to the house, in through the door, and saw a tiny woman with a blonde pixie cut cooking in the kitchen.

I walked up to her to introduce myself. "Hey, I'm Melanie, who are you?" My voice came out quite loud.

She looked me up and down with judgmental eyes. She said, in English, "I know who you are." She was wearing quite elaborate clothing and dangly earrings, that bounced when she turned her head away from me.

"What?" I said as I kept facing her. "Did Ratna say something?"

She just looked down at the food she was preparing and nodded her head up and down. "She really doesn't like you." This woman had a familiar accent. Perhaps French? "I heard what you did. Ratna was mad that all you volunteers were just hanging out all the time, on the terrace. Never working, never offering to help. She said it was the worst group."

I knew I had to explain myself to her, to get her on *my* side of the issues with Ratna. I just didn't know how. She didn't know me, and she wasn't here while we were working. Of course, Ratna would say we weren't working hard enough. That night over dinner was awkward.

The next day Ratna approached me and asked me to make some mango jam for a conference she had to go to, and also to bake some bread for the people to eat with the jam. I nodded, accepting the task. I wanted to get on her good side. I stayed up very late that night, not only making dinner, but baking the bread, making the jam out of mangoes I gathered myself, and with Lara's help, packaging it in tiny plastic bags that wouldn't seal properly, stacking them in wicker baskets. At least I was beginning to convince Lara I was a hard worker.

The next morning, Ratna took the bread and the basket of jam to the conference. Before she left, she told me to "make sure everyone gets food today" and water the garden and take the water buffalo up the mountain in the day to graze and bring them back at night, oh and also, "make more jam, okay, Melanie?"

That day Lara and I tag-teamed the projects around the property. I explained a lot of my difficulty in connecting with Ratna as a person. "I'm a pleaser," I told her, "but even trying my very best to please her isn't getting me anywhere! She is so short with me. I do everything she asks me to do, but she usually doesn't ask me to do anything. When she does, it's a really big request and I feel a little like she sets me up for failure."

By the evening I was completely exhausted. Ratna arrived back at the farm as I was making dinner for everyone, as I had promised her I would do, while stirring the batch of jam I had made that day.

She walked into the kitchen and started complaining immediately. "That jam wasn't packaged well," and, "that bread was not good." She laughed, as she took my fried rice out to the dining room. I laughed too, and then I realized she was laughing at me. Lara came in to help me and asked if I was okay.

"Yeah, I'm fine," I assured her with a smile, rubbing my forehead with the back of my hand. "Don't worry."

We plated up the food at the table. A group of men, all strangers, joined us for dinner. They must have come back with Ratna from the conference. They helped themselves to generous portions of my vegetarian fare. Ratna was speaking English at the table with us, explaining what had happened at the conference.

"Oh, the bread was so bad. The people ask me, 'Why you have this bread, Ratna?' They ask me why it's not good." She shoveled the food I'd made into her mouth and laughed aloud. "I tell them, 'no, it's not my product! It was made by an American!'"

She kept eating her meal and I sat at the end of the table, staring blankly at my plate. A tear slipped out. She went on about the poor packing job as Lara looked at me sympathetically.

I finally interrupted her. "OKAY! You didn't like the bread? The French people like the bread. Maybe you don't know good bread. You didn't like the packaging? You gave me the wrong size bags, they didn't even seal properly and that's not my fault. I did everything you asked of me." I stood and bolted out the door.

I sat on a rock by the lake by myself, unsure of what had just happened. I'm not an angry person. I don't even know if she understood what I was yelling.

About an hour later Lara came out of the house to find me. "Are you okay?"

"No," I sighed. "I think I'll leave soon."

Lara, a new Polish volunteer named Robert, and I all decided to leave together. Perhaps my personal frustration with Ratna had influenced the other two volunteers. Yet, we were all overworked and exhausted, and we didn't feel satisfied with our accomplishments. What had we even done for her, other than help her make things to sell? What had we learned?

As the three of us waited for the boat to arrive, Ratna's mother sat next to me on a stone. She put her arm around me. Then, the boat arrived. Lara, Robert, and I boarded. Ratna pushed the boat from the dock.

"Bye," she called out after us coldly.

We looked back at the farm silently. I had never felt so worthless before. On our boat ride, we reflected on our experiences with Ratna. I confided in them that perhaps it was easier for me to connect with the volunteers than it was to connect with her. Maybe I had given up on trying to have a personal relationship with her. I understood when I arrived that I'd taken on the perspective of the other volunteers, rather than immediately attempting to understand her. I'd let their own negative experiences affect my time with her—giving up, in a sense, before even trying.

Turkey
Daddy Issues

From Indonesia I went to visit my Aunt Kim and her family in Qatar for a few weeks. They were so eager to host me that they paid me back for my old flight out of Doha and bought me a new flight so I could stay longer! The country was a total cultural shift. Although it was just as hot as Indonesia, the people were heavily clothed as modesty is so ingrained in their culture. It was so sweet to have a break from "work" and stay with people that I knew!

And now here I was, plopped in warehouse-like bus station in Turkey was a flurry of middle-aged businessmen standing in front of small booths with colorful, foreign words advertising tropical destinations. They were chuckling, leaning back against the counter, smoking cigarettes. Their local banter sounded authoritative, yet familiar like the Arabic I had been surrounded by in Qatar.

As I approached a group of men, they went silent, surely surprised to see a young foreign girl alone in front of them. I wrote down on a piece of paper where I wanted to go and held it up to a few of the them. They looked me up and down, put out their cigarettes, took my backpack, grabbed my money, and pushed me into a nearly empty coach bus with two other men.

The ride got us a bit out of the city, into a landscape similar to the Midwest. Gently rolling hills and deciduous trees melted my apprehension. Here, thousands of miles from home, the vegetation felt familiar. Half an hour later the bus stopped for a weathered man with a moustache that covered his mouth. He looked around the bus eagerly and chose the seat next to mine. I awkwardly moved my purple backpack to the tiny floor space between my legs and the seat in front of me. He had an over-sized fisherman's jacket and fingers that looked like sausages. He smiled timidly but seemed curious about me as I was obviously was not a local. He pulled out a tiny flip phone to show me pictures of his farm and his family. I wondered to myself how he was able to push the buttons when his thumb alone was the size of a light bulb. What if I was the only foreigner he would ever meet in his life? It was beautiful that he was so proud of his life that in our few minutes together he wanted to share photos of his personal life.

He got up at the next stop, turning his bulky body around and waving frantically at me to say goodbye. I waved back, fixed my gaze out the window and rode on, not knowing where I was going, not knowing when I would be getting off. After some time, the bus driver looked in the mirror at me, yelled something and waved one hand in the air.

"Me?" I yelled back, ignorantly using English. He just maintained eye contact in the mirror, as the bus idled. I grabbed my backpack and got off the bus onto a rainy street with small shops on either side. After I descended the steps, I looked back at the bus driver. He pointed to a little glass shelter across the street, then closed the door and drove off.

I walked over to the bus stop and looked for information. Everything in Turkish. Yeah, sure, being lost is exhilarating, but it was now late afternoon and I was exhausted. The adrenaline I'd felt earlier while deboarding my flight had dissipated and now the stress was beginning to set in. Was I going to find the farm and have a place to sleep tonight?

I went up to a building behind the stop, which appeared to be a hair salon, entirely made of glass. Inside, one man was standing behind one lone stool, reading the paper. The lights weren't on, so the shop looked gloomy and gray. The man saw me, put down his paper, and beckoned me inside.

I grabbed the door handle and pulled. It didn't open. I pulled harder. I looked at the man, and he started walking over to me. I kept fussing with the door, until finally he pulled from the inside. He pointed at a small sign on the door, where some letters must have said PUSH in Turkish. Mistakes like this have a universal language. I chuckled awkwardly, while he maintained a stoic expression.

After I showed him my travel itinerary, a piece of paper with my destination written on it, he walked me back outside, to the little bus stop, and went right back into the shop. I sat there for half an hour, alone. A large group of women covered in head scarves, clothing bundled around their bodies, filtered in, surrounding me. They kept attempting to make eye contact, but remained silent. When I would look one of them in the eyes, she would look down nervously.

Finally I asked the space between us for the village I was going to. "Kadapa?"

The women all started giggling and looking at each other. Were they laughing at me? I put my hands together in an act of desperation, begging. "Kadapa. Please?" I couldn't believe I hadn't studied more Turkish. Why didn't I at least learn the word for please?

One of the women approached me and looked at my itinerary. She said, "Ooh, kahh-dah-puh" and all the women started laughing. I had been pronouncing it wrong, and with a simple shift in accent, the locals could understand.

A car showed up with the name of my village written on the dashboard. I thought I was supposed to take a bus? Maybe this is a bus here, for this tiny village. I just needed to move away from this place where I had worn out the novelty of being a lost traveler.

There must have been at least seven men inside, so the quarters were tight. One of the women pointed into the back seat, muttering under her breath. I looked at her, smiled, and climbed over the men. I squeezed my petite body between two of the them. Someone threw my backpack in the trunk, and off we went.

The car-bus took us into the countryside for a few minutes and then eventually rolled to a stop. The passengers around me all started to chatter and then went silent. A man turned around to stare at me. I took the hint and wiggled back out of the vehicle. I held out a few coins (which the driver rejected) and grabbed my backpack just as the car sped off. I approached a sign that said the name of the farm. "Narkoy."

I walked past the wooden sign and spotted a tiny man pacing back and forth with a dog. He had a full black beard, a short, thin frame, and a colorful wool sweater. I can still remember exactly how he spoke, low and heavily accented English, unlike any speech I had ever heard. "Hehh-low!! Melanie? We are waiting for you all day! Welcome!"

This was Sallih (pronounced "sahl-lee"), the young man I had corresponded with to arrange my stay. After a frantic day's journey, not knowing where I was or which road to take, doubting every second of riding a bus or a car in a direction I was unsure of, and finally arriving at my destination where somebody knew my name? It felt almost as good as coming home.

I easily got into a rhythm on the farm. Sleeping in the dense goat-skin tent was rustic and foreign. It was early March in Turkey and the climate was cloudy and cold. Eight fuzzy cats created warm spots on my bed through my layers of wool blankets. When the soil was mud and our clothes were soggy, the most anticipated part of our routine was bedtime. We would stoke the fire with hazelnut shells; the nuts were one of their biggest regional crops and the shells were a necessary bi-product. We would take off our heavy winter apparel, and crawl into dry, warm beds.

The farm was owned by an older set of siblings--two sisters, a brother, and their spouses, who managed it as a team. They utilized the WWOOF organization and had been hosting volunteers for years. WWOOF participants usually offer free room and board in exchange for 4-8 hours of work daily, depending on the difficulty of the activities.

The family cooked and ate every meal with us. After our morning work, as our stomachs growled, we would gather around the woodstove clenching our mugs of hot herbal tea, chewing our tongues in anticipation. A bell would finally ring, summoning us to the window of the house, where steaming bowls of food would emerge. We lined up and carried the food to the oversized oak table in our dining room

Everything spoken was in Turkish during mealtime. We usually kept to ourselves, not wanting to dominate the vibe with our intrusive English. We would smile at each other and try to understand what the family was speaking about.

However, the occasional volunteer would take it upon himself to entertain the other English speakers. Those stories would shake the peaceful lull of the local banter. I hated that. It felt rude to overpower this communal family time with our own stories. Sitting here and being a part of this, as a simple observer, was exactly what I had set out to do in my travels.

The brother of the family, Mumtaz, had an incredible ability to control an audience. I never understood more than a handful of Turkish words, but I could gather that whenever he spoke, everyone wanted to hear what he said. Mumtaz would sit quietly for most of the meal, pick up olives and spit the pits into his hand as he watched the family speak. When he would reach across the table, he would catch my gaze and smile gently. When he had something to say, he would clear his throat and everyone would immediately hush and look at him. This man had so much power. He had the voice of a father. Loving, yet decisive and with finality. I instantly respected him, too.

The other volunteers were from around the world. We had German, Italian, American, French, Australian, and it was so fascinating to meet them and hear their stories. One French man was traveling by bicycle exchanging seeds. Turkey was near the beginning of his journey, and he spent two whole years traveling around the world with his bike. An Italian volunteer, Gemma, learned a bunch of Turkish after only three weeks, and she was learning about traditional farming practices in Turkey for her vegetable farm back home.

The more volunteers I met, the more inexperienced I felt with travel. It was so exciting to meet people who had seen much more than me, and I was easily inspired. An added benefit was the ubiquitous traveler courtesy of casually exchanging email addresses. Invitations to visit "whenever you're in the area" become the norm.

Our group of volunteers at this farm changed weekly--different ones coming in and others leaving.

Mumtaz was the one who worked the most with us. He spoke a bit of English and had a lot of experience with plants and animals, taught us interesting techniques for growing potatoes, and favored strange plants and herbs I wasn't aware were edible.

He was proud of his skills, but his simple clothing and relaxed attitude made him familiar to talk to. He had a strong figure and arms the size of my thighs. He was fun, easy to be with, and he was always happy to see me. He complimented me on my work ethic and my abilities.

I wished he was my father.

I wrote that many times in my journal. My real father never gave affection or admiration or love, unless I begged him with my questions. "So, do you think I'm doing a good job, Dad?" Or, "do you think I am beautiful?" Or, "do you think I am talented? Do you think I'm good at my job?" My dad would glance casually across the street and avoid my question. "Wow-weee, such a beautiful day! Good to see the neighbors cutting that grass." He would take a puff of his corn-cob pipe, and sip his mug filled with cheap wine. Gruff and cranky, he always put one ice cube in his red wine, and had a knack for avoiding personal inquiries.

Sometimes after our evening meal, the volunteers would walk to a tiny village just down the road, to catch the sunset from the southern edge of the Black Sea. We would buy cookies, beer, and cigarettes from a tiny shop along the way, and we'd perch on rocky cliffs to discuss our futures. Sometimes, on the walk home, we would be surrounded by street dogs, or a stranger would pick us up and give us a lift back to the farm. I relished those nights, just hanging with the volunteers. Not only did we have treats and a beautiful view, we also had isolated English speaking.

The Italian volunteer, Gemma, showed me how easy it can be to learn a language if you simply express interest. I pointed at things and asked the family for the Turkish word. Before I knew it, I could count to ten and I knew most of the names for the vegetables.

Attempting to prove myself as a hard worker, I stayed late to clean the dishes after every meal. I would dance my way over to shovel horse shit in the barn and sing while I hoed between the rows of lettuce. My enthusiasm and prior experience seemed to put me ahead of the other volunteers. Eventually I was given more responsibilities and resembled somewhat of a peace-keeper. If there was a dispute between the volunteers and the farm employees, I would often be called to resolve the issue. And I was very helpful--I could say "no" in Turkish.

This trust that the family and employees had in me was exhilarating. The other volunteers seemed a bit jealous that I was given so much more acknowledgment. They didn't earn favor like I did, I thought. I was rewarded with smiles and easier jobs as the weeks went on. When the family would say "thank you" to us, in Turkish, each night after dinner, it seemed they looked specifically at me. Competitive through my core, I relished the feeling of being a favorite.

Eventually Mumtaz, man of the farm, started to single me out. He would assign the other volunteers to go shovel the horse shit, and he would ask me to help him transplant some seedlings. He would invite me to his house after dinner to play games. He excitedly showed off pictures of his two adult daughters who had moved away from the farm, and he used charades to explain their lives to me. He seemed really proud of them. His wife had orange-ish hair, a petite physique and glasses you would find on the nose of a librarian. She made a variety of incredible vegetarian foods, enough to feed fifteen people. Sometimes they would eat meat, but only when it came from their own animals. Mumtaz's wife would never accept appreciation, she would just shake her head and look down at the floor. Flattered, yet humble and subdued.

One day Mumtaz invited me for a walk, alone. We set off down the hill and he pointed out where they grazed the goats, where they grew the barley and the oats, where the best hazelnut trees on the farm were located. He took me under barbed wire fences, through mud puddles, and up to the top of a hill for the best view of the farm.

In simple English he told me about his former life as a politician. After years of endless work, dealing with the public pressure became too much. He was grateful for his simple life on the farm. He put his arm around me, and I leaned into him, eager for affection. We stood for a minute like that, and then made our way back to the farm. While we walked, he grabbed my hand. And I let him. However peculiar this felt for me, I also thought that perhaps I didn't do sufficient reading about Turkish customs. Maybe holding hands is normal when you feel a connection with a person here. I remember in Nepal, men who were friends would hold hands. Maybe he wants to express friendship, I wondered to myself as we walked. I was on the other side of the world; I knew nothing here.

One of the volunteers, a German girl, was leaving from the train station in the nearest city, a fifteen-minute drive from the farm. Mumtaz offered to drive and invited me to come along. He gathered us and tossed a busted metal watering can in the back of the truck.

We arrived at the station and she turned around for one last look at us. We had a three-person hug and tears started rolling down her cheeks. How was this possible? She'd only been on the farm for ten days. I felt some glimpse of pity for her. I felt superior and favored, and she was crying because she would miss this place? She didn't even know the farm or the family like I did. I was part of this family, and I had been here over two weeks. She was older than me, yet when she hugged me, I had an urge to pat her on the head and tell her everything was going to be okay, like a reserved older sister.

Mumtaz and I casually drove off. He asked me when I was leaving, and I said I had to leave in three days to make my flight to Czech Republic. He laughed and told me to stay longer. He started talking about how good I am here, how I am part of the family. We pulled up to this little shack in a grungy area of the city. There were huge metal drums, scraps, cans, and chains scattered around the shop. He haphazardly parked the truck, pulled his watering can from the back, and motioned for me to join him. I followed him inside.

As we entered the metal shop, we saw no one. However, in a matter of seconds, workers started materializing from shiny piles of junk. Before I knew it, ten men with aprons surrounded us, calling Mumtaz's name. He smiled and gave one of them the watering can, and another led us to the back of the shop.

"Come, Melanie," Mumtaz cooed, with his gentle voice, grabbing my hand and leading me to follow him.

We entered an office space with windows, a TV, a couch, and a space heater. I sat down on the couch where I had a view of the shop. I felt out of place. The shop employee asked if I wanted a tea and I accepted. He and Mumtaz spoke gently in Turkish for a few minutes, and then he disappeared, leaving Mumtaz and I alone in the little room.

After we had sipped our tea and watched whatever sport game was on the little TV for a few minutes, I saw a man walk into the shop in his suit and tie. He stumbled around the store, calling out for assistance, and no one came.

I looked to Mumtaz and he was just staring at the TV screen, appearing oblivious. The man glanced behind the piles of junk and some time passed before anyone in the shop made their presence known. In contrast, I looked at the two of us. We were wearing farm boots, pants with mud and dirt on them, ragged hats and holey gloves. Why did we get so much attention?

Our aide came back with the watering can. Mumtaz tossed him cash and we got into the truck together.

Maybe Mumtaz has respect here because of his former life as a politician, I thought to myself. Do the people here actually like him or are they just giving him attention because of his power? I chose to believe he was popular because of his good nature and character. He seemed to be simply *well-liked* by everyone.

We drove through the small roads and the tight city streets and left the chaos behind. Ahead of us, the roads were empty and the sky transformed from dull gray to light blue, with beautiful cloud tufts. Mumtaz looked at me and smiled, and he reached for my hand. He held it for a moment and then he brought it to his mouth and kissed it. Then he kissed it some more.

He gave my hand back and slowly put his hand on my thigh. He squeezed it.

I glanced over to him and smiled, embracing his affectionate offering, stifling the part of me that said this was weird.

I looked out the window at the hills, the beautiful farms perched perfectly between the fields and the forests. What a beautiful place I'm in, I thought to myself. Mumtaz moved his hand further down my leg.

I laughed, like a giddy schoolgirl getting attention from a boy she likes. A mixture of flattery over the physical affection and denial that this man had that kind of motive. This must be a dream. I looked at him and he was just staring straight ahead at the road, with a huge grin on his face. I looked down at his hand as he moved it where it would only go with intention.

My eyes widened; my heart stopped. I allowed his hand in the space between my legs for seconds before my blood starting pulsing and adrenaline rushed through me. My expression went from neutral to irate. I grabbed his hand and shoved it back at him. He chuckled awkwardly. I looked out the window for the remainder of the ride.

When we arrived back to the farm, I got out and slammed the door. He called out after me, but I just ran back to the tent. Langston, a young Jewish-American volunteer was inside, stoking the fire.

"Help me, Langston," I called, desperately.

He stood up immediately. "What's wrong?"

My body shook as I explained what happened. He was a good listener, and when the story concluded, he got very angry and protective. He told me I could leave. I should leave, in fact, to retain my dignity. He had been under a similar trance, he said, as he had watched Mumtaz treat me like a daughter. "He didn't seem like he would ever do that to you. I mean, I thought he was a good man."

We sat there together on my bed in silence. As youngsters, we want to believe in the goodness of our elders. We crave guidance and respect and affection from those who have earned it themselves. We seek attention, consideration, approval, and love.

I was 20 years old and a virgin. I grew up in a conservative environment that didn't teach me enough about sex. In fact, I had no idea why his hand went where it did. I believed sex was something that came after marriage, and ignorant as it sounds, I truly didn't realize people wanted it from you even if you weren't married to them.

This whole situation confused me. I wasn't angry anymore, just actually confused. Why trust someone? I certainly didn't ask for this. Did I? Was that supposed to be pleasurable for me? I didn't know I had to draw a line with him, because I had never before connected my relationships with men to sex. His actions opened my eyes to a new reality, that people want sex.

I remember writing a very long email to my sister Khaiti, explaining te trauma I'd experienced, the first time a man had pursued a sexual experience with me. Minutes later she emailed back.

> *"Get the fuck out of there!! Sometimes men start things and they want to finish them!! If you have to stay there tonight, sleep with a knife under your pillow!"*

Langston encouraged me to tell someone. "You could leave," he said kindly, "but if you say nothing this could happen again to someone else."

The rest of the day I spent like a hermit crab tucked into a shell. I wrote in my journal, going over the details. I got my things together and planned to leave the next day.

Dinner was strange. I didn't look anyone in the eyes and sat down at one end of the table. In my peripheral vision I saw Mumtaz enter, and there didn't appear to be a change in his demeanor. He walked in confidently, smiling and joking with everyone at the table as if everything was normal. He caught my glance and I looked down immediately. Otherwise, I made no acknowledgement of his presence. In fact, I felt violated that he had re-entered my environment. After dinner and washing dishes, I went to visit Nar, an owner of the farm and Mumtaz's older sister.

I rang her doorbell and her husband greeted me, bewildered, as it was out of the ordinary for a volunteer to come to Nar's house. He invited me inside and into the kitchen, where Nar's short, plump figure was leaning against the countertop behind her. She had wild white hair that surrounded her face, and some tiny little bangs just above her right eye. Her large glasses had thick lenses that made her eyes look bigger than they were. She smiled, kissed me on the cheek, and invited me to sit.

She and her husband knew some English, but because I wanted privacy, I asked if he could leave, please, because this is a woman's discussion. Her husband looked slightly offended but left the room.

Nar sat down on the couch across from me. I spilled out everything, probably too fast for her to comprehend. All my thoughts, my good experiences with Mumtaz, and finally what had happened earlier that day. Tears started pouring down my cheeks as the reality of the situation set in. Mumtaz isn't my friend. He never was.

Nar took my hand and held it for a long time. Then, without speaking, she got up and made us some Turkish coffee. She sat down across from me again, with two little espressos and some small candies. "Have you ever had Turkish Delight?" She asked, with a gentle smile. I shook my head no, as I wiped my cheeks of the tears. We sipped our coffees and nibbled on the candies as she began to explain what she was going to do.

In her simple yet metaphorical language, she compared this situation to a book. After I left the farm, she said, she would open the book with Mumtaz. She would give him twenty-four hours to tell his wife, and then in their family meeting she would tell this story. "It needs to be open," she said, "or it will never change. If we close it and put it back on the shelf, we forget. And then I'm responsible for when it happens again."

She promised she would address the situation and she was so sorry for me. She hugged me for a while.

The next morning, I walked around the farm to say goodbye to all the family members, volunteers, and employees. The women who worked in the kitchen, women I hadn't even associated with during my stay, kissed me cheek after cheek, for minutes at a time, insisting that I must come back. I wished I could. Nar's husband came up to me, apologizing for what happened. I guessed Nar had filled him in. He offered me a ride to the airport and I accepted. As I walked from the tent to the car with my backpack, Mumtaz stopped me. He had a shovel in his hand and was wearing a sage-colored sweater. His expression was empathetic.

He put the shovel down and approached me. I closed my eyes and stood still while he enveloped me in his arms. My shoulders shrugged in and I opened my eyes, fixing my gaze beyond him, waiting to be let go. I didn't hug him back. He pulled away and held me in front of him so he could look me in the eyes. His eyes were glossy. He said nothing, just smiled and let the teardrops roll down his cheeks. I walked away from him and got into the car.

Reflecting on this man's impact on my life was not easy. I learned the value of maintaining a proper balance with my hosts. What am I to them? A guest, a friend, a volunteer, an employee, or a vessel for physical touch? I had to evaluate my impact on the people I stayed with. I was volunteering to work and to learn. Not to explore my sexuality.

Czech Republic
A Difficult Language

My green sweater and purple backpack illuminated me in sea of Europeans wearing drab, dull tones. Their faces were stoic; mine wore its perpetual smile. The lighting inside this Serbian airport was strange, filtering all the images around me through a black and white camera lens. As I wandered through ticketing, I spotted one woman with bright red hair and reached out to high-five her. She furrowed her brow and stared at my outstretched hand. Did she just roll her eyes?

The gate to my flight would be opening soon. Departure was in a few hours. After I got my boarding pass, I perched on a black leather couch and opened my computer to browse the internet for a place to stay in Prague, the first city I would visit in Czech Republic. I had two nights in the city before heading east to a tiny village to find my next farm. I reserved a hostel online for $5 USD and scribbled the address and some basic directions on a slip of paper. I folded the note and stuck it into my wallet, where all important things belonged.

In Prague, I was suddenly surrounded with people covered in tattoos and bright clothing. I was relieved to be back in a big, vibrant, diverse city, where the absence of restrictive cultural norms lightened the air.

Consulting my note, I took a few different trains and buses to arrive somewhere in the neighborhood of my chosen hostel. I wandered the streets in the darkness, approaching strangers to ask for the occasional nod in the right direction. Nobody recognized the name of the hostel, and the sole light for reading my chicken-scratch note was the all-too-rare overhead streetlamp. Finally, I found the name of the street and followed it until the name of the hostel appeared, brightly lit, before me.

I opened a large wooden door and walked up a few steps to a reception desk with three young men standing behind it. They smiled at me. "Welcome," one of them said, "welcome to Prague! You need to sleep here tonight?"

"Thank you," I said as I tossed my bag at my feet. "Yeah, I made a reservation here a few hours ago. Melanie. . . Hallstein?"

"Okay, yes, I see here," one of the guys said as he ruffled through a few drawers and tossed me a key with a room number on it. He explained the layout of the hostel. "And the bar, it's downstairs," he instructed with a wink.

I smiled in response as I grabbed my bag. "Perfect. I'll be back."

I climbed the stairs to get up to my room. Inside were bunk beds, four beds tall, with red ladders. Two girls sat on the bottom bunk and looked up as I walked in the door.

"Hey," I said in English. "How's it going?"

They smiled back kindly and spoke in American accents. One of them had a beautiful curly black mess of hair on her head, a sparkling blue dress, and colorful earrings; she looked dressed to go out.

"I can't believe how cheap this place is," I said, as I climbed up to the highest bed. "It's awesome."

"Yeah, girl, you should check out the booze here too," Party Girl said. "It's, like, cheap."

We spoke for a few minutes about our travel objectives. Both talked excitedly about how low-budget and undiscovered Eastern Europe was. I told them about the farm I was going to, and how I was excited to learn about sustainable food production in a religious setting.

"You should totally, like, go to Eritrea. That's where my family's from," Party Girl said, as she pursed her lips in the mirror to smooth on some color paste. "I think they actually cut themselves off completely from the government."

Neither of them wanted to join me for a beer in the basement, so I went down alone. The bar had rock walls and descending the few steps into it made me feel claustrophobic. As if I were entering a dungeon.

The bar had few patrons, and the bartender smiled at me as I walked in. A bit older than I, he had mousy hair tucked into a bun and bordered by a red bandana, a fair complexion, and freckles all over his face. We started talking about travel as I pointed to a beer.

"And you stay in Czech for how many months?" He asked with his thick accent and a gentle smile as he poured the beer and set it in front of me.

I took a big sip and counted on my fingers. "I think about two weeks. We'll see!"

"Oh! Not so much time. But maybe it's enough time to learn our language. It's easy for you, I think," he said with a sideways grin, as he handed a drink to another customer. He came back to stand across from where I sat at the tiny counter. He gave me his full attention once again, setting his hands on the bar to extend his arms. "Where are you going to go?"

I smiled. "It's a farm in a little village. They are almost like Amish, I think. Religious people with organic farming."

He raised his eyebrows. "Wow, sounds crazy! I hope you come back to explain me everything about this Amish farm," he said, with a low chuckle as he picked up a rag and wandered away from me.

I wrote the name of the village down on a slip of paper. Mšecké Žehrovice. I tried to read it out loud for the first time. I could hear the bartender laugh below the counter where he was cleaning something. He stood up. "Before, I make a joke. Actually, I will be impressed if you learn to say this in Czech language. It's really a difficult language for everyone."

He told me about himself. He and his wife had done a bit of travel and were saving up to do more; they had just come back from driving around Peru and Bolivia for a few months. He pulled up a picture on his phone of "The Most Dangerous Road in the World."

"And you survived?" I asked him. "Wow. So you can do anything now?"

He smiled broadly in response, nodded his head, and disappeared into a back room.

I turned away from the bar and started talking to a man standing by himself, leaning against the wall. He made a joke about coming here to sleep with women. My cue to leave. I turned around to face the bartender again. "Well," I said, as I tossed back the rest of my beer and set a few extra coins on the counter. "Gotta get some rest."

"Really? You should have another!" The bartender responded, as he polished some glassware behind the counter. He gestured at the coins I'd left as a tip. "Also, this is not normal here, you don't have to give more money. I do my job."

"Thanks, but you deserve it." I smiled back at him as I got up from my seat.

"No, no, Dekuji," he corrected me. "It's 'thank you' in Czech."

I looked serious and nodded my head like a child being reprimanded. "Deh-koo-yuh," I said, as I walked out the door. As I walked up the stairs, I heard him chuckle softly to himself.

As always, connecting with local people was my objective. Aware I didn't often fit in with typical hostel-goers, I felt validated in connecting with the bartender instead. I never understood why so many young people would travel to hang out with someone they met in a hostel, someone who speaks their language and dresses like them.

That night, before sleeping, I read online about small breweries in Prague and what to do with my vacation day. I was apprehensive about spending a whole day just walking around looking at things. What do I do as a tourist? Spend money and take pictures? I made a list of ideas, folded it up, and stuck it in my wallet.

The next morning I woke up and approached the front desk to ask for some advice.

"Where can I get the best pastry?" I asked the receptionist.

Her glossy, green earrings bounced as she laughed loudly. "Czech Republic is the best place! Everywhere you go have a good pastry!"

I asked her how to say please in the local language ("pro-seem") and I followed her directions to find the place she recommended most. I picked up a few goodies and went back to the hostel to have a coffee and journal about the last few days.

That day I watched the "changing of the guard." It turned out to be just a church tower's clock adorned with miniature soldiers that moved when the clock announced the arrival of the afternoon. I took a photo of a sewer cover in the street because the language and all its accents mystified me. I was alone the whole day. I love experiencing things by myself, but it can be oddly boring if you don't have anyone to laugh with, or feel you have nothing in common with anyone you pass on the street. When I saw two girlfriends giggling on a park bench, or a family taking a photo together, an occasional wave of homesickness washed over me.

I walked into a tiny brewery with two bar stools. An old man stood behind the taps with a face like a white canvas. I pointed to one of the two beers he had on tap. I smiled sweetly and said the Czech word for please, "Pro-seem?"

He looked me up and down, maintained his unenthused expression, and poured me a beer. I looked around the room as he watched me drink it. Trying to divert the attention away from myself, I pointed at a small clock on the wall. I nodded my head in approval, lacking any of his language to make a legitimate comment, and I drank some more.

When my interactions with shopkeepers and bar patrons all had a similar feeling, I chalked it up at first to unfriendliness. Later, I came to see that yes, the locals here seemed reserved and distant, but perhaps they weren't seeking approval from strangers as my efforts prove I do.

The next day it was time to return to the farming lifestyle. I took a city train and then a long bus ride out of the city. My next farm host, Alon, had agreed to pick me up at 2 PM at a train station in a village near to his farm. On the bus I listened to Turkish music on my iPod nano as I watched the cityscape slip from view. An older Czech couple started talking to me from their seats across the aisle. We exchanged a few words in English about where I was trying to go. They nodded and smiled in apparent recognition. Awesome, I thought, maybe they will tell me where to go when I arrive.

After our conversation reached a lull and an hour of silence passed, we arrived in a small village. I saw a sign on the bus stop structure as we approached. The sign said the name of the village where Alon had agreed to meet. I stood up and tossed my backpack over my shoulder.

The old couple descended the bus steps before me and waited patiently together at the stop as I paid the driver. The lady put a large sun hat with a pink ribbon on her head as she squinted into the sun to wave good-bye to me. They nodded in recognition and pointed somewhere. Were they trying to show me where to go? "Choo-choo!" I called out, flailing my arms in a hap-hazard train demonstration.

They smiled and turned their backs on me, locked arms, and hobbled away. I called after them and raised my hands in the air to show I needed help. Either they ignored me, or they were hard of hearing.

Frustrated, and feeling slightly abandoned, I sur-veyed my surroundings. I didn't see anyone walking around, and there were only a few small brown build-ings. One building stood out—a door was open and I could see colorful things inside. I needed some direc-tion, so I started towards it.

I maneuvered my petite body and backpack through the mounds of items on display and called out to no one in particular, "pro-seem?" A woman with pursed lips and a stoic air appeared behind the counter. I was somewhere in rural Europe, lost amidst people who did not speak English. Time for charades.

"I . . ." I said, as I pointed to myself. "Look," I said, as I held up my hand as if to cover my eyes from the sun. "For train!" I said, and pumped my fist up and down in the air.

She looked back at me blankly.

"Choo-choooo!" I tried, again pumping my fist in the air and moving my body forward.

She shook her head slowly, bemused. I sighed loudly and stomped out, increasingly frustrated.

I walked along the road, looking everywhere for any sign with wording resembling "train," or even railroad tracks or an illustration of some kind. Alon had said we were going to meet at the train station. Wait, had he said train station or just station? I racked my brain to recount an image of the email he had sent me, with no smart phone or internet to confirm anything. Here I was, yet again, completely lost, doubting myself, and at the mercy of strangers who couldn't understand a word I said.

A man in a dark jacket with a painter's cap appeared on the other side of the road, walking the opposite direction. I crossed the street and approached him excitedly, beginning my charades routine. He cut me off with a hand out, right before I yelled "choo-choo."

"You can to speak English," he said in a heavy accent and a gentle smile. He had a weathered face and tufts of white hair peeking beneath his cap. "I can try speak English."

Relief flooded my system. Finally. I explained where I was trying to go. "Oh, trehhn?" he said, smiling. Seriously? The word is that similar in their language? He pointed behind him and explained which road to follow. I took his advice and walked another half hour down a hill to the old railway station.

I plopped my backpack on the cracked concrete next to the station. I reached into it pulled out an orange I'd purchased in the city. I sat down, peeled the orange and tossed the skins into the bottom of my pack to keep it smelling fresh.

I had a little alarm clock to tell the time, but I wasn't sure of its accuracy from all the time changes I had zipped through. I ate my orange as I tried to do some air math, to figure out if I had crossed a time zone recently. After a few minutes of getting nowhere with my speculations, I went inside the station to ask what time it actually was.

There was one woman at the counter. I pointed to an imaginary watch, and in response she swished her hand in my face. She came out from behind the counter and shuffled me out. I scanned the room for a glimpse of someone's watch or cell phone. No such luck.

She slammed the door after me. Did she think I was homeless or something? Asking for money? I rubbed my forehead and pulled my journal out to complain to my future self.

I heard a honk and turned my head as I saw a worn-out pickup truck pulling into the parking lot. I quickly got my things together and approached it. A tall man with a scruffy beard and a dark sweater got out of the driver's seat.

"Hey," I called out to him. "Alon?"

He smiled and whistled two tones, a gesture I didn't understand. With his hand in the air, he beckoned me over. I approached and he reached out to shake my hand. "Melanie?"

I smiled, nodded, and sighed aloud. "Thank you for coming to get me," I said. He nodded and grabbed my backpack to toss it in the bed of the truck. He hopped in the drivers' side and I opened the door to the passenger seat.

After a brief ride through the Czech countryside, we passed a sign that said the name of the village, "Mšecké Žehrovice," which Alon read to me out loud. I tried to say it after him, and we both laughed. I would eventually learn how to pronounce it correctly.

Czech Republic
Baby Christian

Alon and I entered a long driveway, bordered by beautiful cherry trees in bloom. The sky was gray and there was a slope off to the right, where I could see children in long dresses and bonnets, carrying woven baskets and chasing baby goats inside a large pasture.

We pulled up to the house just as the sun came out. Women with clear complexions and simple, loose clothing poured out of the house to welcome me. "Melanie?" They asked, in a thick accent that reminded me of German. I smiled in recognition as they took turns touching my hand and spewing their names.

One of the women was tall with long, brown hair and thin, circular glasses like a professor. She took my backpack and said, in English, "Come on, we'll show you our castle."

The woman went ahead of me, and a teenager with blonde braids joined her. They were speaking a language that I didn't understand. She hopped ahead to skip along the path with the teenager. They both had large sweaters and brown pants that were fashioned in a style I had only seen paired with saris of the women in Indian culture. We came upon an airstream trailer. The professorial woman opened the door for me, and I walked inside. There was a miniature kitchen with an assortment of teas and coffee mugs, a shower, a big bed, and a small sofa with a plethora of pillows, a few folded clothes, and a woven basket, full of treats.

"Welcome to our life! I'm Hassiah," the woman said, as she plopped herself on the bed at the end of the trailer. "This is my daughter Hannah," she said, as she pointed to her smiling girl with braids and rosy cheeks. "We have lived in the community for ten years."

The girl, Hannah, sat next to her mother, who gave her a long affectionate look. Hannah had a chubby face, with crystal eyes and perfect, ivory skin. She looked about sixteen.

"Okay, we'll leave you to get settled," Hassiah said, as she and her daughter stood up. She motioned to a pile of clothing sitting on the couch. "This is for you! We offer our loose clothing, as we want you to feel comfortable with us. After you change and get settled, will you please come to join us for afternoon worship? It's in half an hour. Come back to the house and go up the stairs." She clapped her hands together excitedly. "Everyone will be there!"

As the door closed, I pulled everything out of my bag and sat down on my new bed for a minute. What have I gotten myself into here? I peeked through the basket of treats. There were a few apples, a bag of granola, and a few cookies in plastic wrap. My stomach grumbled and I ate one of the cookies. Should I change into these clothes? I grabbed another cookie and decided not to change. I couldn't quite abandon my clothing yet; was this place worthy of compromising my individualism?

I obliged Hassiah's invitation and followed the stone path back to the communal house. I went through the door into the kitchen and up the stairs to a room filled with a large circle of people. Everyone wore loose clothing, and the heads of the women were adorned with jeweled caps. The familiar man who had picked me up at the station, Alon, sat on a chair with a guitar in his lap. All the others sat on the floor, looking up at me curiously. Alon said, with his strong German accent, "Ahnd dees ees Melanie, I hope dat you haff dee time to speeek vit her."

Hassiah and Hannah smiled at me, beckoning for me to join them. Hannah scooted over to make a place for me and I sat down next to her. I listened intently to their speech, all in English. As I would discover, they were a mix of Germans and Czechs. Their organization was a branch of Christianity, although it followed the Old Testament ideology. It felt somewhat like the Jewish religion, yet they would take offense if you accused them of being Jewish, which at one point, I made the mistake of doing.

Their worship entailed Scriptural readings and the sharing of thoughts from the community. There was singing involved, and even some dancing and clapping. In the tiny room filled with strangers, I abstained from joining their dancing. Also, my conservative religious upbringing had taught me not to worship with someone unless we shared the same faith. Thus far, I was fairly certain we did not.

Time passed rapidly at this farm, as my daily tasks were always the same. I began to blend in with the community members, even wearing the strange loose cotton clothes to appease them. As a Christian, I was eager to see a connection between love of God and love for creation, treating animals well and taking diligent care of the earth. However, on this farm, I spent most of my time in the kitchen.

I helped entertain the children, chop carrots and onions, prepare the coffee for morning worship. I accepted it initially, assuming it was just a temporary placement, prior to my real work—outdoor farm tasks, the intention behind my visit.

I helped the women assemble lunch before noon, when the men would come in from working outside. Sweaty, with dirt encrusted hands, they would lead us in prayer, and then gobble down their meals. After they had been served, I would plate up my own meal like the other women and sit down. I would spoon my meal slowly, watching the men enviously. Why didn't I get served food, like them? They would clean their plates, thank us for the meal, and leave a mess behind. For us to clean up. I was jealous of the fresh air that wafted in on their bodies when they entered the dining room.

They certainly had a structure here—who-did-what was dependent on each person's gender. Unfortunately in today's world, the Bible is interpreted in countless ways. This community's men assumed the role as the providers, earning the "daily bread" and working in the fields. The women were valued for their attention to detail and had bodies created to rear and care for children. This is what I saw, anyway, and I hated it.

One morning after worship, fed up with chopping onions, I asked Alon if I would be able to work outside. "Of course, Melanie," he said with a gentle smile.

He introduced me to a lanky man named Jehu ("Jayhoo"). He had curly white hair and a tie-dye bandana holding it back. "Come with me, Melanie," Jehu said. "I'll show you what I'm doing in the greenhouse."

Jehu had exactly the transparent vibe I needed. Someone had to explain what this place was. Someone who seemed to be an actual real person. I had been trying to fit in, stay under the radar, and hopefully understand their lifestyle from within. Yet so far, I hadn't found any adequate understanding. Jehu had a hippy vibe, offering me hope that perhaps, finally, I would get some answers.

Jehu showed me where I could do some weeding, where to rest my knees so they wouldn't get too strained from the weight of my body when I bent down. We weeded beets and spoke about our shared passion for the environment.

After an hour of work and light-hearted who-are-you-and-where-did-you-come-from-type conversation, I had my relatable factor. I had proven my worth to him through my hard work and my great conversation skills. Now, I thought, I could approach the burning question.

"Uh, so," I began timidly. "How did you find yourself here?"

Jehu stopped weeding for a second to make eye contact. He smiled fully.

"It's a great question," he said, as he chuckled to himself and looked back to the plants he was tending. "You know, I traveled for a long time. I was searching for something. I didn't even know what that was." He leaned back to sit on the ground. "I got caught up in this world of hippy thinking. I fought for equality and role-reversals, smoking marijuana, and protesting anything that restricted society. I thought I could make sense of the world and who I was by exploring and meeting new people, defying anything that held humanity back."

His eyes glazed over as he focused on something behind me. A moment of silence passed as he stared, and I studied his face. "I was really, really lost," he said, as he reached up to rub his forehead. He chuckled and made eye contact—seemingly, suddenly lucid.

"Then, somehow, this place appeared. I had always hated religion. The rigid organization of telling people who and what to believe, well, it disgusted me. The best way I can explain it is that after twenty years of confusion and soul-searching, finally I am at peace. I have jobs here and I know my place." He looked up and smiled at me. "I'm happy here. I have a purpose."

At that, he left me alone in the greenhouse to finish weeding the row of beets. He seemed very convincing. Why was I so skeptical?

I found myself searching for any small error in their community structure. I wanted to find a way to categorize them as a cult, run away, save myself and write a book about it later, entitled "Checked out of the Czech." But so far, everyone seemed really. . . Fine. Happy, even.

Sometime later, Jehu came back into the greenhouse to give me a new task. Would I mind moving some compost? I nodded my head emphatically. I'd been eating too much anyway and craved the exercise.

Jehu walked me over to three different mounds.

"We use humanure here. You know that outhouse?" He pointed behind him to the tiny shack where the community members went to relieve themselves. "We scoop it out and put it here, mix it around with some dirt and sawdust, and then after some time it becomes rich dirt!"

He left me alone after showing me where to put what, how to turn the piles, the best way to handle the shovel, etc. I cursed under my breath as I worked at it for an hour. It didn't smell very good. And it was weird to see chunks of white toilet paper in a pile of dirt, an eternal reminder than all this was from an outhouse.

"Time for lunch!" Jehu called out to me from near the greenhouse. I wiped my brow and stuck the shovel in the shit-dirt. I walked back to the house, just in time to be a part of the line of men coming in from their outdoor tasks.

One of the women set a plate in front of me, and I smiled at her and said thank you. She smiled back timidly. I was surrounded by men scarfing their food down, and I followed suit. After the meal, I wiped my mouth, satisfied and smiling, and headed back in the line of men returning to their work. Alon stopped me before I walked out.

"Melanie, we could use your help in kitchen for the afternoon," Alon delegated. "There are many things to prepare for Sabbath this night."

I nodded my head slowly in submission. Confused, yet at the mercy of these strangers, I obliged. Should I consider myself lucky to have escaped from the kitchen for just one morning?

As I found my place again among fussing children and cutting boards, I saw Hannah, my young room-mate, peeling garlic at a table. Usually, in the after-noons, she taught the children. Infinitely curious about this lifestyle, I perched myself next to her.

I grabbed some garlic from her pile and asked about her previous life outside the community and what she remembered. She laughed.

"Well, I was young, so I don't remember much. But my mother couldn't work enough to support us." She set the garlic down and wiped her hands on her apron. She leaned back against the bench and her eyes fixated on the cutting board in contemplation. "We were strug-gling, and this place took us in." Then she looked up at me. "We call it home now, the people are good here."

I nodded my head and returned my attention to the garlic. She got up to go to the compost toilet and left me alone with my thoughts. It still didn't make sense to me. Why were these people so cut off from the out-side world? In their worship services they talked about setting an example for others. They spoke of the power they had in being good Christian people. But who were they an example for? They were completely, intentionally separated from the rest of society. They produced most of what they consumed and rarely went to the store to purchase anything.

Then it dawned on me. Perhaps they invited strangers into their community to make them see their beautiful lifestyle. And be converted?

The community members I had spoken to in private conversations seemed open to discussing their past lives. But when they did, they had the same empty expression on their faces and a strange, glossy look in their eyes, as if they were confused. They were thinking back, and the common theme during all their reflections was how lost they were before stumbling into this society.

Raised within a very conservative branch of Christianity, I pursued experiences in life that broadened my perspective. Always believing in God, Jesus, and the Holy Spirit, I fought to connect with the world around me and fit in, while maintaining my truth, inside myself. After my strict upbringing, my beliefs had shifted from being defined by church attendance to being defined by my connection to a higher power.

I had always fought against "feeling" God. My teachers and mentors at my religious school had encouraged me to stay away from that. Yet as a young adult, old enough to travel, I was very aware that God was with me, seeing what I saw, and watching out for me. Before I'd left to see the world, I had a Christian fish tattooed on my arm, the symbol Taylor had identified with in the airport in Los Angeles. The scripture below it read, in my handwriting, "Your mercy, O Lord, endures forever." I can't really hide the tattoo, and that was the point: never be ashamed of your beliefs. Wear them loud and proud and welcome the commentary.

One night, before falling asleep, Hassiah told me about a huge controversy their community had suffered a few years before. They were a German organization and had fled Germany because of the progressive mentality enforced across the country. Their community follows traditional methods of physicality with unruly children, Hassiah explained—they believe a swift spank on the behind is effective in discouraging a child's bad behavior.

When the community was in Germany, a young volunteer had come to stay with them. "He seemed to fit in so well," Hassiah recounted to me in the darkness. "He left after only a few days, much earlier than we had expected him to."

As with any volunteer who leaves early, the hosts were concerned about their actions, but had eventually shrugged it off. "Our lifestyle doesn't appeal to everyone," Hassiah explained.

However, a few weeks later, some footage of the community members spanking their children was released to the media. "He must have put cameras in the houses," Hassiah said sadly. Defying the new German laws, and probably fearing repercussions, the community fled to Czech Republic.

After my third day of staying with the community, Alon approached me. "Melanie, after evening worship, we can have a talk? After three days with every volunteer, I sit down with them, to make sure all is okay."

After evening worship that night, Alon walked right past me. We ate dinner and nothing happened. He must have forgotten. I went to bed. The next day he said the same thing, "I'll check in with you after evening worship." Yet once again, when our time to connect arrived, he was caught up conversing with someone else.

While I was cooking in the kitchen with the women, I asked Hassiah what he wanted to talk to me about. "Oh, you know. He wants to make sure you're happy here. It's something he always does, talk to the volunteers privately about their stay," she said, as she measured dry millet and tossed it into the large soup pot. She stopped mid-pour and set down her measuring cup. "You know, I overheard him talking to someone this morning about you." It was as if she had just suddenly remembered. "He said he feels that checking in with you isn't necessary. He said that you're a happy WWOOFer!"

I suddenly felt a wave of nausea. My ears hurt from being around whining babies. I wanted to be outside! I had accidentally cut my thumb the other day while chopping celeriac for a soup. The women had swarmed around me and put the thin slimy layer between onion skins on the cut to coagulate the blood. It functioned in halting the bleeding, but the bandage on my thumb kept getting soaked when I did any dishes or washed my hands. Somehow, I was feeling responsible for not enjoying my time.

I knew I wouldn't be staying as long as I had planned to. I wasn't happy here. Yes, I always had a smile on my face, and accepted any task I was granted, but I didn't come here to learn about prepping veggies or silencing children. I came to help outside, in the gardens, with the soil and the animals. I wanted to learn about how these people transformed Christian principles into a sustainable lifestyle.

After I had been with the organization for less than a week, another volunteer appeared. She was Czech, she told me, and spoke a bit of English. She was short and very thin with large, brown eyes. Upon our first meeting, I asked how she had discovered this place.

"You know, it's a special place," she began in a timid voice. "I see online, and I send a message. I know nothing about religion, so I think maybe it's interesting for me. I need a change for my life. Alon says yes and it's easy!"

I figured she would last a few days and get bored like me. What woman could possibly like this place?

During her first evening worship, she took a Bible and looked around the circle, completely doe eyed. She smiled and blushed when she was introduced. She even danced with them when they asked her and tried to sing along, even though she didn't know the songs.

After that first night, she fit in perfectly. She wore the same swooping pants and unflattering long tunics that I was forced to wear, but she wore them with a fulfilled smile. Before I could blink, she was carrying babies on her hips, joking with the women in the kitchen in their shared native language, Czech. She accepted the role she was given with no hesitation. She sang along loudly in their worship services. She looked around the room smiling. When her eyes would catch mine, she would look away instantly.

After seeing this volunteer fit in so effortlessly, I had to reflect on my own performance within their community. Was this place good for me? Is submission really something that God wants for women? As a stubborn, outspoken young woman, I'd struggled with this concept my whole life. Was I supposed to stand behind men as they spoke? Was I supposed to serve the food and let them do all the fun stuff? Perhaps this was the point of my journey here: I was to learn to be more submissive.

This other volunteer, why did she fit in so well? Perhaps my upbringing made me a little more guarded when it came to facing new religious perspectives. This volunteer, however, didn't have one to clash with theirs. I was jealous of her, whether or not I even wanted to fit in here.

After much thoughtful contemplation, and ample tears shed over diced onions, I decided to leave the next day. My last night, in evening worship, I thanked everyone for showing me a humble lifestyle. The members of the community engulfed me in a large hug before we headed down the steps to eat our dinner.

One of the most outspoken men and I got caught in a conversation.

"I'm so glad you are happy to find us, Melanie," the man said. "You mentioned you are a Christian yourself?"

"Yeah, I grew up Lutheran. I went to a school above my church, and went to a private Christian high school," I declared proudly. The glass of water I was holding sloshed onto my hand as I talked animatedly. "I was even part of a choir that toured the country singing religious hymns for small churches. Religion has always been a big part of my life."

He gave me a knowing smile. It was as if he saw through me. "Oh, okay. So, you are. . ." He held up his finger in a moment of revelation. "Baby Christian."

I choked on a sip of water and set my glass down without breaking eye contact. "Wh-what?"

"Well," he continued, "you grew up in conservative religion. You knew nothing of the true meaning of the Bible. This makes me even more happy that you come to us. You know," he said, as he leaned in, his voice switching to a whisper, "God wants to save Christians, too."

I smiled without my teeth and backed away from him slowly. I brought my water glass to the sink and said goodnight to Hassiah, who was finishing her plate of food. I wandered off to our airstream and cuddled up on my little couch-bed to get some sleep before leaving in the morning.

The next day I left early and found myself in a tiny Czech bar in the nearby village. I drank an afternoon beer and smoked Lucky Strikes as I did some reflecting in my journal. Through the smoky haze, I could see a cluster of middle-aged people standing at the bar, laughing heartily. Having been here for twenty minutes, I felt more comfortable than I had throughout my entire stay with that Christian community.

I had been under an illusion about them being open and friendly and warm. Suddenly, I realized I was being judged and they had been trying to make me see the True Way, their way, of following God's book. They were doing it right, and I had been doing it wrong the whole time. Perhaps, by their standards, even thinking these thoughts would be condemning.

Now that I knew where it was, I went back to the station, and hopped on a train to Prague. I had a few extra days to use before I would head into Germany to meet my cousin. From Prague I caught another train to a small village in Southern Bohemia. I walked into a random hotel and got a room for two nights.

I hiked four hours up the highest point in Czech Republic and found a smoky bar at the top, where people were tossing back local beers and laughing jovially. The owner of my hotel sent me to explore the old center of witchcraft in Southern Europe, a white building taped off and deemed by the locals as "the birdhouse." It was a half-hour walk through the forest, and there was no one else around when I arrived, but I doubted the credibility of its power. I could picture it, though— a huge bonfire at the base of this wooden tower, flecked with peeling paint. People would have been dancing and hooting around the fire, tossing strange things in and doing chants and lighting candles to reach out to the Devil. Why would you want to make friends with him?

One night, after hearing Gypsy music pouring out of the entrance, I wandered alone into a tiny doorway that led to a bar, like a dark cave, so small that the end of a clarinet blasted in my face as I danced and drank my beer. I also found a restaurant in the city that had recipes from an old cookbook written in Czech over three hundred years ago. I had dinner by myself, hot honey mead and a pile of cheese and bread.

After a few days, I went back to my original hostel in Prague for a night. I put my things in the room and went down the steps, once again, to the dungeon bar. When I went so many places and experienced so many things in a short period of time, people I met a week ago could feel like best friends. Especially when I could speak to them in English.

"Hey, girl!" The bartender called out; his face lit with recognition. "You're back! How was the farm?"

A rush of emotion flowed over me and I sat at the same barstool from a week before. "Um, it was . . ."

My voice trailed off as I caught my breath. He finished pouring two beers, set them in front of me and disappeared. Then he came out from behind the bar and sat next to me. He gave me a nod as he handed me one of the beers. "Good to see you, my friend!"

"Wow, thanks." I smiled, licking the heady foam from my lips. "You remember I like beer!"

He smiled back. "So the farm was . . .?"

I poured it all out. My feelings of frustration and confusion, working hard and feeling under-appreciated, having to work like a woman when I wanted to work like a man. I showed him my dried-out hands as proof. He laughed. Then he asked me to pronounce the name of the village.

"Mšecké Žehrovice," I said proudly, with a nearly passable accent.

He patted me on the back. "It's good, you can be Czech now. Maybe don't go to the farm, you can stay in the city! The people here are better."

"Yeah, I do like the Czech people," I told him, as I finished the last sip of my beer and set some coins on the counter. "Smiling, serving beer, asking questions."

He picked the coins up and put them back into my hand, shaking his head.

"You're the best Czech," I told him as I stood up with a wide grin. "Dekuji."

Holland

Weeding Yoga

A few hours train ride brought me into the bustling city of Amsterdam. I had planned to take another few local trains to get into the farming area of Lelystad, where my next farm was located. I had been corresponding frequently through email with Piet and Renee, a Dutch couple with a bio-dynamic vegetable farm. Their attentiveness to me, a simple young traveler whom they hadn't yet met, gave me expectations of a good experience with them.

Being in any Dutch station was confusing because everyone looked like they could be American. But they were speaking what sounded like gibberish. It was the strangest language I'd ever heard: heavy like German, but melodic like some Scandinavian language.

This train from Amsterdam was a much shorter journey. So instead of sitting, I stood with my backpack, looking out the window to see the names of the train stops so I wouldn't miss Lelystad. If I looked away or was lucky to meet a chatty stranger, I ran the risk of missing my stop. And without a phone or a map, that would be the difference between arriving ten minutes early or a day late.

A man in a business suit with a briefcase boarded the train and stood next to me. After a few minutes passed, I made eye contact with him and smiled.

"Leh-lee-stahd?" I said, my best attempt at a Dutch pronunciation. I had never actually heard the name spoken aloud. The man raised his eyebrows in acknowledgment yet shook his head in confusion. I tried again, and he chuckled. After a minute of frustration, with no recognition from the man, I pulled out my ticket where the name of the city was written.

I pushed the ticket into his face and pointed to the word. He chuckled, "Oh, Lay-lee-schtadt!" He started speaking English. "It's the next stop. I'll show you." He sounded almost American.

The train screeched to a stop and I saw the city's name inscribed on the wooden plaque at the station. The man standing next to me leaned down and said gently in my ear, "It's this one."

I rolled my eyes confidently, as if I never needed help in the first place. He smiled at my sarcasm and we waved goodbye. Butterflies bounced in my belly as I exited the platform and looked around.

I walked over to the parking lot and saw a tall, scrawny man with a pile of fluffy white hair on his head. He had a wide smile, and his teeth pointed in different directions. "Melanie?" He called to me softly as I approached.

"Yeah, that's me!" I said as I raised one arm in the air, widely waving.

He cleared his throat before he kissed me on one cheek. He was wearing an oversized fleece and loose cargo pants. I got into the passenger side of the car with him and was relaxed by that familiar farm-car smell. Piet introduced himself as "Pete," as we pronounce it in America. We drove off together in near silence.

After just a few scenic minutes, passing farms in all directions, we arrived, parked, and walked into a tiny blue shack. In the kitchen were three women. One of them, tall, with flat, short silver hair and a big mouth, was wearing hard-working farm lady attire. She had a broad chest and long arms, and kissed me on the cheek when I walked in. "Welcome, Melanie," she said in a surprisingly low voice. "We hope you like it here! An American!" She covered her hand with her mouth as she glanced at Piet candidly. "We don't get many of those," she chuckled.

"Are you Renee?" I asked.

She chuckled again and spoke from the side of her mouth. "Who else would I be?" She held out her arms dramatically.

Behind Renee was a young, tanned woman with a smile eclipsing across her face. She had faded, simple clothing and caramel hair that framed her face perfectly, sassy yet sophisticated. She reached forward to greet me and put her lips on my cheek.

"I'm Yu-dit," she said, pronouncing Judith with a foreign accent. "I'm a volunteer here, I go to a bio-dynamic school so sometimes I work here to get the extra

108

credits." Her smiled remained pleasantly on her face, even as she concocted sentences.

She sat down in a nearby chair, making me feel a little less short in the presence of these iconic tall Dutch people. "Good job picking a farm," Judith said. "Piet and Renee do such a good job. It's really a nice place." She glanced at Renee and smiled endearingly. She looked back at me and squeezed my hand gently, "It's nice to meet you!"

Another young woman was sitting down at the table behind them all. She hadn't introduced herself yet, but I had caught her watching me intently, with an inscrutable expression. My gaze shifted to her. She smiled confidently and stood up. "I'm Anneliese," she said in a perfect American accent. She asked me a few questions about who I was. Everyone listened politely.

After a minute of exchange, I had to ask her. "Are you American?"

Anneliese laughed dismissively. "No, no. I'm Dutch. When I was in school we learned English from a young age. Most people in our country speak English," she said as she flipped her blonde ponytail, not a hair out of place. "I also worked in America for some years. So, thank you for the compliment on my accent, I suppose," she said. The air filled with her intoxicating perfection. She only asked me questions that would give way to a stupid answer. Or at least that's how it felt. Yeah. I was totally intimidated by her.

When I finally told her that I had been traveling for nine months, her face lightened up a bit, "Oh, that's cool," she said. Her skeptical expression lifted and she looked a bit more human.

Renee took me to my room, which was a tiny trailer behind the kitchen. Judith was staying on one side of it, as she would come for a few days to work and then head back to her place in Amsterdam. I was offered the other side of the trailer. After I got settled in, Anneliese disappeared and the remaining four of us made some dinner together. Then they walked me around the property before the sun went down. They had about seven hectares (over ten acres) and cultivated nearly all of it. It sounded like they grew any vegetable you could imagine, and they had efficient techniques of working with nature instead of against it. Following biodynamic principles in vegetable production meant that they could grow their produce without any chemical intervention. It also symbolized a connection between healing the earth through gentle cultivation of the soil and healing our bodies through ingesting the by-products.

It was the middle of April when I arrived on the farm. Currants, lettuce, strawberries, asparagus, greens, and peas were right around the corner. Together, these people had been farming vegetables off this land for over twenty years. For all those years, they were able to live comfortably off their hard work. I was impressed. This was the first time I had volunteered on a farm that wasn't surviving from a supplemental income. That is, most of the farmers I'd worked for were either retired or had a job on the side that supplied them with extra funding, enabling them to experiment with a "sustainable" lifestyle. These guys were the real deal.

Piet and Renee's land was also originally part of the ocean. A levy, also known as a dyke, had been built to cut the ocean out from most of northern Holland and extend the amount of arable land space. Since their land had been under the ocean many years ago, the soil was sandy and filled with bits of seashells. It was the perfect soil for root vegetables, which require good drainage to prevent the roots from sitting in too much moisture and rotting before reaching ample size.

On this farm, we would get up early and start the day with a small task, take a coffee break, work again, have another coffee break, work, then eat lunch. We'd have an hour rest time (for a nap or a walk) and then we'd work again until the afternoon. The tasks were simple, I just had to follow instructions.

For example, I joined the lettuce-planting assembly line. First, Piet would drive the tractor over the soil to create uniform holes in the ground. On our knees, accompanied by a little scooter with wheels, Renee, Judith, and I would follow the tractor's grooves in the soil. The scooter had a flat of baby plants. We followed Piet's tractor and transplanted the seedlings into the holes he had just created. It was an ingenious system.

I felt relieved to be sucked back into the daily grind of farm life. Renee showed me how to weed strawberries the most effective way, with a Dutch hoe. Piet showed me the best method to harvest asparagus and how to plant corn.

Within a few days I felt right at home, a valued part of the crew. They had been hosting WWOOFers for over five years, and had many volunteers come from the land school where Judith was studying.

A young Scottish man had been staying with them for a few weeks and had gone away on a biking trip for the weekend when I arrived. He returned to say good-bye to Piet and Renee and to pick up the rest of his belongings. Renee had written him a little card and had packaged up some gifts for him. He opened them like a child on Christmas Day, exclaiming how excited he was to be able to bring things back home with him as mementos from the farm. I felt a bit intimidated by their closeness to him. Seeing the potential in how open they were to creating lasting relationships with their volunteers raised the standards for my stay.

Piet and Renee had two fulltime employees: a middle-aged go-with-the-flow kind of couple. John had birth marks on his face, an off-kilter smile, and always wore a patterned bandana. His wife, Lidia, had curly gray-streaked brown hair and eyes that pointed in different directions. They asked many questions while we worked in the fields together.

"I think maybe the farm will come to us when these guys are done with it," Lidia said over one morning coffee break. She cracked her *stropwaffel* and dipped it into her coffee.

"You keep a-wishin'," Renee said with a smirk. "I'm not planning on quitting anytime soon." She leaned over in her seat to bump shoulders with Lidia.

After about a week on the farm, Renee took me for a walk through some local flower gardens and explained the nature of her relationship with Piet. They had been married for quite some time when they both realized they weren't attracted to each other anymore.

"All we ever talked about was when to harvest the squash," she began. "Squash! Talk about romantic!" She chuckled as we passed by a cluster of bright blue flowers. "We knew things were dull if that's all we had. Then we just decided to break up."

I knew they shared a house on the farm, so I pried her for more details. "I have a girlfriend who lives about ten minutes away," she continued. "Piet and I still live together as farm partners. It's been like this for quite some time now. We rely on each other for help, but we aren't married anymore."

Renee and Piet hosted a farm market once a month in the driveway of their property. They would invite all the city people to come buy veggies from them and other farmers in the area. Piet and Renee spent the morning finishing up some harvest of beautiful lettuce and radishes. Piet bundled up asparagus and set out some description cards, naming all the produce. Renee asked me to make a WELCOME sign with pictures of the seasonal vegetables and their Dutch names. I spent a few morning hours on the sign. When I was finished, Renee commented on my cursive writing of "sla" (the Dutch word for lettuce).

"It looks like it says 'sea,' Melanie," Renee said with her low voice, her lips almost closed. She could probably pick up ventriloquism. "People are going to

113

come here asking to buy the sea from us. We're going to have to say no."

I raised my eyebrows and opened my mouth. "Oh Renee," I chuckled, tilting my head to the side to inspect the sign. "I did *not* invent this language, okay?"

We swept the pavement and set up tables for the market and customers appeared. They were sweet and mindful, asking endless questions and often paying more than the asking price for the vegetables. They brought their children and stayed for an hour or so, just looking at the produce we'd harvested and cleaned and catching up with their farmers.

Judith, the other volunteer, spent a week on the farm, overlapping with my visit. We'd work mornings together, braving the chilly, mud-muck spring weather with huge water-proof suits and heavy rain boots. We'd weed the endless rows of carrots, conforming our bodies into various positions to find comfort, and giggle about how it was free yoga. We'd spend our evenings drinking tea together in the kitchen, discussing our personal lives back home. She seemed to be very well-acclimated to farm life, even though she lived in the city. She was from Germany, she told me, but her school was here, so she and her German boyfriend lived in Amsterdam.

Most evenings it would just be Piet, Renee and I. We would all cook together. One night, Renee invited me to see her friend's choir rehearsal. We drove through the countryside, and she told me about the history of tulips in Holland.

She pointed out the fields filled with tulips flowering. "They cut off the flowers," she explained, "so the tulip bulb can retain all the energy it would put into the flower. Then the bulb dies, and they dry it and sell it internationally."

I stared at her in shock. She looked over at me. "I know," she continued. "It doesn't make any sense to cut off the flowers. But people want to buy the bulbs so they can grow their own flowers! The bulbs have to grow somewhere first. And tulips grown in Holland, you know. . ." she said as she looked over at my slyly. "People say they are the best tulips in the world."

We made an unexpected stop at the grocery store. "I have to buy yeast for my bread machine," Renee muttered under her breath, as she shut off the car engine. She led the way to the cashier and called me over to join her.

Her towering figure stood in front of me in line and next to her I felt like a 10-year-old. Yet, *she* was the one whose eyes lit up when she saw a package of chocolate eggs on clearance from Easter. She turned her head back and shot me a mischievous smile. She grabbed a few of them and tossed them onto the moving conveyor belt.

"Oooh, they have orange-flavored ones!" She added a few more to the pile and looked at me wide-eyed. I stared back at her blankly.

She shrugged. "They're on sale!"

She didn't fit into the conventional, grocery store persona at all. Seeing someone I admired casually buying a few cheap chocolate eggs in packaging on the clearance rack was as refreshing as watching my sister in Wisconsin buy tortillas from the dollar-store. It was out of character, sure, yet in both situations I was reminded of their humanity. Renee would laugh if she thought I put her on too high of a pedestal that buying processed chocolate was out of character for her.

We arrived together at the church where her friend's choir was singing. We walked in quietly and the whole altar of the church was occupied with faces. We were just in time; they were about to begin. Renee and I took a seat in a pew near the front row. But it didn't matter, we were the only people in the audience. The music began. The choir was a mixture of old and young faces, and there was a plethora of instruments that created some of the strangest-sounding music I'd encountered. It was all in Dutch as well, and that never helped a person understand anything.

Most of the choir members were women, but most of them had cropped hair cuts and wide shoulders. They all, excluding the children in the front few rows, had weathered faces and deep voices. As the music began and I scanned the crowd in front of us, Renee seemed to have read my mind.

"I know all these women look super butch-y," she whispered in my ear. She looked at me sideways and continued speaking quietly, through closed lips. "This is just a farming community. All the women are big and strong and have short hair. It's just more efficient that way," and she tousled her little gray tufts at me. We giggled together quietly.

116

After the rehearsal, a group of the women greeted Renee. They pulled up chairs and made a little circle. Renee introduced me to all of them in English. They looked at me curiously. They began to question my lifestyle, my dreams, my goals, my travels. I was so flattered by the attention and I could see out of the corner of my eye that Renee was beaming at me.

Back on the farm, there was a young guy from Judith's agricultural school who came to help. His name was Geiss. We got along like good friends, and he was just a few years older than me. He invited me to come with him to a free music festival one night in Zwolle, and Piet and Renee encouraged me to go so I could see the land school and meet his friends.

Geiss and I caught the train together. He'd brought a few beers. "We can drink beer on the train?" I asked, insecure about breaking the law. He laughed at me.

"Of course we can!" He laughed. "It's not a problem. Everybody does it here," and he pointed at a man in a suit drinking beer from a can, just a few seats from where we were sitting. I cracked my beer open and fell even further in love with this country.

We arrived outside the festival and waited for his friends to meet up with us. "They're around our age," Geiss said. "And they all work at school with me. I think you'll like them." A few young people arrived and greeted Geiss. We got in line together.

Someone had brought some plushie animal hats and tossed one of top of Geiss's head. One of his tall, blonde friends caught my eye. He was chatting with everyone else, using his hands and raising his eyebrows with intense facial expressions.

We entered and grabbed a few beers and set a blanket out on the hill in the sun. Everyone spoke Dutch until they realized I was American, then they fluidly transitioned to English. They told me about their goals at the land school and what they did there. They passed around a few joints—like public drinking, marijuana is legal in Holland.

Eventually the blonde guy, Sebo, and I started talking. He asked about the fish tattoo on my wrist. I told him I was Christian, and I got the tattoo to break down my fear of speaking about religion in casual conversation. He smiled, "Yeah, I'm Christian too. I just try and live like Jesus did, though, I don't listen to a lot of the Old Testament."

I was feeling generous, so I bought him a beer. "I like your attitude," I told him confidently. "I wish I could get to know you more."

He sent a sideways glance from where we were standing together at the outdoor bar. "You can if you want. It's up to you." We smiled at each other for a moment and grabbed the beers to return to the rest of the group.

I ended up staying late at the festival. We danced to the music and lost track of time. Geiss and Sebo told me I could stay with one of their friends. They would take me back to the farm in the morning. I borrowed Geiss's phone and called Renee to let her know.

She was laughing through the phone, excited for me. "Thank you for calling," she said. "Have fun!"

I stayed with Sebo in his tiny dorm room. He had five baby chicks under a heat lamp next to his bed. He turned on some music and closed the door. He suddenly started kissing me. When he tried to lay me down on his bed, he explained quietly. "Yeah, I'm Christian, but God forgives, so whatever. I don't think it's a big deal to keep my virginity. "

I retracted and looked into his eyes. "Well, I do."

We ended up making out in bed for a while, clothed, until we fell asleep.

The next morning, we sat in his living room, waiting for his friend to give me a ride back to the farm. Sebo offered me some coffee, which I refused. I sat there in awkward silence, trying to figure out the details of the night before. He sat looking at the floor.

"I think I'm getting sick," Sebo said.

"Oh really?"

He sneezed. I saw a piece of mucus fly from his nose, through the air, and onto my shoe. I closed my eyes and tried to ignore it. I had to get out of here.

Moments later his friend appeared and the three of us got in the car together.

"Bye, have fun at the farm," Sebo called out the window as they drove off. I didn't mention it to Piet and Renee, and immediately got back into my routine. When they asked me about the festival, I said it was awesome. I made no mention of my awkward night.

I hadn't taken a day off since I'd begun working for them and had already been there for almost two weeks. Renee kept telling me to sleep in one day or go for a walk and do something for myself. I didn't want to.

119

One day when I came into the kitchen for breakfast, she and Piet were standing there waiting for me.

"You are not working today, Melanie," she said in her commanding voice. "You have all day and you are *going* to explore Amsterdam."

I shook my head laughing, trying to explain how staying here didn't feel like work, I had so much fun with them.

She grabbed my arm roughly and pulled me outside to find a bicycle for me. "This one has good brakes. Piet, could you fill the tires for her?"

Piet nodded silently and took the bicycle into the garage. Renee got her wallet out and handed me 25 Euros, a train pass and another special ticket. "I'll show you on the map where you can go. It would be such a shame to be in Lelystad and never see Amsterdam. It's less than an hour by train. You'll have so much fun."

I looked at her blankly. She nudged me with her elbow. "Geez, lighten up. Take this money for your food, have some wine or something, and use the ticket so you can bring the bicycle on the train with you."

She sent me off for the day and told me I didn't have a curfew, but if I wasn't going to be home, I needed to call her. I laughed. "Of course I'll be home."

I got on my bicycle and started riding down the driveway. "Thank you so much," I called behind me as I rang the bell. Renee waved.

I biked a half hour to the nearby town of Lelystad, where Renee had told me to go to see all the sales. It was Queen's Day, a celebration for the entire country.

Everyone wears orange and brings items out of their houses and displays them on blankets for sale.

They were unofficially called "shit sales" by Renee, as she had described them to me earlier that morning in disgust. "Why do these people have so much shit in the first place?"

As I saw firsthand, all the businesses shut down and the whole town of Lelystad became a big festival. There were people everywhere in the streets and I walked around to look at the merchandise available. A red bag with an apple cartoon and some large, Dutch lettering in a "bubbly" typeface caught my eye. I bought it as a practical, usable souvenir.

As Renee had recommended, I biked from Lelystad to the train station and brought the bike onto the train with me. I went further east to Haarlem and an older village filled with beautiful, wooden windmills, the structures you think of when you hear about Holland. I took the train west to Amsterdam, where I biked around everywhere, slowly getting my bearings. I spent four or five hours seeing many beautiful buildings and people watching, eating lunch with the money Renee gave me and biking over the canals.

Amsterdam is filled with bike lanes. Not only are they on both sides of every street, they are jam-packed with cyclists. I'd never seen such a tremendous number of bikers in one place! I joined them as we waited for a stop light to change. When the light switched to green, I flew down the path and scoffed at tourists who were crossing the bike lane too slowly by foot. I rang my bell at them and exchanged disgusted looks with other cyclists around me. Stupid tourists.

When I got home that night, Renee was excited to hear about my day.

"What happened today?" She said, as I walked in the kitchen where she and Piet were drinking tea around the kitchen table. She got up to give me a hug, "We missed you."

I explained all the activities I had occupied my day with. She listened intently with a big smile. "Well, I'm proud of myself for making you go and have fun," she said, as she punched my arm lightly.

On my last night my loving farm hosts invited me out to dinner. "We don't do this for everyone, you know. Only the special ones," Renee said, with a wink, as the three of us piled into the car together.

They brought me to a Buddhist community a few minutes away from the farm. It looked like suburbia. Once again, Renee read my thoughts and offered a preface: "I know this looks weird," she explained, "and it is a strange location. But they are good people who make good food."

We entered the room. I observed Tibetan prayer flags all across the white walls of the dining area. We signed into a guest registry at the front desk. "Here you can write your name," Renee instructed. "And you can put here that you're from Minnesota!"

The food was simply set on the table in hotel pans, buffet-style. Renee ducked her head low while we walked up to the food so she could whisper in my ear.

"They're all Buddhists," she said. "We took you here because it's donation-based."

I turned around to make eye contact. "You mean, it's free?"

"You didn't actually think we would spend money on you, did you?" Renee said with a low chuckle as she looked back at Piet. I made a mock-angry face at her as she reached over to pinch my arm in jest. Then she took out a twenty Euro note and tossed it in the donation box.

The next morning, an Australian volunteer arrived, with thick purple hair. As I brought her with me to do some weeding near the house, she told me she had never volunteered on a farm before and that she already loved it.

"It seems like Renee and Piet really enjoy you," she said with a smile. "I think they're going to miss you when you leave." My cheeks got pink as we worked side-by-side. I knew how she felt. I had felt the same way when I saw the love and affection that Renee had given to the Scottish man. I'd felt a bit intimidated by the closeness of their relationship and didn't think I could ever compare.

"You're going to fit in here," I told her confidently, "before you know it, they will treat you as well as they have treated me. That is, if you are a hard worker," I laughed.

We had our last breakfast together before my timed departure. Renee had made a card for me and wrapped several small gifts, just as she had for the other volunteer. She looked down at the items on the table as I unwrapped them. She set her hands in her lap as I laughed at what she wrote in the card. She gave me a coffee mug covered in vegetable drawings ("I don't know what you're going to do with your life, but you're certainly going need to think about it over a cup of coffee," she had commented), a bag of dried mangoes and some chocolate caramels ("for the trip today"). She hugged me tightly and choked out some parting words, "We will miss you a lot. Send us some updates when you arrive in Italy."

Renee and Piet walked me outside. Lidia and Anneliese were driving together to the train station so they had offered me a ride, as I needed to go to Amsterdam for the night. We drove away and I started sobbing as I looked out the window. Renee and Piet just stood there under a large umbrella in the pouring rain, waving as they watched the car disappear.

In the car with Anneliese and Lidia, I reflected on my intense emotional connection with Renee. "I don't know why I'm crying," I said between sobs, "I just love her. She is so amazing." Anneliese reached back and put her hand on my leg to comfort me.

"You'll be okay," she said, with a gentle smile. Her kindness caught me off guard. She had only seemed cold and judgmental. Now here she was, expressing affection.

I just stared out the window, wondering why I did this to myself. I allowed such amazing people into my heart and letting go of them was always so painful. Especially older women like Renee. (If she read that, she would be mad I just called her old.) What's the point, if all my wonderful experiences end in heartbreak?

My chaperones dropped me off at the familiar train station in Lelystad and Anneliese gave me her email address, as she was planning to be in Amsterdam the next day. She had a pass to see the Van Gogh museum and offered to lend it to me for the day. I took the pass and promised to meet back up with her to return it. I thanked them both and said goodbye.

I took the train to Amsterdam once again, where I had arranged to meet up with Judith. She had emailed me with an offer to stay at her place before I caught my flight the next day to Italy. I took her up on the offer. We met up for a beer at a tiny plant-filled cafe. It had been over a week since we'd seen each other, and I expressed my sadness in leaving Renee. Judith was sympathetic and sweet, assuring me that Renee felt the same way about me. She paid for my beer and we went outside in the rain.

She walked up to a bicycle and opened up the lock. She gave me her bike helmet and patted the little basket on the back of the bike. "Get on," she said.

I looked down at the basket and back at her, confused. "What? On the back of the bike? What if I break it?" I said. "I have my backpack and everything!"

She laughed. "My boyfriend has sat on here before, many times. He weighs much more than you. Come on, let's go get some food! I know a great Indian place for take-out."

After her insistence, I sat on the basket awkwardly. She biked confidently through the rain as I sat clinging onto her slippery blue rain jacket, my body swaying with the turns in the path. Finally we arrived at the Indian place and she ordered multiple vegan items for us.

We were an odd sight as we made our way to her apartment. I was still holding tightly onto her back with my left arm, I had my backpack on, and my right hand held a plastic bag filled with food in Styrofoam containers. We went to her place and sat on cushions on the floor of her apartment, giggling about our time together and how much fun we'd had getting to know each other. We ripped off pieces of roti and dipped it into the various curries we'd ordered. She told me about her boyfriend and what they wanted for their lives together. They were going to rent a van and travel through South America. I told her about the next day and my travel plans, and she wrote down directions to the Van Gogh museum where I planned to visit the next morning. We went to bed early in the evening and I slept on the couch.

When I woke up and walked into the kitchen, I found a sweet goodbye note on a little postcard with bananas making kissy faces and the Dutch word for kisses, "Kusjes!" She had left early for work and apologized for missing a chance to say goodbye.

I ground some coffee beans in a vintage wooden coffee grinder and made a cup of coffee in her metal mocha pot. I emailed Anneliese from Judith's apartment with a time to meet outside of the museum, took my backpack, scribbled a gracious note back to Judith, and left.

I transferred from a few buses to make my way to the Van Gogh museum. I don't often find myself attached to artists, but Van Gogh's painting style was a perfect mix of intent and disarray. It resonated with me strongly, the clumps of paint on his original pieces spoke to me as unfinished, a new perspective. It was a refreshing way of feeling art.

I went outside and found Anneliese there waiting for me. When I'd met her on the farm, she had seemed overly confident and perfect. Stuck-up, even. Here she was, inviting me for a cup of hot tea in the city center.

We sat down as a small metal table and she complimented me on my ability to travel so far and for such a long period of time. We talked about her life and her desire to continue work in sustainability. The time flew by and suddenly she asked, "What time does your flight leave?"

"Uh, I don't know. Maybe in a few hours?" I pulled out my ticket and it said I had exactly two hours before the flight would leave. I read my schedule out loud and glanced up at her. She looked shocked.

"Are you serious? You're so calm about that. Don't you get nervous? If I were you I would already be at the airport. Do you know how to get to the airport from here?"

"No," I chuckled, "I was hoping you could tell me." She obliged and gave me some directions, which bus to take and which direction to travel. We hugged good-bye. She pulled back and held me at arm's length from her face.

"You are really a unique traveler to have such emotional connections with strangers. But your visit is so short! It's an inspiration for me. And it really was great to meet you." She kissed me on both cheeks.

I set off through the drizzling rain, meandering around the dedicated cyclists, accepting that I *absolutely* looked like a tourist. I took the city transportation and got to the airport in time, checked into my flight, and boarded it with a throng of strangers. As the plane lifted off, I looked out the window in wonder, anticipating seeing Gemma again in her home country. And I couldn't forget to tell her about Mumtaz.

Italy

Café Americano

My flight descended over the Alps and arrived at a tiny airport in Torino. I looked out the windows at the snow-capped mountains as the passengers in front of me began disembarking. An all-too-familiar voice in my head asked me what I was going to do when I got off the plane. Although my Italian friend, Gemma, had agreed to meet me here, I wondered if something would go wrong.

Italy was where so many food traditions originated. I had heard references to it my whole life, and it had always seemed so mystical and unattainable. The intricate language and the wholesome cuisine, the beautiful people and way of life seemed so very out of my league. Excitement coursed through my veins as I anticipated having an Italian girl, a friend of my very own, come to meet me!

I entered the arrivals area. Tiny European airports usually didn't have much of a customs department, so I didn't receive an Italian stamp in my passport. I walked past a few faces I didn't recognize, and then there was Gemma, with a huge smile on her face and her arms out wide. We hugged and she kissed me on both cheeks. We went outside as we waited for the bus, and I started rambling in rapid English, explaining how beautiful my flight was.

She held up her hand and closed her eyes, "Please, Melanie!" She opened her eyes and reached for my hand. "My English is sleeping. Now I need wake up. Please, slowly!"

I giggled and responded, "How. Are. You?"

She smiled and glanced toward the road. We were standing in what appeared to be a parking garage. "So, I wait for you here, maybe ten minutes," she spoke fluidly, using her hands in the air for added emphasis. "People came first, a big woman with short, like, brown hair? And after, a big woman with long hair and glasses and a big smile. I think, it's Melanie? But no, it's not possible you get so big in one month."

I laughed out loud. "No! I work on farms, remember? Muscles!" I flexed my small arm sarcastically.

We boarded a bus together, and she insisted on paying my fare. "You're a guest Melanie, it's normal." We sat side-by-side and I smiled as she spent the half-hour ride telling me about her village and her family.

The bus dropped us off right outside of the city. A Gumby figure emerged from a small blue car. He approached us with a huge grin.

"This is Eugenio, my brother," Gemma said proudly, as he stood before us. "He's studying English. He's my little brother."

I laughed and looked him up and down dramatically. "Little?"

"It's a problem, I'm smaller than him but he is the baby!" She stood on her tiptoes to reach up and pinch his cheeks. She taught me how to correctly say his name. Italian is similar to Spanish in that most letters in the words are always pronounced the same. I tried to say it like her, "ee-oo-JAY-nee-oh." They just giggled at me as I shrugged my shoulders.

"Oh, like Eugene!" I exclaimed and clasped my hands together. "With an Italian accent!" Again, they laughed, and I leaned forward to give him a hug. He stopped me and kissed me on the cheeks instead. Oops, I forgot. Just because I felt comfortable with these people didn't make them my American family. Hugging isn't normal here.

We got in the car together and Eugenio drove us through the narrow Italian roads, between tall buildings and tiny cars. We arrived in front of a tall apartment building with terraces covered in plants and flowers. They invited me inside and we walked up the stairs and into the apartment. As I took off my shoes by the front door and Gemma and Eugenio greeted their parents, I became suddenly aware that I knew no Italian. Absolutely none. I strode into the kitchen where the family was clustered.

Gemma's mother Suzi was pale and petite, with cropped black hair. She avoided eye contact, and sheepishly peeked her face forward to kiss my cheeks when Gemma introduced us. Her father had been looming in the back of the room but also came forward to kiss me.

"Happy . . to . . meet . . you!" He exclaimed, dramatically with his arms out in front of his body. "Me," he said as he pointed to himself. "Amelio."

He was tall and thin like his son, with an expressive face and cropped black hair. I smiled at the family as they spoke in Italian. Gemma held her hands out as she spoke loudly. Her brow furrowed and her face blank as she spoke, she seemed upset. Yet she turned to me with a smile and pulled me out of the kitchen.

"Are you okay?" I asked, as we walked into a bedroom. "You have a fight with your family?"

She looked back at me and the smile wiped from her face. "What? No."

"You seemed angry?"

"No, I only speak about my day! I am happy!" She said, assuring me with a big smile, as she set a blanket on the bed. "You sleep here, in my room."

"I can sleep somewhere else!"

"You're my guest, Melanie, it's normal," she said again, which became a common theme of our discussions about who gets what.

She walked out of the room and I put my bag down and sat on the bed for a moment.

I went back into the kitchen and watched the family speak some more. Gemma was a very outspoken young woman, a few years older than me. She was vegetarian and didn't shave her armpits like me, our original connecting factors when we met back in Turkey.

132

She had shaved the left side of her head and wore one large feather earring. Her asymmetrical hair was a perfect representation of her personality. She referred to herself as a former "metal head" and usually cocked her head to the side while she listened. When the conversation would allow for her interjection, she would emphatically bob her head around while she spoke, the one earring dancing along.

No one looked at me as they spoke in an aggressive local tongue. I felt like a fly on the wall. I couldn't understand them, so I stood there allowing myself to be completely submerged into their lifestyle. After a few minutes, we went out to the covered porch where we sat around a large table, set for dinner.

"Vino, Melanie?" Amelio asked me.

I nodded my head up and down enthusiastically. Why didn't I learn how to say "of course" in Italian?

He chuckled and said something in Italian to Gemma as he filled my glass with red wine and gestured at me. "Good, Melanie." He said in deliberate English. "Ver-r-ry good."

Gemma's mom, Suzi, rushed back and forth from the kitchen to the table, presenting us with more and more food, giving me the impression of a feast. As the platters multiplied, spreading across the table before us, Suzi reached for my plate. She looked at me timidly and scooped a mass of white mush with green peas onto my plate. She set it back down in front of me as I smiled at her. She pointed to the plate as she cowered over the table. "Ri-sot-to," she said in slow Italian. She looked at Gemma for translation.

"I understand," I assured her, as I nodded and put my hand on my heart. "Thank you."

The rest of the family helped themselves to the steaming food and we all began eating. The warm risotto had a heavy texture but a gentle, sophisticated flavor. Creamy, tangy, soft.

As the food began to disappear, I remembered my wine glass. The family watched me intently as I reached for it. Relishing the full attention of the room, I took a small sip, closed my eyes, and for full effect, swished the wine around in my mouth. Not knowing what to expect, I swallowed the wine and opened my eyes. The whole family was looking at me.

My experience with wine had been limited to a few glasses of red on family holidays, my dad's stash of boxed Franzia that he kept hidden under his bed. But this was authentic Italian wine; nothing could have prepared me for the experience of this sensuous, blood-red liquid. "I LOVE THIS!" I yelled across the table.

The family started laughing and looking at each other. Amelio and Suzi exchanged a few words in Italian and Gemma spoke over them, "It's a cheap wine. From the region."

"It's amazing! How much does it cost?"

"Maybe three Euro at the corner store?" Gemma said, with a giggle, and she translated for her parents.

I laughed and took another sip, closing my eyes and letting the warmth of it fill my body.

After we finished eating and cleaning up the meal, Gemma and I sat on the patio and smoked a cigarette together. She spoke to her mother who was in the kitchen, as I leaned against the wall and watched her mannerisms. She looked angry when she furrowed her brow and said simple things like, "this is red," or "it's cold tonight," or "she is funny."

We finished our cigarettes and Eugenio invited us for a walk. I put on my green sweater and said good-night to her parents. We filed out of the apartment building into the dark streets, illuminated eerily by streetlamps above. The paths were made of bricks, un-even and perilous in the night. We wandered into a small valley of a park and sat on a bench. Eugenio rolled up a joint and offered it to me. I smiled and took a puff. Is this legal in Italy? Who cares.

We walked out of the park back to the streets, past gelato shops and boutiques with dresses hanging in the windows, up small hills that dominated the village landscape. And then we reached the top, where an im-posing stone building looked over the whole village.

"This was a castle before," Gemma explained, as she led me on a small path around it. "Now, they make it an exhibit for the art. It's a museum."

We ran around like kids and danced along the tiny path, giggling. Then we retired on the edge of the rock wall bordering the castle, perched like pigeons with an incredible view of the village lit up below us.

"Thank you for inviting me, Gemma," I said as I reached around to put my arm across her shoulder. "This is really a beautiful place."

"You haven't seen anything yet," she said, as she pushed my arm away. "I will show you real Italy, then you can say 'thank you.'"

I stayed a week with Gemma's family. One of the first few days, she invited me to go rock climbing with her friends. "We'll go climb the Alps," she said nonchalantly, like that was something everyone did.

We got in her car and picked up a few of her friends, one of whom was named Alfredo. They all spoke in loud, melodic Italian over the car stereo. Through the window, I watched as the mountains get closer. We arrived and hiked a bit into the forest.

I volunteered to go first. The only time I'd ever gone rock climbing was inside an outdoor supply company with a plastic wall covered with small knobs. If you fell off the plastic wall, you would fall onto something like a plush mattress. Here, you would fall on nothing but rocks and prickly bushes.

Gemma and her friends laced me up in intricate knots and special shoes that felt too small. I grabbed the wall hesitantly, until I learned to propel myself up off the strength from my legs, not my arms. I made it about twenty feet up the wall. Suddenly overcome with terror, I wailed, convincing them to let me down.

"Great, Melanie! Good work," Gemma said, as she helped me descend the face of the cliff and the ropes twirled about my body. "You don't get high, but you try. You aren't scared, it's the most important."

I smiled proudly back at her. My body quivered and I leaned against a rock.

After everyone got a turn to climb and we took a group picture, we went to Gemma's house to have dinner with her family. It was pizza tonight, with homemade crust, sauce, and vegetables from Gemma's garden. Suzi even topped the pizza with fresh mozzarella. It was incredible.

Then after the dinner, the climbing guy, Alfredo, walked in the front door. He invited us to a party in the forest. "For dancing," he said, as he used his fingers to make an "o" and moved it up and down. Dancing in the forest? I looked at Gemma for clarification.

"Yes?" She checked in with me. "It's okay for you, a rave tonight, Melanie?"

Laughing, I nodded my head. Why not?

Gemma, Eugenio, Alfredo, me, and another friend of Gemma's, Carmen, all crammed into a little car for a two-hour drive through the winding mountain roads. At some point we were driving behind another car on the dark highway. The car pulled over and so did ours. The group of people from the car approached us. My heart stopped. Everyone was speaking Italian and talking over each other. They sounded aggressive. I looked at the faces of my friends. No one was smiling or laughing.

Yet, a group of twenty-somethings leaned in through the windows and high-fived us. When they got to me, I just smiled awkwardly at them and reached out to high-five them, too. Gemma explained something about my name and "American" and the group of youth nodded and got back into their car. We drove behind them the rest of the way, and I saw cigarette butts being tossed out the window of their car onto the highway, sparkling on the asphalt.

We arrived in the middle of the forest and drove down a narrow road surrounded by pine trees. Then there were cars, parked in a line like sardines along both sides of the already-too-narrow road. We eventually found a place to leave the car and walked over a hill and down a small path to where we could feel the bass of the music resonating on the earth.

There was a cluster of colored lights in an other-wise-empty valley. People had set up tents, where they sold food, liquor, and hippy clothes. We sat down on someone's blanket and beers were passed around. The moon was full and lit up the scene: a man in a loose coat approached. He had a few pills that he held out to Gemma. She shook her head and he walked away.

"What was that?" I asked her.

"Oh, sorry, did you want E?"

"What? Like Ecstasy?" I asked as she nodded her head.

"Oh. Okay. *No*," I responded. She laughed as she grabbed my hand and pulled me to dance.

Each person had his or her own way of interpreting the strange techno music that was blasting through the speakers. Lovers slow dancing, children bouncing around, young people looking completely drugged and out of it. An old man with neon lights hung all over his body kept dancing from side to side, swaying his hips as he moved around. I wasn't a confident dancer, I was sober, and this electronic trance wasn't my thing, so I just mimicked other people's movements.

After what felt like an entire day of swaying our bodies to the music, Gemma and I walked past the party people into a huge expanse of field. The lights and the sound receded as we laid in the dew-covered spring grass and admired the moon.

"You think you have kids, Melanie?"

"One day, maybe. You want?"

"I think yes, when I am old and have nothing else to do," Gemma responded with a sigh.

We left before the sun came up and went back to Gemma's family's apartment.

She also took me in a bus to the city center of Torino. She pointed to the direction of the museums and architectural marvels, and then of the markets and the local people. She asked me where I would prefer to go. I looked down as if I had a confession to make.

"Um, Gemma, I just want to spend time with you. I don't care what we do. I want to see your city." I pointed to a billboard advertising the museum's Egyptian exhibit. "If I wanted to learn about Egypt, I could go to Egypt."

She put her hands on my shoulders and turned our bodies in the direction of the markets down the street. "I hoped that you would say that!" She responded, and then she taught me the classic south Italian phrase, "Ah-moan-eee!" Let's go!

We explored the markets, feasting our eyes on the first tomatoes of the year, Italian greens and cucumbers, grapes and figs imported from the nearby Arabic countries. We found a place to get falafel and ate outside on the patio. After the meal, we ordered coffees. As our waitress walked away, I called out to specify,

"Americano!" She turned back around and nodded her head in recognition.

The coffees arrived and sent us into a fit of laughter; they were identical. We had no earthly idea which coffee had more water added to it.

"You can learn the Italian way, Melanie," Gemma said, "Espresso is better than the big American coffee that needs one hour to drink!"

We took a city train to a park. I got a beer; Gemma had a cup of water. We perched on a hill, surrounded by strangers playing instruments and lovers rolling around on blankets. I had a lot to tell her, and finally we were alone. I explained the whole story about Turkey, how much I had trusted Mumtaz, and what he did to me. She laughed as I got to the punchline.

I paused mid-sentence, offended.

She smiled and explained herself. "Before you came there was another young girl, like you." She looked down, rolling blades of grass between her fingers. "Happy, interesting, active, beautiful. She had something similar with him. He took her as a daughter, so sweet with her. One night he invited her to his house for games with his wife. After, he tried to kiss her. She left the next day. She didn't tell anyone then, but she sent me an email a few weeks ago to explain."

Now I was shocked. I felt a mixture of frustration and anger, as well as a bit of jealousy. I thought I was someone special to him. He treated me like I was his favorite person, exchanging meaningful glances over our tahini breakfast toast. He sought me out to show me the lay of the land and teach me things. Hearing that I was not the only special young girl to him somehow deepened the blow my heart felt.

"I can't believe him," I said to Gemma as I glanced across the horizon. "He tricked me."

"I'm so sorry for that, Melanie. Now, it's over, that is good." She stood up and smiled, eyebrows raised. "Now, ready for more Torino?"

I held out my hand so she could help me up.

Another day Gemma and Eugenio invited me to hike up a mountain with a monastery on the top. On the way up the mountain I saw some glossy green leaves with small, delicate white flowers. The texture of the leaf reminded me of the wild onions my sister and I went hunting for in the Wisconsin forests. I pointed to it, as Gemma caught her breath from the walk. "Yes, it's a famous one, but my mother doesn't like the flavor. She says it's too *forte*."

When we finally arrived at the summit, we could see the snow-capped Alps in front of us, close enough that I entertained the idea of reaching out and picking them up, stuffing them in my backpack to show them to my family back home. I took a few photos instead.

Back at the house for dinner, Gemma's father, Amelio, was excited to practice his English with me. He proudly showed me pictures of his monthly excursions skiing in the Alps. He told me about a special liquor he made with his son, Eugenio, from a piece of juniper only found on a specific, regional mountain. The more he spoke to me, the more English he seemed to remember.

"Only walk, no car," he said, as he shook his pointer finger at me. "No roads. And, the juniper? It's very small." He symbolized with his fingers how much you could take. If you took more, he explained, maybe next year it's *finito*.

After dinner that night he invited me to try some. It tasted like gin, but it was sweet by itself, and they would occasionally drink it with their coffee after the evening meal.

I was also invited to help Gemma with her small vegetable gardens near to her family's apartment. She used to work for a man who owned a big greenhouse, and he allowed her to use his backyard to grow vegetables. She had a walk-behind tractor to turn the soil and used black plastic tarping to keep weeds down. She didn't use any chemicals, and she went out to visit the farm about once a week. It was nestled in the hills preceding the snow-capped Alps. She had strawberries, lettuces, and baby pepper plants growing.

She also had a plethora of chicory. After a day visiting the gardens, when she would walk into the kitchen with a giant mass of chicory, her mother Suzi would groan sarcastically.

Gemma looked at me. "I don't understand her! She doesn't like! It's so delicious!"

Suzie glanced at me, pursing her lips and shaking her head. Then she pinched her fingers together and said the Italian word, *amaro*. Bitter.

One night before dinner I took a shower, changed, and came out to the patio where the family was setting the table for the meal. Gemma's dad, Amelio, saw me

142

and smiled, and in pristine Vanna-White style, he gestured with his arms toward where I was going to sit. There were two glasses filled with an inch of red wine.

Gemma saw me looking at the place setting and rolled her eyes. "He wants to see if you are Italian yet," she explained. "He put two different wines for you to taste. One is cheap, one is expensive. Can you tell which is which?"

I laughed, as Amelio came behind me and put a blindfold over my eyes. He guided me to the seat as I heard the rest of the family settle into their places. Her dad handed me each of the glasses individually to taste. Both were dry and full-bodied, yet one tasted empty. I guessed which was the expensive and which was the cheap and indicated my favorite.

Gemma's dad stood up from the table and started clapping. "Good, Melanie!"

"I still prefer the original one, the Barbera," I told Gemma. Amelio understood and laughed.

Gemma interjected, "My parents prefer this one, too. It's a secret. The expensive ones here are not as good. This one, Barbera, it's cheap and good quality."

Amelio just stood there beaming at me for another minute. He reached across the table to shake my hand.

On our last day together, Gemma drove me to a small town called Avigliana, near a picturesque lake, Lago Piccolo. We went for a bit of a walk and found a restaurant with a patio. As we walked into the restaurant, we passed a long table filled with old people.

"Gemma?" Someone called out.

143

My friend and I turned around to the origin of the voice, back to the table of the elderly. One such gentleman stood up slowly to wave to her, and her face lit up. She called back to him and we approached the table. Everyone started talking to her excitedly, and she introduced me as her American friend.

We got a table for ourselves and ordered food. "Those were your friends, too, Gemma?"

She laughed. "Yes, I have friends everywhere, so *popular*," she giggled sarcastically, as she flipped her hair around her head. "I know this man from an art project. He's a good guy."

We got back in the car and she dropped me off in the city, where she had arranged a trip for me to France through a rideshare organization called "Blablacar". Gemma paid 10 Euro for my ride ("you're my guest Melanie, it's normal") and we said goodbye as I got into a car with a quirky old Italian man. She shoved a bottle of Barbera in my hands

"It's a gift from my parents. They say they will miss you. Come again, when you want."

I smiled and thanked her, as I closed the car door and waved to her through the window.

While we navigated through the narrow roads that twisted their way through the mountains, he spoke to me about his family life, his house, his brothers. A typical Italian, he used his hands for emphasis as he spoke. Driving seemed to be no exception for him. The car was consistently crossing the white line on the side of the road, where there was no barrier between us and the cliff. When I asked him what his house was like, he pulled out his phone to show me a picture. I felt nervous, never comfortable with a driver on their phone. Being in the mountains made it worse. I kept silent for the rest of the ride.

France

Je Suis Heureux

Descending the Swiss Alps into France from the east, I watched the pines *whoosh* past the car window. We entered Montpellier; road signs suddenly switched from familiar Italian to French, with strange new letters. The chatty Italian man and I arrived at the station where Gemma had instructed him to drop me off.

He asked to look at my train ticket. I pulled it out from where it had been folded neatly in my wallet and he scanned it casually. When he found the departure time listed, his eyes bugged out of his head.

"Oh, no," he said. "It's a very small time!"

Well-versed in casual travel, I was sure he couldn't be serious. I smiled calmly and took the ticket back. "Okay, thank you for the drive," I said, as I folded it up. "It was nice to meet you."

"Go now," he interrupted as he pushed my left shoulder. "Quick!"

I got out of the passenger seat and opened the door to the backseat to grab my backpack. I hobbled across the parking lot, without having had the time to strap it on properly and waved sideways as his car sped off. I approached the station ahead where Gemma had told me to catch my train. By the time I reached the glass-walled waiting area and removed my ticket from its quarters, I had two minutes to spare.

I bounced from foot to foot in anticipation amidst a cluster of strangers of all different ethnicities. This was my first time in France; ignorant as it may sound, I had only expected to see white people. I listened to their conversations eagerly, my heart bursting with nostalgia for that French accent that reminded me of Yola and Molly. But first I was headed to see the Dutch couple from Indonesia who had invited me to visit.

After our shared experience in Indonesia, our frustrations with attempting to connect with our Ratna, I'd felt bonded to Lia and Pim. That tiny eco-village was also my first truly *rustic* volunteer experience, so it felt natural to bond with the volunteers who'd shared the challenging experience with me.

Lia had kept in close contact with me via email, asking with genuine curiosity about each new farm I visited, wondering how I interpreted all of the experiences. When she invited me to come visit, I agreed. How could I turn down a free place to stay with people I already knew? As I had discovered earlier with the bartender in Czech Republic, sharing time with someone while traveling and being able to reconnect with them meant temporarily putting your heart back together. It felt like being a kid sent off to summer camp, coming home to share your stories with family.

A train arrived and I looked around frantically. I compared my ticket to the voice over the intercom; French pronunciation is so strange, nothing written in this language seemed to match how it sounded.

The doors slid open and I called out to the nearest stranger, "Please help! I am American!"

A man with an afro and large headphones looked me up and down, glanced at my ticket and nodded his head. "We, we," he said.

Was he saying yes in French or encouraging me to go with him? He pushed me in the direction of the train's opening doors. I slid into the cabin and sent a quick wave in his direction. The train looked like a space shuttle. Gemma had told me about these French trains; hyper-fast and quite new, they could fly down the track at over 100 mph. I took a seat near the door so I could watch the names of the train stations we passed. On my ticket, I had the departure and the arrival time. Using my best air-math, I had a few hours to ride the train before arriving in Lia and Pim's village.

The train doors closed and I set my backpack onto the ground at my feet.

Molly and Yola, the other two volunteers I had connected with, had also insisted on hosting me. After spending so much time talking with Molly, naturally I felt closer to her than I had felt to Yola. However, after they left the eco-village and I sent them both emails, Yola was the one who responded.

After consulting a map of France, I thought it would be more economical to visit Lia and Pim first. After staying with them, I could travel further west to continue my journey without having to back-track. I shared my plan with Yola via email, and she had responded wondering if she could join me at Lia and Pim's house, and we could drive back together to see her family! She'd sent me this email a few weeks earlier:

"So it's ok for me I stay to Lia and Pim place until 20 may. You can stay at my place for 1, 2, 3......100...days if you want, no problem!"

I remembered how reserved she was face-to-face in Indonesia. Perhaps she had acted that way because she had been intimidated by all the English spoken there. But in our emails, she seemed like a different person. I sent the news out to Lia and hoped she would accept having an extra guest.

It was early afternoon as the train glided through the French countryside. Sunshine lit up the landscape, casting a golden glimmer across the grapevines and the fields of crops. I watched cows and tiny farmhouses fly past the window. I saw farmers wandering around with blue overalls and janky pick-up trucks. Somehow I felt at home, though I had never been here before.

Nearing a station, I looked out the window and recognized the name of their village on a wooden plaque. I snapped out of my relaxed state and grabbed my backpack. I exited the train alone, sure this was where

Lia had promised to meet me. I stepped onto the platform. I was the only passenger who had gotten off the train.

I wandered around into the parking area and heard someone calling out my name. I turned around and there they were, Lia and Pim.

Lia bent her knees a bit, hollering, "Mel-a-nie!" It was as if she was calling to her stumbling grandchild.

I called back a greeting as I ran toward them. The sun was beginning its descent. Pim was standing behind Lia, his face illuminated with that same golden light from the sunset behind me and suddenly I was enveloped in a group hug. "We're so excited to have you," Lia exclaimed, as Pim took the pack off my back and tossed it into the backseat of their van. "How was your travel?" Lia asked, sitting in the passenger seat with her torso turned toward me, smiling eagerly.

"It was so easy and fun!" I laughed to myself and held up a finger. "I will never again ask an Italian man questions while he's driving—especially not while in the Alps!"

Pim and Lia laughed as we pulled into their driveway just a few moments later. Their gray house was surrounded by bushes and flowers, a well-tended garden. There were large windows and a front door of dark wood. Lia walked ahead to open the door for me. "Welcome, welcome to our home!" She said excitedly.

The house smelled fresh. Everything looked pristine. They had a large kitchen area with an island, a grand fireplace and a plush couch. Everything looked like it belonged. On the mantle of the fireplace was a large collection of pictures of Lia with a bunch of little boys in Africa, a volunteer trip she took a few years back and had told me about in Indonesia.

Lia joined me. "Oh, I see you found my pictures!" She said as she came up behind me. "I have something else you might like to see," she said, as she wandered away. "Just a moment."

Pim set my backpack down and smiled as he sat down on the couch.

Lia came back holding a wide book with a picture of Ratna's house on the cover. "It's a photo book I made of our experiences in Indonesia! There are pictures of you inside, too."

"Wow, awesome," I said as she handed the book to me. I sat on the couch next to Pim and turned the pages, reminiscing.

"It was difficult for us, yes," she said as she leaned back into the couch and Pim put his arm around her gently. "But it's important we still have some good memories. And it's also good you were there."

They showed me to their guest room; I would be sleeping on a queen bed. "Thank you so much for your hospitality, Lia," I said as she set my bag down.

"You are so sweet," she said with a smile. "We are happy to have you. Get settled, and we'll make some dinner, okay?" With that, she closed the door and left me alone.

I sat on the bed in silence, piecing together my impression of them in a conventional setting. How different this experience would be from our rustic days in Indonesia.

When I entered the kitchen, I admired the view from the windows. The sun had already disappeared, but the remaining glow illuminated the outdoors just enough that I could see their patio and a pond off in the distance.

"Wow, is this all your property?" I asked.

Lia came up behind me. "It ends there, a bit beyond the pond," she said. "I'll show you tomorrow when we have more light."

Together we prepared a yellow curry. I marveled at their selection of ingredients. I had anticipated a much more primitive household, based on the experience we'd shared of bathing in Lake Toba, brushing our teeth and scrubbing our bodies in our bathing suits, sharing the water with the fish and the lobsters and the local people.

We plated up the meal and ate together, bringing up old memories and laughing at our luck to be together again. They pushed me for every detail of my travels they could think of. Did I like the Italian wine? What did I think of the French people so far? Did I miss Ratna? (Ha, ha.) Was I planning to visit Spain?

I felt I had two parents intrigued by my observations and experiences, wanting to understand my perspective. It was refreshing to feel valued and respected for these things that had just *happened* to me. I made a mental note to call my dad. Although I didn't expect him to act as curious and interested as this wonderful couple was, I still felt a wave of nostalgia for a true family connection.

As we finished eating, I explained how things had worsened after they had left the eco-village. I was the outsider to the other two volunteers; it had been my word against Ratna's about what happened. "Sure, it didn't take long for Robert and Lara to side with me," I explained, "but I felt like 'the bad guy' having to defend myself and my actions."

Lia and Pim nodded enthusiastically in agreement. Lia pushed her dinner away from her without finishing the meal. Pim smiled and looked down at his now-empty plate. He wiped his mouth with a paper napkin and his Anthony-Hopkins eyes fixed on mine.

"And your hands?" He asked in his gentle way, reaching out to look at them.

I chuckled and sighed. I placed my hands on his and cocked my head. "Well," I said, pursing my lips. "They are completely gone!"

He raised his eyebrows and opened his mouth in awe. He gently touched the small circular scars where the warts had been.

"This is amazing," he said with a proud smile. "Your hands look near-normal. But who wants normal anyway?" He said, with a wink.

Then his brows furrowed as he continued to inspect my hands. "You should know you will always have the virus," Pim said with a quiet voice, as if he was sharing a secret. "That will stay with you forever. Once you have it, you have it. But it is in your power to stand up against it and never allow it to control you again. It's your body, and it's your responsibility."

I nodded earnestly. "I understand," I said, as I cleaned my plate and leaned against the back of my chair. "Being here feels like coming home, even though I've never been here before."

Lia smiled. "That's because you're family."

We cleaned the kitchen and then Pim retired to the couch, where he turned the TV on with a remote control and called me over. I sat on the other end of the long couch, and Lia offered me a coffee from the kitchen.

She brought the coffees and opened a small wooden box filled with dark chocolate on the coffee table. The three of us sat together in silence on the couch and watched an old cop movie about alligators in Florida, letting the chocolate melt in our mouths.

After the movie, we said goodnight and I crawled into my way-too-big bed and thought about tomorrow. Yola was coming to visit!

The next day began with coffees and more chatting. Eventually I got changed and helped outside with a few small garden projects. It was late spring in France and the weather was perfect. Lia led me to the backyard, where there was a small pond and a tiny vegetable garden surrounded by a wooden fence. She showed me her baby tomato plants.

"And my secret for vegetable gardening . . ." she said, as she bent down on her knees to inspect the small plants. She weeded a few tiny sprouts around the base of the tiny tomato plant and looked up at me.

" . . Is that every time I transplant a tomato from inside to the garden, I make a hole, and I put a banana

154

peel inside. I put the tomato plant on it, and it's magic!"

Her Dutch accent was familiar now, her words filled with breathiness. Yet she had French influence as well, which made her speech even more peculiar.

As we sat in the garden, admiring the plants, we heard a car horn honking. Pim came out of the house to beckon us inside. We ran down the path to the house and tossed our shoes by the back door. I ran through the house, slipping across the stone floor in my socks as I approached the front door. It wasn't my house, however, so I waited for Lia and Pim to be the ones to greet their guest. I stood behind both of them when Lia opened the door. There was Yola, in a huge blue sweater, her dark hair twisted eloquently on her head and fastened with a clip.

"Yola!" I yelled, lacking ability to exercise restraint. Her eyebrows shot up and she smiled big as she tried to kiss me on the cheeks. In my excitement, I forgot her French customs, hugging her tightly, as I would any close friend back home. She squealed and tried to push me away, laughing. "It's so good to see you!"

She giggled as she held my face and kissed me on the cheeks. "Melanie, you forget, you are in France now. No more of this," she said, as she imitated me hugging her. "The people here think you are crazy if you do this."

"It's okay, I *am* crazy!"

We all laughed at that as we shuttled her into the house. Lia and Pim went back into the living room as I showed her the room where we were staying. "I have to sleep with you?" She turned to me with a blank expression.

"Uh, no, the bed it's for me," I said, quickly switching into my broken English to be more easily understood. "The floor, it's for you."

She laughed dramatically. "Oh, ha-ha, Melanie. You forget, I am the guest."

I sat next to her and laid back against the pillows. "Actually," I clarified, "I am the guest and the American. I expect to be treated like a queen. You can have a pillow," I said jokingly, tossing a pillow at her.

As we talked in our room, in private, I couldn't believe how differently I felt around her now. "It's okay for tonight," I said to her. "You can sleep with me. But then you have to teach me some French. So when I meet your family, I can talk to them."

We giggled as we exited the bedroom and sat at the kitchen table with Lia and Pim.

"You would like a coffee, Yola?" Lia asked her in English.

Yola nodded her head and said something back in French. Suddenly they were speaking French and Pim raised his eyebrows at me. "I think they forgot about you," he said as he patted me on the back gently.

We all fell back into English conversation and a few hours passed easily. They showed Yola around the house and the yard; I dedicated myself to making dinner. Yola and I were both their guests, and neither of us spent a single Euro while we stayed with them. European hospitality is only fully understood when you get yourself over there and find someone to know.

One night, Lia and Pim made fondue for us. We ate outside on the patio, dipping small chunks of bread and fresh bell peppers into the melted, gooey, white cheese. After cleaning up the dinner, Yola and I sat outside smoking cigarettes and talking. I was flattered to see her make such an effort to communicate with me in English. When we went to bed that night, I asked her how to say "nice to meet you" in French, so I could impress her parents. She laughed.

"Uh, no, in France we don't say this," she said dismissively.

"Well, then," I said, as I shut off the light and crawled into bed next to her. "How do you say nice to meet you in French, without saying it?"

She giggled and pulled the blanket up around her face. "Well, I can translate directly, maybe, but I think my parents will laugh at you."

"*Sil vous plais*, Yola," I said. Please, in my terrible French accent.

She said a long phrase, which sounded guttural and nasal.

"That sounds horrible. I can't say that, I think it will make them angry. I thought French was supposed to be beautiful."

"I tell you! Melanie, *this* is what I tell you! It's not a good one!"

We laid there in silence for a while and I asked her to repeat the phrase again. Then I tried it. I fell asleep that night practicing the French phrase, while Yola stifled her laughter into the thick blanket.

The next day we went to a tiny market in a nearby village and made a big dinner together. During the meal prep, Yola and I announced we were going to go to see her family the next day.

As they sat down to dinner, I ran off into the bedroom. I came back with the bottle of red wine that Gemma's family had given me as a parting gift. "I want to share this with you," I told them. "This is the best wine I've ever had. My friend's family gave it to me, and I think even the French will be impressed."

Yola rolled her eyes at me. "You forget, in France we have the best! Italy? *Hmph*."

I sat down next to her laughing. Lia smiled. "Well, we have to try it to see."

She popped the cork and distributed the bottle among four glasses, with a bit to spare. We clinked our glasses, Pim raising a toast in classic French, *chin-chin*! We all made eye contact as is custom and sipped our glasses. Yola swished it dramatically in her mouth, closed her eyes, breathed in deeply, and swallowed. Then she opened and closed her mouth.

"Hmm," she said as she set the glass gently on the table. "It's not bad for Italy wine."

We finished our meals and the neglected bit in the bottle. Then Lia asked if I wanted to call my Dad. "I have free international calls, so it's no problem."

I smiled politely. I hadn't spoken to my father in a few months, but since I was traveling, one month felt like a year. Sure, I'd sent him post cards and letters, but I didn't even honestly know if he was alive. "That would be nice, maybe. Thanks," I stood up from the table as Lia disappeared to retrieve the phone.

She showed me how to dial the country code before punching in the American number. The phone started ringing and my heart stopped beating in anticipation. Wait, what time was it back home anyway? Is he even in the house or sitting on a chair in the driveway, blasting jazz from his car stereo?

He interrupted my thoughts. "Y'hello?"

"Dad?"

"Who's this?"

"Mel!"

"Mel? Oh, wow. Where are you?"

I sniffled into the phone a bit. "Uh, I'm in France now. I'm staying with some friends from Indonesia. We just had wine and dinner and they offered their phone so I could call you."

"You sound clear. Are you sure this is Mel? It sounds like you're just right outside," he said, as he chuckled.

"Thanks. How are you, Dad?"

"Oh, you know. Things are fine. I got a new Mustang. I have a girlfriend now, you know. Rita. She likes classical music, too. She is just wonderful."

A tear rolled down my cheek as we spoke a few more minutes. He didn't ask me any more questions, but right before the phone call ended, after we said our goodbyes, he said quietly, "Love you Mel."

I ran back into the house from where I'd been perched on the porch, not wanting any distraction from listening to my Dad. The combination of the Minnesotan accent and his voice brought crazy emotions up inside me. I came back to the kitchen table where Lia, Pim, and Yola were still sitting.

"He has a new Mustang!" I exclaimed, tears rolling down my face. My body was shaking from the adrenaline. "And he said he loves me!"

Lia and Pim looked at each other, and then Lia reached out for the phone. "He doesn't usually say he loves you?"

I shook my head awkwardly, as I put the phone in Lia's hand.

Yola smiled sweetly at me and patted the chair next to her. "What else? A Mustang. It's a car, no? Expensive? I think this man, your father, it's a crazy guy."

I laughed as I wiped my cheeks with my sleeve. "Yeah. I just thought he would be dead or something. I didn't prepare myself to actually hear his voice." I leaned forward onto the table, resting my head in my hands. I peeked back out as I wiped my eyes and held a hand up in the air. "Oh, I forgot to tell you," I said, laughing to myself. "He has a girlfriend now."

"How is it, Yola," I said as I put my arm around the back of her chair, "that you and I, young and ambitious and happy and *young*, we are single? My father, angry and wrinkled with 70 years, he finds a girlfriend?"

I encouraged them to laugh with me over my father's relentless ability to defy odds. He'd already lived thirty years longer than anyone expected, shoveling in cans of beef stew from the dollar store and laughing in the face of our homemade vegan lasagna.

160

He'd take me to Burger King. I'd order French fries and he'd get a Rodeo Burger.

"And you know Mel," he'd whisper across the table, as if he was sharing a secret I was interested in learning, "at Cub I can buy ten slices of cheese, you know, Swiss cheese? For one dollar!" He pulled a plastic-wrapped, flexible, white slice out of his pocket. "If I order a cheese on my burger here it's another fifty cents!" He chuckled as he lifted the bun smothered in barbeque sauce and set his processed, pre-pocket-warmed cheese on top of the burger.

He's got it all figured out, driving around in his new Mustang and flouncing around a way-out-of-his-league girlfriend. What does she see in him anyway?

Eventually Yola and I retired to our room again, both of us muttering to ourselves in French. I was still practicing the phrase she had taught me. As I slipped under the covers, I said it one more time.

"That!" Yola exclaimed from where she was turning off the light. "Melanie, that one was perfect. The French men, wow," she laughed. "They will love your American accent!"

"Thanks, Yola," I said as I rolled over to face her. "If you come to America and speak in French, I think the American men will fall on their faces for you."

We spent a few days with Lia and Pim and eventually headed out for a day of driving to Yola's family home in Dordogne, France. We blasted music on the stereo and rolled cigarettes and talked about the differences in our societies as the sun streamed in through the open windows and the wind whipped our hair into our faces.

France

The Fire-Breather

Yola's family home was nestled in the countryside, between sparse wheat fields and horse pens, an area of mostly forested hills. She slowed the car down as we passed the edge of the forest encroaching on the narrow driveway ahead of us. The sun was beginning to set, and she parked the car. A golden retriever came up to greet me, slobbering and whining for attention as I attempted to exit the vehicle.

"Tilia—" Yola called out to her, and then yelled some frantic French, while pointing her finger sternly. Tilia sat down, wiggling, glancing between Yola and I eagerly. We grabbed our bags and walked in the side door. I reached down to pet Tilia and she whimpered for more.

We entered through the pantry, past a wooden shelf crowded with glass jars and pots and pans hanging on the wall. We passed through some door beads from the pantry into the kitchen, where her two brothers and parents awaited us. When they saw us, they burst into rapid French, kissing me on the cheeks like family.

Yola's mom, Eva, was half-Spanish and petite with fluffy brown hair, tanned skin, and a raspy voice. She had voluptuous lips, small hands, and a timid demeanor. As they all spoke, she made curious eye contact a few times.

Gilles (pronounced "Jill" like a girl's name) was Yola's father. He was bald and quite short, and although I understood nothing he said, he was the clown of the family. He made jokes about having beautiful hair, using a brush or a comb to sweep across his bare head. His nickname was "gee-loo" and he immediately teased Yola about her clothes and the amount of time it took for us to get here. Then they all turned to look at me in rapt expectation, as if waiting for me to speak French with them.

"Juh swee . . ." I said slowly, as suddenly everyone's eyes were on me. Yola looked shocked, as she bit her lip in anticipation. I continued. "Oo-roo-zuh doo voo rahn-cohn-tray." I tossed my arms out at the end of my phrase, and Yola smiled encouragingly at me. Her family looked at each other.

"Go-o-od, Melanie! Nice!" Yola said confidently, as she squeezed my arm. I narrowed my eyes at her, expecting sarcasm. Yet her smile remained.

I smiled proudly and clarified in English, "Nice to meet you!"

Then the family laughed. Eva, Yola's mom, came up to my side and put her arm around my back. "Bienvenue," she welcomed me in French.

"Puedo hablar en español," I said to Eva, letting her know I could speak in Spanish.

She looked thrilled. "Ah, Melanie! Bon," She said, as she raised her hands in the air.

"Mira, mira," Eva said to the rest of her family. Look, look. "Melanie puede hablar en Espanol." Melanie can speak in Spanish.

The rest of the family laughed at her. She was mixing up her languages, speaking Spanish to them when she should have been speaking French, and speaking French with me when she should have been speaking Spanish.

It became a common theme, Eva having some ditsy moments, her family always erupting into laughter. I made a mental note that teasing was acceptable, invited behavior in this household. Eva slapped her head in response and said, "oye," the Spanish equivalent of "oh shit." She was digging herself deeper in the hole.

Guilles came up beside Eva and kissed her on the forehead, gesturing grandly as spoke French with a sweet inflection. Yola smiled at me across the broadening scene.

Eva had thick skin. She shrugged off any teasing from the males in the family with snarky wit. She spoke to them in rapid French, laughing about how lucky she was to have an opportunity to practice her Spanish. From that moment on, she became a self-proclaimed translator for me, and explained every bit of French to me in Spanish. It would prove to be unhelpful but certainly entertaining.

Yola's two brothers were Yoris and Nils. Yoris ("Your-iss") was the oldest of the family, a too-cool-to-look-you-in-the-eyes sort of guy, attractive and aware of it. He had dark hair and steely blue eyes, he appeared to have forgotten to shave, always sporting a half-smoked cigarette.

Nils ("Kneels") was in the wonderful pubescent stage of life, scrawny and growing legs, not too cool, but too young to make meaningful eye contact. He wasn't around much during my visit, just occasionally playing the soundtrack to Amelie on the piano in the living room.

Yola was the middle child. She brought her two brothers together. Her hunched posture and deeper voice around her family hinted to me that she felt more comfortable associating with boys. Although they were speaking French and I had no idea what they were saying, it was obvious they were an easy-going family, not unlike mine back home.

The house was filled with musical instruments, wooden furniture, and a huge stereo system. Plants filled the windowsills. A fluffy black cat sat outside in an apple tree. The house was mostly made of wood. Above the kitchen was a little loft space where Yola and I would watch a French film together one night, with the roof hatch open to the starry sky. That was where I smoked my first cigarette during a movie.

Her family invited me for a beer and we sat on their patio facing the setting sun. In a trim green pasture, two horses watched us. We sat on comfortable patio furniture, the whole family clustered around a coffee table, chatting.

I learned that drinking before dinner is very typically French. It's called *aperatif* and it is where the word "appetizer" originated. Wine or beer is served with a snack before the meal, but the alcohol could be of any kind, and the snack could be nuts or crackers, cake or pate.

I had learned to drink alcohol when my friends and I wanted to get drunk and act crazy. This family treated alcohol as part of their regular lifestyle. They drank to enjoy their day, not to get wild and forget about it.

That night Eva was kind enough to make a vegetarian pasta, to accommodate my diet.

Yola told me in English, over the chorus of laughter at the table, "My mother is not so good cooking. She make the pasta one way, like worms, or tomorrow, like --" she made a crunching sound as she held an imaginary noodle and pretended to crack it in half. Eva scoffed at her and snapped something in French as she set food on the table in front of us.

Gilles had been to South America for a few months when he was in his early twenties, so he liked to practice his English.

"She say . . uhh," He stuttered as he pointed at Yola, "*She* . . no good . . cooking."

Everyone started laughing, especially Yola and I. "Merci, Eva," I thanked her in French. "C'est bon," I commented on the food. Yola smiled encouragingly.

After dinner, Eva brought out a box of red wine and a wooden platter of cheese, the *fromage*. She explained to me in very slow, deliberate Spanish, that it is typical French to have wine and cheese after the meal, to help with digestion.

Someone poured me a glass of wine from the little plastic spigot on the bottom of the box as I reached to unwrap the individually packaged cheeses. I am primarily vegan while traveling, but this was France and I knew I needed to make an exception.

I unfolded the paper around the different shaped, smelly packages. There was a firm yellow one, a soft stinky one, a crumbly white one covered in black, and one that tasted like cheddar cheese, but it was white. The family had only a few pieces, but I continued. More wine, more cheese, and fifteen minutes later I noticed that everyone else had finished.

"I think maybe," Yola began, as she washed down the cheese with a hearty slug of wine, "we need always *fromage* here, for you, Melanie."

I giggled, wiping my mouth. "Oui," I said.

After we cleaned up the meal, Yola and I poured some more wine and retired to the porch to have a cigarette together. We set our glasses on the coffee table and rolled our cigarettes in hurried silence. She lit hers and leaned back against the cushion. "You want, we go to party tonight?"

I took a drag of my cigarette as I contemplated. What does party mean in France? I shrugged my shoulders in response and laughed gently. "Of course!" I said, as I took a sip of wine. "But it's late now. When does the party start?"

She looked off into the distance. "I think maybe now. Or, after to smoke?"

I nodded into my glass of wine. We wandered into her room with our cigarettes trailing smoke behind us. Yola tossed some clothes onto her bed, trying to decide what to wear.

"What you think girl, this one?" She said as she held up a dark sweater.

"Yeah, it's a nice color," I said. I was content with my infamous green sweater. It had holes, unabashedly displaying pit hair anytime I got excited about something and threw my arms up.

"Did you want to use my clothes? You can take, as you want. It's mine, it's yours," she said, as she snuffed her cigarette into an ashtray in the windowsill and tugged the sweater over her head.

I smiled and shook my head. I perched on the edge of her bed, watching her change and look in the mirror, trace her eyes with a bit of dark liner and spritz some perfume. After a few minutes, she looked at me. "We can to go now?" She asked, her hand on the light switch, anticipating my response.

I shot up from the bed, where she had left a pile of clothes and followed her down the hallway as a wave of insecurity rushed through me. What kind of party was this? A dancing party, a house party, or just a circle of friends drinking in the forest? Why had she put on makeup? She never put on makeup. Was I underdressed? Whatever, I consoled myself. Who do I have to impress? I already have a friend.

We kissed goodbye to her family, and I held myself back from hugging them. Tilia whimpered at us as we piled into the car.

Yola yelled her name to silence her. Tilia backed up and whined some more. I closed the door slowly, careful not to catch her slimy nose, and we backed out of the gravel driveway.

We drove through the winding roads, hills on either side of the car. The sun had set and no other cars passed us. "So, who's house is it?" I asked curiously, searching for clues of what kind of group to expect.

"Oh, Maniya and her family. My friends," Yola said nonchalantly. I low-key transitioned the conversation to a discussion on local geological formations.

Almost half an hour later, we arrived along a line of cars parked haphazardly on the road. Yola parked her car past the cluster of vehicles and we walked down some steps in the dark. She reached out for my hand to lead me, and she opened the front door.

Light and techno music streamed out of the house. I saw a long table covered in food, booze, plates and glasses and packs of tobacco. The whole house seemed to be one large room, separated only by furniture. There was an aquarium in the back of the room. A disco light flickered red, green, and purple spots across the empty space in the middle of the room.

There were about twelve people sitting along the table, all different ages, each with a different style. They yelled out in acknowledgment, waving and hollering over the music in French. Yola started making her way around the table and offering her kisses in greeting. She yelled something in French to an older man at the head of the table, something including my name. A few of the people waved at me. I awkwardly tried to follow Yola and kiss all the strangers' cheeks, but the space was too tight for me to wiggle through. Is it offensive to just sit down without kissing them? I plopped down at the first empty chair I could find.

As I scanned the table, I could feel the eyes of many party guests glancing across me. I felt awkward. Yola wasn't introducing me. I didn't know what to do. I couldn't just assume anyone here spoke English, and I certainly couldn't speak French.

I had questions for everyone, like a good party guest would, but do I ask them in English? Or do I ask them in charades?

Yola approached me with a smile, interrupting my thoughts with a hand on my shoulder. "It's okay for you, Melanie?" She asked, and I nodded. "Something to drink, you would like?"

She brought me a beer. Somehow five or six or seven hours passed. During the evening, Molly, our mutual friend from Indonesia, showed up. She was cavalier with me, making her way around the table after just a quick few kisses on my cheeks.

During the night we all whirled our bodies around to some trancey, electronic music. There were people dancing in all different styles, like a robot or like a little girl running in a meadow. The creative liberties I saw inspired me to also dance however I wanted.

Yola drove home that night, or early morning. We crawled into her bed and slept. I woke up around 11 and wandered out into the living room, where Eva was making coffee and Gilles was sitting at the kitchen table. They smiled up at me in acknowledgment and asked me a couple things in French. I smiled awkwardly, shook my head, and rubbed my hair like a crazy person sleeping in the street. "I'm hungover," I told them in English, and laughed. "I'm sorry," I said, as I put my hand over my heart and focused my gaze on the floor.

Eva brought me a mug of coffee and said some sweet things in Spanish about taking it easy and relaxing today. I squinted my eyes at the light filling the room and accepted the coffee. I wandered out to the porch to sit in the cool breeze. Gilles called out to me from the kitchen table, "Too much . . . uhh, drink Melanie?" He held up his hand in imitation of a bottle.

I chuckled and stared into the grassy pasture.

I finished my coffee and went back inside to find my journal. Both Eva and Gilles went back to work. I sat on the patio by myself for a while, writing about my impressions of the French people. I liked them.

Yola crept out of her room a few hours later and stood in the doorway of the patio, wrapped up in a blanket.

"Good morning!" I said eagerly, a few hours ahead of her in the process of sobering up.

She sighed to herself as she wandered back into the kitchen and poured herself a cup of coffee. She came back to the patio hugging a steaming ceramic mug and sat on the patio couch next to me. She rolled a cigarette slowly and lit it as she leaned back into the cushions and closed her eyes. I sat next to her and reached for her tobacco.

"So," she said, as she slowly sat up a bit straighter and opened her eyes a crack. "What we do today, Mel?" She asked, puffing out a cloud of smoke and sucking it back in.

"I'm ready now. Maybe we can go for a walk? Or to see the neighbor's farm?" I said, as I compartmentalized my journal, coffee mug, and pen into a neat pile on the coffee table.

"Oh, ha-ha," she laughed dismissively. "Slowly, slowly. It's the morning. I need time for wake up. For take my cahhhh-ffee," she smiled at me, "for smoke."

I sighed loudly, pulled my journal out of the pile of my items on the table and rifled through it. I set it back down and picked up the coffee mug, destined for the kitchen to get myself some more.

Each day I stayed with Yola, I would get up hours before her. Eventually her parents became concerned that I was bored. After a few days, they decided it was time to find an activity for me. After so many morning walks in the woods with Tilia, they must have figured I needed more.

"Good . . uh . . morning, Melanie," Gilles said, standing in the middle of the kitchen with his arm out expressively. "Uh . . Yola . . Ana . . farm?" He concluded, slowly. I knew the French accent now, and my heart filled with fondness. I felt so welcome when anyone made efforts to communicate with me in English.

Gilles was speaking about Ana, a Spanish woman who had moved to the area years ago. Yola had told me about this woman, who grew and sold vegetables to her parents and other local families in the area. She had offered Ana's farm like a WWOOFing opportunity for me as she had lots of work to do. Ana was also Spanish-- so I could put my three years of high school Spanish to the test!

I thanked Gilles as Yola came out of her bedroom looking groggy, as usual. She was not a morning person, I had quickly learned. She had her thick, dark hair twisted and casually clipped together in a beautiful mess on the top of her head, and her slim figure was covered by a black shawl that she had wrapped around her body. "I'm cold," she said, as a greeting.

She invited me for a coffee and we went to the patio for a cigarette to contemplate our plans for the day.

"Today, as you want, we go to Ana farm," she said, as she sipped her coffee and wrapped the shawl tighter around her body.

"We go now, Yola?" I asked her, eagerly, slugging my coffee down.

"Slowly, slowly, you remember, Melanie?" She giggled as she smoked her cigarette and looked across the yard pensively.

A few hours later we left together. After about ten minutes of driving, we arrived at a long gravel driveway. There were three plastic greenhouses on the left and a few old stone houses in front of us. Yola parked the car next to one of the buildings and we got out.

"Ana?" Yola called out and said something in French. There was no one around, so she kept calling her name as we wandered over to a field of vegetables.

A woman in overalls, with curly black hair and glistening olive skin, peeked her head up between rows of garlic. "Bonjour, Yola!" She called back and stood up, wiping her dirty hands on the denim.

We walked over to her and kissed in greeting and they spoke in French. Yola kept looking at me and mentioning my name, so I could gather they were formulating some kind of plan. I watched Yola's face as she spoke expressively, smiling. Ana was also smiling at me, looking back and forth between the two of us. She had a gap between her two front teeth and short, curled bangs just flopping around on her forehead. I gazed across the landscape, admiring the farm. It was idyllic, as romantic as a farm in Southern France could be. I overheard "Español" and looked over at Ana, who was clapping. Yola must have told her I speak Spanish.

We had a bit of a tour, mostly in Spanish. I was too nervous to speak Spanish with Ana, so I just nodded my head and pretended I understood everything she said. Hopefully I wasn't leading her on to believe I understood more than I did. When she asked me questions, I focused on the small vocabulary I did know, like "month" and "vegetable" and "where." *Speaking* in Spanish was always easier than *understanding* it, for some reason.

Ana asked me to come the following morning and help tie up the tomato plants. Maybe if it goes well, it can be a regular thing, she said in Spanish, smiling.

Gilles could drop me off on his way to work, and Yola could pick me up. It was perfect.

Yola and I went back to her family's house and spent the afternoon lounging about. Molly called Yola's cell phone, asking if we wanted to join her family for a late lunch. We got ourselves together and hopped in the car again, headed to Molly's house.

The two of them had grown up together in this same small village with a population of around 200 people. We pulled into the driveway and walked into their wooden home. Molly was there, reaching forward eagerly to kiss our cheeks. "Bonjour, Melanie," she said with a wink, and stepped back to place her hand on her hip. "Parlez-vous français?"

I laughed out loud and shook my head back and forth. I had only been in France for a week, I told her, laughing. Eric, Molly's Dad, peeked his tan face out from the kitchen.

"Bonjour, Melanie," he said with a gentle smile that offset the dark circles around his eyes. He had been washing dishes, so he wiped his hands on a rag as he came out of the kitchen. He kissed my cheeks.

"Boo-jourh," I returned the French greeting. Eric and Molly fled gracefully back to the kitchen, beckoning us to join them. We followed and Molly offered us something to drink.

She pointed to the bottles of wine on the counter and offered water as well. Trying to remain neutral, I pointed to the pitcher of water sitting on the counter. She smiled at me and poured me a glass. Then she got out a wine glass for herself, poured white wine from a box and splashed a purple liqueur into it.

"What's that, Molly?" I asked curiously.

"Oh, it's a white wine, with some syrup liqueur from this berry," she pointed at the label, a colorful sketch of elderberries.

"Oh yeah, I know that one! Elderberry, we say in English."

She smiled at me and gestured to my glass of water. "You would like some too, Melanie? You are in France. It's a French experience, drinking all the day."

I laughed. "That would be lovely," I said, as I took a sip of water. "This has no flavor, anyway."

Yola pulled a few more wine glasses out. I guess she wanted some too.

They showed me the meal they were preparing, some sort of roast and potatoes. "The potatoes have no meat," Molly said proudly. "We make them special for you. Also, Yola says you like cheese?" She opened their tiny fridge and a plume of odor filled the air.

"Ah, sheeeet. I always forget this stinking cheese," Molly said, as she tossed a container out of the fridge onto the counter.

Yola raised her eyebrows. "Mmmh, smell good for me!" She said, and I nodded in agreement.

"This is disgusting," Molly said, rolling her eyes. "I don't know how you like the French cheese, Melanie. Even me, I am French, and I don't like the cheese."

We brought out all the food from the kitchen out to a table on the patio in the sunshine. We brought our glasses of purple-tinted wine and plates and silverware. We sat around the table, and the three of them spoke mostly in French as they dished tremendous plates of food. I happily piled potatoes and salad on my plate.

During the meal, periodic social shifts were made from gorging ourselves to sitting back in our seats and smoking cigarettes. I felt quite relaxed after my wine glass had been filled a few times. After we concluded the main course, Molly ran back into the kitchen to grab the long-awaited cheese. She came out with a flourish and tossed the Tupperware across the table and a long baguette on top of it. She started back to the kitchen and said, "Okay, enjoy, and call me after, when you finish," she joked and made us all laugh. She waved her hand in the air and sat back down, away from the cheese.

Molly ripped off a large chunk of the baguette and started munching it, while Eric emptied the table's ashtray into a plastic bag, blowing in the wind, filled with cigarette butts, tied to the patio fence.

I opened the Tupperware, excited to discover what kind of cheese *this* household had. I found a few familiar ones, and Yola snapped the *chevre* from my hand; clearly it was her favorite. It was a crumbly goat cheese, rolled into a log and covered in a layer of dark mold. You could slice pieces of it off and rub it into a large chunk of French bread. I reached for a hard cheese instead, and shaved off the outer wax layer, which I tossed into the ashtray. I sliced a large chunk off and piled it on a chunk of crusty bread.

After the meal, we leaned back into our seats and looked at each other in beautiful silence. Drunk and stuffed, nothing was left to be desired.

After I got my bearings with Yola's family and friends, I began to have a routine of my own. Most mornings I would go to Ana's farm to help. My tasks varied from tomato plant maintenance to picking garlic, arranging boxes to sell to her customers or weeding the artichoke patch. Ana and I became close, as we spoke only Spanish together and she pushed me to remember everything I knew in her language. She asked me questions about my family and insisted I respond only in Spanish. Ana would tell me to take my time formulating sentences, as we harvested lettuce together and complained about the massive quantity of zucchini that was coming in.

Some days I would wander along a small forest path in the early morning and arrive on the road near Ana's house. I have memories of fog surrounding the cattle huddled together in the nearby fields. It was gorgeous country landscape, and I felt so very lucky to have tasks and my own purpose here, while also reconnecting with my dear Yola. I helped Ana at least three times a week, and would sometimes see her off the farm, at community parties with Yola's friends.

Ana and I had such an easy time working together that she was inspired to begin regularly accepting farm volunteers like me. I helped her get her farm listed online and become part of the WWOOF organization.

Yola had a part-time job working as a waitress at a small restaurant nearby. One day while she was working, her parents, Ana, and I took a few canoes out on a murky brown river. There were beautiful rock formations on the sides of the river, ancient drawings, and caves once inhabited by people long ago. After a few hours of pleasant paddling down the river, we reached our destination. We pulled the canoes up and walked to a restaurant.

It was always tough to imagine what was happening around me without a common language. I'm sure Yola's parents had been talking about going to visit Yola while we were canoeing down the river, but I wasn't able to understand much of anything in French! So, we sat at her table and asked her for some wine. Another day, her parents invited me to a party. I was happy to be around them anytime; they made me feel like such a part of their family. We all got in the car together after dinner and drove into town where people were standing in the street outside a bar drinking beer out of glasses.

We walked into the bar and it seemed everyone we passed pulled aside Eva or Gilles. It was such a tight-knit community here. Everyone looked at me curiously, and I would often just step in without introduction, kiss their friends on the cheeks and spurt out my name, followed with a poorly pronounced "nice to meet you."

When someone would ask me something in French, however, I would freeze up. My French responses were limited to "how are you" and "I am Melanie" and "I am hungry," so I hadn't quite learned how to navigate the larger vocabulary these strangers used. Perhaps they were asking simply who I was or where I was from. Yet without subtitles in front of these faces, I was completely clueless. My default was just to say "super" with a French accent. Occasionally that was acceptable. Other times they would just stare at me blankly, waiting for me to continue an explanation. Then I would smile and find someone else to have a quick exchange with.

This evening I walked into the bar after a few awkward exchanges, rubbing my cheeks against people I thought perhaps I should know. I saw Ana standing at the bar with a tall man. She greeted me as I approached and asked me, in Spanish, what I was doing here. I explained that I was here with Eva and Gilles, and I had no idea what we were doing here.

She laughed. Then she continued in Spanish, telling me about the music that was about to begin, and she motioned to the man standing with her. "El es Gael," she said.

I smiled at him and leaned forward to rub my cheek against his. Instead, he kissed my cheeks gently, intentionally. "Guy-elle," I pronounced his name slowly. "Je suis Melanie."

"Oh, French and Spanish?" He asked in English.

I blushed. "No, no, no. Only English. I pretend sometimes."

He laughed and kept looking at me. I patted Ana on the shoulder and leaned away from them to order a beer. I held up my finger and pointed to the beer I wanted, and the bartender served me. I tossed a few coins on the counter and took the change. Tipping in France is about as uncommon as it is in Czech Republic. That is, unless you're in Paris, where they're accustomed to serving wealthy foreigners.

Grabbing my frosty glass, I waved to Ana and Gael and pushed through the cluster of people to sit near the stage, where Ana had said there would be music. We ended up staying late, and a few English speakers presented themselves.

The next day when I was at Ana's farm helping sow lettuce seeds, she told me about the guy I had met, Gael. Apparently after I had wandered away, he told Ana that he thought I was beautiful and *sympatica* as the Spanish say. He had asked if Ana could please connect us, he wanted to get to know me better. She raised her eyebrows.

"He's a gentleman," she explained. "He loves women. Especially foreign women."

I laughed and agreed, and she jotted down his number for me on a piece of paper. She winked and told me I needed to call him when I got back to Yola's house.

After a few more hours of putzing around in the rainy muck, Gilles picked me up from the farm and brought me home. Yola was still lying in bed. I peeked my head in her room and asked to borrow her phone so I could call Gael.

"Wait, you have a man now?" She said, as she pulled the covers from her face and rubbed her eyes. "A French man? Did you speak your French for him?"

"Well, no, only a little bit of Spanish," I said, as I sat next to her in bed and held out my hand. "I don't know who this guy is, but if he wants to see me, why not?" I shrugged my shoulders. "But, please, your phone?"

She rustled around near the bed, pulled her phone out and set it in my hand.

I called him and was delighted to discover he spoke better English than anyone else I'd met in France. We set a date for the next day and he offered to pick me up at Ana's farm.

"Ooh, Melanie! You have a date," Yola called out as she heard me finish the phone call.

That night we had another party somewhere with Yola's friends and their alcohol. Some of her guy friends dressed like women, putting on makeup and stuffing oranges down the bodices of brightly colored dresses. We danced with them, swirling around in circles, spinning each other. We stayed out way too late, as per usual. We all piled into a car later, drunk, and ended up at another crazy party where a crowd of people surrounded a man who was also surrounded by drums and props. Yola and her friends wandered around socializing, and I just sat down on the damp grass to watch this strange man perform.

In the darkness, I couldn't see the performer very well. Then he started lifting things up off the ground and breathing fire onto them, and tossing them in the air, catching them in his bare hands. I was mesmerized.

The next morning, I went back to Ana's and found her in the garage, washing off French black radishes with a spray hose. Gael is a gentleman, she assured me. He just wants to get to know you.

Near the end of the morning, as I was pulling weeds between the rows of green onions, I heard a car pull up. I peeked my head up from the vegetation and saw a small yellow car in front of Ana's house. It looked like the mail cars I had seen driving around in this region of France, so I went back to my work. Ten minutes later I heard Ana yelling my name, and I saw her standing with a man by the car. "Melanie!" She yelled, beckoning me over. "Venga!"

I candidly wiped my muddy hands on my pants and approached them. It was Gael. He had thin glasses on today. He smiled and asked, "ça va?" It's French for "how's it going?"

"Sah-vah," I answered, in typical response. Meaning, "I'm good." If I had the intonation of a question, then he would have had to answer, too. How are you? How are you.

Ana stood there beaming at us. I apologized to him for ignoring the car when it arrived. "I thought your car was the mailman," I said, embarrassed.

Ana and Gael started laughing. "Really? Strange," Gael said, as he smiled at me. "Do you want to come with me? We can go for a drive?" he asked politely, in his heavy accented English.

Ana was behind him and she grinned widely, shrugged her shoulders, and gestured for me to go with him. Then she turned around to get back to work. I ran to the garage to drop off Ana's gloves, and came back to where Gael was standing next to the passenger side of the yellow car. He opened the door for me as I approached.

I waved goodbye to Ana and sat in the car. We took off down the narrow country roads. The sun was shining brightly across the countryside. Gael switched the car stereo on to classical music. I giggled.

"Oh, you don't like this music?" He glanced over at me with uncertainty, as he turned the volume down.

"No, it's good!" I looked out the window awkwardly. "It just reminds me of my Dad."

Silence cascaded over us as Gael drove about five minutes. Suddenly he caught sight of a huge tree that had fallen down and was half rotten. He pulled over on the side of the road and turned off the car.

"What are you doing?" I asked him.

"It's a beautiful wood."

He got out of the car and surveyed the logs. He came back dragging a large piece, about the same size as him. I got out to help him toss it into the car.

"Wow, beautiful and strong?" He said with a wide grin as he wiped his hands together.

He started the car back up and told me he liked to use the wood to decorate his apartment. We set back off on the road. I wondered to myself who in the world I was with: a mailman with a passion for classical music and rotted wood?

We drove up a small hill, and he parked the car next to a huge field. He took off his seat belt and popped the trunk. He grabbed a blanket and asked me to come with him. I waded behind him through the tall grass. We arrived at a lookout point, where you could see the whole valley where Yola and her village were. He laid the blanket down on the grass under a lone tree in the field, and we laid down together and looked up at the beautiful blue sky.

After a few minutes of silence, he stood up. He took his shirt off, to reveal a surprisingly muscular body. He opened a small bag he'd brought with him and dumped the contents out on the blanket. Inside were little balls connected with string. He stood there, in silence, tossing the toys around in the air, twisting them in mesmerizing ways about his body. Suddenly something clicked. I had to ask.

"Were you the guy breathing fire last night?"

"Yeah, that was me," he said, as he continued twirling the objects. I'd never had someone create quite a display of whatever this was to impress me. Like a rooster courting a hen.

He put his toys back into the bag and laid down next to me. "Why did you bring me here?" I asked him.

"Well," he reached for my hand and held it gently. "I was hoping I could kiss you. Now I'm worried it's too late."

I laughed and leaned my lips into his. We laid there on the blanket, under the blue sky, next to the apple tree, hidden in the tall grass, kissing for an hour. He tried to push me for more but twirling some toys around in the air doesn't get you into my pants.

We went back to his apartment together and he made a vegan squash soup for me. He sold tea that he imported from China and practiced tai chi. His kitchen was filled with branches hanging from the ceiling and

186

logs propped up on the walls, as impromptu shelving, to display small Asian trinkets--carved wooden elephants and tiny tapestries.

We sat on cushions on the floor and ate our soup and French bread in silence. He seemed disinterested in me, perhaps after realizing I wasn't going to give him any sex. After I finished my meal, I asked if I could call Yola to pick me up. I used his phone for a minute and said quickly my date was over and could she meet me by the river in Montignac? She agreed. I handed Gael the phone back and he walked me out the door. He kissed me goodbye.

"It was nice to meet you," he said, as he held my chin sweetly for a moment.

Noting his disinterest, I nodded my head and smiled definitively. "Thank you for lunch."

I wandered away from his apartment and went to sit near the river. When Yola pulled up in front of me, she immediately started laughing. "So, Melanie," she looked me up and down casually. "You have a date?" Smiling, she motioned for me to get into the car. "It's good?"

I laughed and walked over to the passenger side. "Uh, yeah, I guess."

"Did you have sex?"

"What?" I slid in the car and strapped the seat belt across my lap. "No!"

She raised her eyebrows and started the car up. She drove through the small village roundabouts and once we were out of the city, she explained herself. "I ask because the French men, they all want the sex. You have kiss this man, Melanie? You like him? It's good guy?"

We laughed together and went back home to her family. We had some beers on the patio before dinner again and watched the sunset. Yola's family pulled out a special *foie gras* for aperitif that night, a French classic that originated from this region. The geese are force-fed so their livers are full of fat. Then they are killed and the livers are processed with seasoning and pureed into a greasy, flavorful spread.

Eva explained to me in Spanish during aperitif, about the one time when Yola went vegetarian. For one month. But, Eva explained, she wanted to eat foie gras. So, she was vegetarian, eating the livers of the geese.

"It's . . not . . vegetarian," Gilles said in deliberate English, laughing, looking at Yola.

Yola shrugged her shoulders and reached for some more condensed goose liver. "It's okay for me, Melanie, I can eat this. I'm not vegetarian now."

For dinner that night, Eva made a classic French soup, "the poor man soup" as Yola referred to it with a scowl. "My mother, she does not like the cooking, so she makes this easy, poor man soup."

Eva nodded at me enthusiastically. She ladled a large amount of the brown broth into a bowl and handed it to me before anyone else. I looked into the bowl. I couldn't see anything but broth inside.

Eva served herself and then offered the ladle to her husband. She had a silly expression on her face. "Ajo," she said to me, the Spanish word for garlic. I spooned some into my mouth and the flavor was incredible.

"Ajo y farine," she said, confirming that yes it was garlic, and then she used the French word for flour. My languages were getting all mixed up.

That night after her family went to bed, Yola and I had some more wine. Both of us preferred red, and we sat on the patio under the stars alone.

"You believe in God," she explained, "but you act like a normal person." She said she was impressed by my laid-back attitude towards religion. "You have a good example. Now I know someone who likes God and is good."

Yola didn't like organized religion, she explained, although she had never met an actual Christian before. She didn't believe in pushing beliefs onto others. We passed a few more hours, drinking wine and chatting under the moonlight.

The next morning I wasn't scheduled to help Ana, so I went out in the forest with Tilia. I saw some bright yellow mushrooms the size of a stick of deodorant. I grabbed them and headed back to the house to show Eva. Her entire face lit up.

"Girolles!" She yelled immediately in recognition. "Gilles, Nils, girolles!"

She was calling for her husband and son to come appreciate what I'd found. She googled it and muttered to herself as she adjusted her glasses on the edge of her nose, scrolling through the Google images to find the best picture. She pointed and said loudly, "Chanterelle. En Anglais, chanterelle."

Ah, that was a mushroom I had heard of! But I had never found in the forest before. It turns out Girolle is another French variety that grows in this region, a bright yellow-orange one.

Eva cleared her schedule for the rest of the day over the phone, speaking urgently.

"Venga, Melanie, a ver," she said in Spanish, and pulled my arm from where I had been looking at mushroom pictures. She grabbed a large basket and tossed me an oversized blue rain jacket. I didn't know what we were going to *do*, but her urgency inspired me.

She tugged me behind her and Tilia came running by her side as we trucked eagerly into the forest. Eva wasn't dinking around. She took me to a few of her favorite spots in the forest and we split up, walking slowly in different directions. Eva carried the basket and a long stick which she used to prop up the dead leaves from the forest floor, to look beneath them. We were officially mushroom hunting.

These mushrooms were bright yellow, but they were also rarely larger than a spool of string. We would call out to each other when we found some, as seeing one means others are hiding nearby. "Mira, mira, Melanie," she called to me asking me to come help her search an area. But we would always leave some small ones behind, to ensure not to eradicate all of them.

After a few hours of wandering, we had collected maybe thirty of the little yellow mushrooms. We set them gently on fern fronds in the bottom of the woven basket.

We came back to the house and called the family together. Yola seemed unenthused, as per usual. Nils hopped off the piano to see our harvest, then wandered back to his instrument to play that Amelie song, again. Eva chopped the chanterelles gently, without washing them, and sautéed them with butter and garlic. She sprinkled fresh parsley and salt on them. Gilles grabbed a few beers from the fridge, and we wandered out to the patio. Eva came out after us, carrying a small ceramic bowl. "Gracias a Melanie," she said proudly, patting me on the shoulder as she set the bowl in front of us.

It looked to be about a standard cup-measure's worth of cooked mushrooms. The mass of them cooked was significantly less than what we began with. Gilles saw my expression and chuckled. "You . . want . . more?" He asked, as he reached for a toothpick to stab a precious mushroom.

I smiled and looked wearily at the bowl. "It's almost nothing!"

"It's normal, Melanie," Yola consoled me. "My mother makes it simple, so we can taste. It's a special one. And we can enjoy with the beer!"

She lifted her bottle of Heineken and knocked it against mine and took a slug. Then she and I reached for a mushroom.

"Wowww," everyone gushed. We ate all the mushroom pieces within a few minutes, licking our lips and fingers and settling back into the cushions. Somehow, those three hours of adrenaline rushing at the sight of a tiny yellow fungus and having maybe four bites of bliss with this family, it all felt incredible.

I had been with Yola's family for over two weeks, much longer than I was expecting. I voiced my concern to her for potentially over-staying my welcome, and Yola laughed at me. "I say to you before you come, you stay as you like! One day, one week, one month," she said confidently. "My house, it's your house."

The next time the two of us went into town and stopped at the grocery store, I insisted on buying a large case of her family's favorite German beer, Leffe. It has a good flavor, but it isn't overly expensive. Yola warned me not to buy it. "You are a guest, Melanie, you buy nothing. My mother won't be happy with you."

When we walked back in the house with it and Eva saw, she just shook her head. She didn't look excited or appreciative. She did thank me in Spanish, but I gathered from her reaction that my contribution wasn't necessary.

Where I grew up in Minnesota, people always said "hi" on the streets or "how are you" casually, in passing. Here it wasn't so. You would just pass people. At first I found it strange. But with time, I realized how much more rewarding it is to know people. When you knew someone here, and you got them to laugh, they weren't laughing out of politeness but out of genuine amusement.

As much fun as I was having, and as welcome as I felt, I also knew I had a few more countries to visit before I returned home. I asked Yola to help me plan my departure. In the meantime, I kept up my routine of working on Ana's farm during the day and hanging out with Yola's family in the afternoon through the evening, and sometimes partying at night with Yola and her friends.

Yola got travel details together, arranging a Blablacar for me online. I told her about my experience in the Italian Alps with the chatty man.

She laughed dismissively. "You forget you are in France. No driver speaks English here."

The day before I was scheduled to leave, the carpool group cancelled on us.

"It's a symbol, Melanie," Yola said, shaking her head, and looking at the floor in defeat. "I suppose now, you must to pass more time here."

I knew she was being kind and welcoming, but I couldn't help feeling a bit restless. They wanted me to just relax all the time, and I couldn't even buy them beer. My integrity felt a bit compromised. Of course, I'd been appreciative after every meal and helped with everything I could get my hands on. But the fact of the matter was, I was their guest. I wasn't a farm volunteer here; I had become part of the family. So, I had an internal struggle with embracing that, a similar feeling to my stay in Qatar.

After a few more days, Yola made me an alternate departure plan with a French man named Martin. "And Melanie, it says here," she squinted her eyes at the computer as she translated. "Martin speaks ENG-LISH!"

I was scheduled to leave the next day. Eva and Gilles threw me a big party. Ana came, as well as some of Yola's friends from our party nights, and their parents who were friends with Yola's parents. I cooked a bunch of vegan food and Eva made a chocolate *gateau* or cake. There were about ten people sitting at the table on the patio, eating together. We got quite drunk and stayed up late, laughing and talking about all the good times we'd had together.

As I walked around the table to say goodnight, each person held me tightly and gave me some parting words of acknowledgment. "You are the moon in the sky," or "you have a beautiful heart," or Eva, in Spanish, "you are welcome back anytime."

The next morning Yola drove me into the nearby city of Montignac to meet up with my driver, Martin. Yola kissed me and I hugged her tightly, I couldn't resist. A tear slid from my face as I hopped in the passenger seat and Martin greeted me in English. I watched Yola walk away and wiped my face.

"Melanie, you are okay?" Martin asked, as he started up the engine.

"Yes, sorry, it's just . . Yola is a very special person." I stared out the window as she got into her car and glanced at me. She smiled as she quickly wiped her face. I waved once more as we sped off.

Martin brought me to Toulouse, and in the car, we spoke about his desire to travel the world, as I had been doing for the past year. When we got to Toulouse, I scribbled down the name of my blog on a little piece of paper.

He took the note, folded it up, and held it between his hands in a prayer pose.

"Thanks for the ride," I said as I got out of the car. "I appreciate your English!"

"Thank you! It was good practice for me." He leaned over the passenger seat as I stood up and tossed my backpack over my shoulder. "Safe travels to you, Melanie," he said with a delicate smile.

Ireland

Gentle, but Firm

I'd arrived in Dublin, and what a cultural shift! Suddenly I was surrounded by English, everywhere, yet it was different than any English I'd ever heard. I passed a small red pub with a door hanging open, filling the street with folk music. I caught sight of a few men playing instruments and knew I had to be there. I went to the hostel around the corner and returned to the pub. I bought a beer and plopped in front of the band. Someone brought me to the back of the room where a man with white hair and leathery skin was tapping a set of spoons on his knee.

My impromptu guide pushed me into the bench next to the old man, yelling over the loud music, "I want you to learn as much as you can while you're in Ireland!"

I sat next to the old man as he peered at me through a half-shut eye. The side of his mouth curled up in an ever-so-slight grin. He stopped tapping them and reached for my right hand. He placed the spoons in them just so and showed me how to tap them on my knee. I tried, but the spoons kept slipping off each other.

He took them back into his right hand and tapped them together on his knee.

"You see? Gentle, but firm," he said, and his face lit up with a whimsical smile. "Like a good Irishman."

I missed the reference. He handed them back to me and I tried again. This time, I had it. A group of more old men surrounded me and cheered me on. Someone bought me another beer and we danced together until late into the evening. They kept trying to buy me beers, but things started to get a bit uncomfortable as they danced around me. I excused myself promptly.

The next morning, I took a few different buses out of Dublin to the Wicklow area, where my farmer had scheduled to pick me up. I sat alone there for over an hour, journaling to catch my future self up on my recent activities. A small, dusty car appeared and I closed my writing to greet a stout woman with curly blonde hair. She exited the car and stuck out her hand. It was smudged with dirt. "I'm Suzi," she said, with a gruff Irish accent. She had a pointy nose on her wide face, and thin wire glasses.

"I'm Melanie," I responded, and felt my lips tilt into an easy smile. "Thanks a lot for picking me up."

She laughed, as she picked up my backpack. "Yeah, usually volunteers just hitch their way in, but not always. No problem."

We walked together back to her car, where it smelled like spices and dogs and raw earth. I felt right at home.

Suzi pulled up to the farm and parked in a small gravel lot next to a huge structure made of what looked like adobe. She took her seatbelt off. "That's the cobb house," she said. "It's a slow process but a steady venture. We work on it every once in a while. Hopin' soon it'll be a nice community space for dances and such."

Vegetation abounded on the property and I saw many trees brimming with fruit. I could hear chickens and a few dogs ran up to greet us. "That's Pip," she said, pointing at the slightly bigger of the two small dogs. He had black hair with layers of brown and gold. I felt an instant connection, almost as if he was a small human. He jumped up on my legs excitedly. "He's the boss around here," she said, chuckling. "If he likes you, he'll let you take charge sometimes."

Suzi walked me past a picnic table as Pip followed closely behind, into a small wooden shack with a sink and a cooler. There was a large wooden dresser; plants hung from the ceiling. Dirty dishes were stacked on the counter. A young woman approached us to introduce herself. "Hey, I'm Steph," she said, barely looking my way, as she reached her hand out. An American, I could tell by her accent.

"Hey, I'm Melanie!" I tucked some stray hairs behind my ear. I needed to cut it soon. "Where are you from?" I asked.

"You don't really sound American. But yeah, Clarke and I live in Maine," she said slowly, as she looked me up and down. She was wearing simple clothes and her thick, straw-colored hair was in a large twist on the top of her head.

Just then, a young man appeared to greet me. "Hey, I'm Clarke," he said, as he reached a skeletal hand out to shake mine. "And I'm Dutch," he said, as he chuckled softly. Tall and slim, definitely the Dutch type. His neutral clothes seemed 8 sizes too big. He had straight, clean brown hair and a goatee.

Clarke seemed genuinely interested to meet me, his smile wide and his body language open. Steph, in contrast, seemed less than enthused. She occupied herself with some task in the kitchen, and Clarke offered to show me where I could sleep.

I obliged and followed him down a narrow path, past a large greenhouse. As we walked, I saw a huge garden encompassed by a wall of small trees. Everything seemed to be made out of wood. I also spotted a circular white tent up the hill a few hundred feet. As Clarke turned around to check on me, he caught me glancing over there.

"Oh, that's a yurt. Ever seen one of those things?" We kept walking as I told him I hadn't. He turned his head over his shoulder to explain more. "They were used in Mongolia. Suzi and Mike went to Mongolia and fell in love with the concept of a big tent like that. So, they made their own! Steph and I sleep there."

After a few more feet we arrived into a small, grassy space with designated open patches, like a small campground. "You can set your tent up anywhere here, wherever you like." He looked around the space and then up at me, smiling. He motioned to one tent up the hill. "It's only the three of us and Theo right now, so take your pick!"

I set my backpack down and bit my lip. "Uh, I don't actually have a tent."

"Really?" He thought for a second. "I don't think that's a problem, I'm sure Suzi's got a spare you could use."

We walked back together to a large outdoor shelving unit and found a spare tent. Clarke went back to his day, disappearing into the greenhouse, and left me alone to set it up. I took all the items out of my backpack and I arranged them neatly along the wall inside my tent, careful to leave myself enough space to crawl in without disturbing my organization.

Then I joined Clarke in the greenhouse, where another guy was helping him water some plants. I called out a greeting to him, and he introduced himself as Theo.

"Where you are from?" He asked, with an interesting accent. He was Asian with dark skin, and he'd grown up in Taiwan. We conversed a bit, as I offered to help them with their tasks. I was handed a clipper and Clarke asked me to trim some of the tomato branches. I knew how to do that; Ana had shown me in France.

We passed a few hours doing garden work in the greenhouse until it was almost time for dinner. Steph called to Clarke and asked for his help with dinner. I stayed with Theo to learn more about him. He had spent the last two years traveling everywhere, and although he insisted he loved plants, this was his first experience volunteering on a farm. He seemed well-loved here. He had a good sense of humor and a can-do attitude.

Dinner the first night was just the four of us, and Steph explained to me that Suzi and her husband and three sons lived in a house just down the hill. We had curry with rice and flatbread. They explained that we alternate cooking meals, and that there was no fridge. I learned that Clarke was a vegan and a runner, Stephanie loves cheese, and the ashtray was for Theo and his Marlboros.

After we cleaned up our dinner, they invited me up the hill to watch the sunset.

Pip ran up ahead, sticking his face into the low bushes, like he was eating something. I pointed it out to Clarke and he laughed.

"Oh, he loves the wild blueberries. In Ireland, they call them 'bilberries.'" Pip turned around, having heard the reference, and smiled at me with his now blue-stained lips. He ran ahead of us again.

We made it up to the top of the hill after a ten-minute jog up boulders surrounded by bilberry bushes. We were there just in time. The last inch of sunlight streamed from beneath the heavy purple clouds trying to push it down for the evening. The scene spreading out before of us was a mixture of grassy knolls decorated with black and white cows and clumps of forest. Everything was lush and green. I picked a bilberry from a bush and felt it *pop* in my mouth. I could see why Pip liked them.

We went to bed early that night, and I thanked them all for their hospitality. I slept well, with a full stomach and some satisfaction with my choice of farm assignments. This seemed like the perfect place.

I had only scheduled a week here. During my stay I got to know the other volunteers and was able to help with cobb building. I learned how to cook much more resourcefully, as there was no fridge to store leftovers. I learned to trellis melons so they would hang from the vines rather than lie on the ground, about companion-planting and how to properly care for baby plants.

In the circular garden, potatoes were developing some form of disease visible on their leaves. When I pointed it out to Suzi, and she nodded her head in disappointment. "Honestly, no one's been able to grow potatoes successfully here since the Potato Blight."

Suzi had cultivated this farm to educate young people about a more sustainable lifestyle. We not only provided many of our own vegetables through permaculture gardening techniques, we were able to learn about "humanure" (composting human poop), cooking, building, and a more primitive lifestyle.

They wanted to do something big to impact the future, Suzi and her husband Mike. They had become frustrated with "the system" and had lapsed into depression before realizing the best thing they could do would be invest in the future. They wanted to steer young people away from convention and technology and get them involved in practical lifestyles.

Once I ran out of shampoo and asked Suzi for some. She told me to use dish soap.

I stared at her blankly. She chuckled. "It's the same! Just think about it. It cleans dishes. Why couldn't it clean your hair?"

One day, a few more volunteers showed up. Clarke and Steph were leaving the next day, so Suzi had put me in charge of filling them in. Their names were Scott and Becca. The sun was out the day they arrived, and they laughed about it. "I didn't expect sun in Ireland," Scott said, with a low chuckle. "We didn't even bring sunscreen!"

Scott was tall and scrawny, with gorgeous glossy hair that fell right at his shoulders. It looked like a golden-brown curtain, reflecting sunlight. He had a wide smile and, as I wrote in my journal, he reminded me of Calvin from the comic strip "Calvin and Hobbs."

Becca was also tall and thin. They'd been in a relationship for almost nine years and were in their mid-twenties. Becca was pale with freckles everywhere and long hair. She had a familiar accent; I asked if she was from the Midwest. She responded, "Oh gosh, yeah."

I took them on a little tour, other volunteers calling out their greeting. I showed them where they could set their tent, and Pip sat by my side as I explained the lifestyle here. "So, I'll let you get settled and then I can show you some plants and what we do around here."

They nodded enthusiastically. Scott said, with his velvet voice, "Sure, sounds great." He made eye contact as he stooped down to pick up his camera. "Thanks!"

Later, I showed them the plants, pointing to the herbs casually. "There's oregano, mint, basil . . ."

Scott stopped where he was and knelt to touch them. "Wait, seriously? That's basil?"

I laughed and was enamored by his curiosity. Then he told me that neither he nor Becca had any farm experience. Perhaps he'd never had any experience with plants, either. I walked back to where he was standing and picked up a mint leaf. "Just roll it in your fingers like this. It smells amazing."

He pointed at the mint plant. "Which one? This?"

I nodded my head patiently. He rolled one of the leaves between his fingers and inhaled. "Oh, my god!" He said, as his eyes rolled back into his head. He opened them slowly after a few moments and a wide grin peeled across his face. "Dude. Becca, you gotta smell this." He put it in front of Becca's nose and demanded she inhale.

"Yeah," she played it cool. "It smells good, Scott."

I smiled proudly. As we continued walking, Scott told me that he was a teacher in Milwaukee. I made a mental note; it seemed teachers liked to learn, too.

Scott had the same reaction when he saw snap peas growing on the trellis, when he watched us make homemade pasta, and when we worked together on constructing the cobb house. Judging by his enthusiastic response to the stimuli around him in this farming environment, you'd think he had no experience in anything. He and I became close very quickly. His earnest reactions inspired trust.

"Wow, you've been to how many countries? What the fuck, dude," he'd said to me, astonished. "By yourself? For how long?" He made me feel recognized and valuable. As if I'd done something cool with my life.

One day I came out of the greenhouse as Scott was sitting at the picnic table, taking a break. He had huge, gaudy headphones on and his eyes were closed. His lips were held firmly together as he bobbed his head from side to side. I sat across from him and watched his face for a moment and started laughing. He opened his eyes slowly.

"Drake is fuckin' *hilarious*, man." He took the headphones off and set them on the table. He laughed harder, held his stomach and tried to catch his breath. "He takes himself so seriously. It's just. Ridiculous. You have to listen to this."

He put the headphones over my ears. I mimicked his face as I listened to the rapper and opened my eyes. Now *he* was laughing at *me*.

Another couple arrived on the farm, a woman in her early thirties who had managed a vegetable CSA farm for ten years and her partner had a small business that specialized in meat production. She had jet-black hair and didn't smile very often; he was a bit shorter than her and held his body so strangely that you felt uncomfortable just looking at him. They had taken a break from their farm in Massachusetts to evaluate their future. She wanted to quit.

"I just hate having to sell vegetables. Like, why should it be hard?" She rolled her eyes. "I hate working for nothing."

Her second day on the farm, she spent the whole afternoon organizing the shed.

"Why do you like organizing?" I asked her.

"I like when I can work hard and actually see success," she said, as she shoved a huge purple bin to the side of the shed. "I hated managing employees. It seems like it makes sense, everyone getting together and helping grow food. It just doesn't. People suck, customers suck and aren't willing to offer as much support as you need."

I laughed, attempting to commiserate. "Yeah, my sister has a farm and she's expressed similar frustrations. I guess I just have to see for myself, though." I smiled awkwardly, trying to stay positive. "I can't wait to have my own farm."

She paused her work for a second to look at me. "It's not even support I needed! I was growing vegetables for *food*. People need to eat. It's not rocket science to pay money for good food. The most frustrating thing is that we just don't value food as much as we should. People don't clean their plates because they don't have to." Her voice trailed off as she disappeared back into the mass of things she was organizing. She came back and reached for my hand. She looked meaningfully into my eyes.

"I know I sound angry. I don't mean to scare you away from your dream. But the sooner you learn that people suck, the easier it will be for you. I don't want you to get into organic vegetable farming and wish someone had warned you about how your customers will act. It's hard work. I don't want to do it anymore." She sighed. "Anyway, can you help me for a sec?"

I tried to shrug off what she'd said that night. I can do it, I assured myself. I love people, I love vegetables, what could possibly go wrong? This farm was fun and we got a lot of stuff done. However, as it wasn't a business, I noted that there was no stress on our efforts to make money or to be successful. All we had to do was grow vegetables to feed ourselves, and practice living a more practical, sustainable lifestyle.

Then one day I needed to find Suzi to ask her something. I walked down the hill and approached a normal house. I peeked around the property, no clothesline in sight, a neatly trimmed lawn. In fact, this looked like suburban Minnesota! I knocked on a normal front door and saw a normal mailbox.

They were teaching us how to live off the land, but they had a washing machine and a dishwasher. They had a fridge and a toilet. Why did they care about cultivating a more mindful lifestyle in young people, but not in their own lives? I was confused.

Is a more primitive lifestyle just an option? I suppose it is in today's world. We can choose the road less-traveled or take the highway like everyone else. The highway is easier, cleaner, and more people are there. But the road less-traveled is the one people used to use, before they had another option.

One night we went down to the local watering hole in Wicklow. Scott, Becca, and I walked together as Scott disclosed a long story about his teaching career, becoming almost famous on a televised music competition TV show, and having issues with his voice. He was a good singer, he told me, and he really enjoyed teaching high school kids. But for some reason, within the last few years, his throat just hurt when he used his voice too much. He went to see doctors and specialists, he was offered many solutions, but nothing worked.

Becca was in the bathroom or talking to someone up at the bar. I shared my Wart Story with him. I told him about the Dutch man I met in Indonesia, Pim, who had taught me that my warts were a manifestation of my insecurities.

"Maybe you're just not using your voice the right way," I said to him, as I picked up my beer to take another slug. He stared into my face, lost in thought. Becca sat back down and we resumed our regular conversation, about Irish people and beer and our lives back home.

My last night on the farm I made a huge dinner for everyone. Scott and Becca had been into town and bought cookies and crackers to celebrate my last night. We had beers and talked about our futures and what we wanted to do with them. I spoke about anticipation of returning home, scared that none of my friends would care about my journey.

The woman from Massachusetts piped in. "Melanie, you have to share your story with your friends. Even if they don't ask." She looked across the simmering flames into my eyes. "If you don't share it, you'll resent yourself for holding it in. If it's important to you that your friends are interested, you need to cultivate their interest. Find a way to make your travels and your experiences relatable to them."

I smiled as I glanced down into the embers. Words of praise and acknowledgment were uttered around the campfire from my new friends. They told me I was so mature, so developed, so independent for journeying alone.

"You are the reason that your travel went well," Scott said. "Don't you forget that."

Part 2

"If you don't know where you are going, any road will get you there."

—Lewis Carroll

Colombia

¡No Me Toques!

I'd always wanted to go to South America. I wrote a report on rainforests when I was in 8th grade. I loved to stare at the vibrant green jungle photographs and picture myself there, in khaki pants and rain boots, exploring with savvy jungle inhabitants. And even with the travelling I'd already done, I was never able to cross that dream off my to-do list.

After a few months back in the US, counseling kids at a Bible camp and working at the state fairs selling fried foods, the weather began to change. It started snowing one day in early November in Shakopee, and I realized it was time to disappear again.

I found a flight from Minneapolis to Cartagena, Colombia for $190. I brought my backpack on my flight as a carry-on, as per usual, and was surrounded by passengers speaking in Spanish. I was entranced.

I needed practice with my second language and wanted to learn coffee and chocolate production. That was the extent of my goal. I had $3,000 saved, but I didn't think I'd have to spend it all. In a tattered, five-cent, garage-sale guidebook, I learned that hostels in most of South America were under $5 a night.

My WWOOF travels had led to now-predictable experiences—I knew what animals were on the farm, what languages were spoken, and a general idea of where it was located. This time, I wanted to explore as much of a continent as possible with NO itinerary.

I arrived in the airport in Cartagena, made my way through security, and watched people catch taxis outside with intention and places to be. I had neither. I smoked a cigarette as I pondered my plan to make a plan. The sun was bright, and the brilliant blue of the ocean was just barely visible beyond the impressive concrete border surrounding the city.

I crushed my cigarette and put it in the trash bin, deciding to go for a walk. My backpack and I navigated across a few wide streets of cars going quickly, and a taxi stopped for me. The driver smiled pleasantly as he rolled down the window to ask if I needed a hotel. I laughed, nodded my head, and hopped in the backseat. He dropped me off in the tourist area for what seemed like a fair price (just a few dollars) and I walked down alleys with green weeds growing between the stones that made up the road. A small, faded sign was hanging outside of a metal gate. Written in English, it said something-something "Hostel."

I could see an inviting terrace with potted plants inside. I knocked on a thick wooden door and someone invited me in. The chalkboard behind the desk was filled with English writing and the man who offered me a room sounded American. He pointed me in the direction of my room, and I walked past a gaggle of other travelers.

I set my backpack down on the floor near the bunk. A few young guys came in and greeted me casually. I talked to them a bit, grabbed my journal, and bought a beer at the reception desk. I wrote in a hammock as the sun began to go down. A few people approached me, along with one of the guys I'd talked to in my room.

"Hey, we're going out to dinner if you want to come," he said, *also* sounding American.

"Cool, thanks." I said, as I closed the journal quickly and sat up. "I guess I'm hungry."

I tied a sweater around my hips and closed the gate behind me. I joined the group of twenty-somethings in the dark city streets. As we walked, a girl caught my stride. She had frizzy brown hair and spoke to me in Spanish, asking what I was doing here and who I am. "I'm just looking to practice Spanish and help on some farms," I told her.

She switched to English and complimented me on my accent, "but your vocabulary needs some work," she said, slapping my arm in jest.

We went to a restaurant and ordered a variety of foods. I felt honored to be included in this group of travelers, but they were loud and seemed ungrateful to the people in this tiny restaurant, who had agreed to accommodate us. As we paid our tabs, the group discussed tipping.

"I don't think we have to," the guy from my room said. "It's not like the *local* people tip."

"Yeah, it's whatever," Frizzy Girl said. "Let's save our money for cocktails. Who's in?"

I declined and went back to my room to get my bearings and some sleep.

I stayed in that hostel for two nights and explored the city by day. I bought a fresh juice at a tiny stand painted with colorful fruits. A man nodded enthusiastically as he tossed carrots, pineapple, ginger, apples, grapes, and oranges in a loud machine. He handed me the juice and I gave him the equivalent of a dollar.

Everywhere I wandered there were festivals in the streets. I couldn't figure out why people were celebrating. The costumes were all various colors and the decorations seemed to match all sorts of different themes. Then some drunk stranger in slurred Spanish explained they were celebrating Mary, the Mother of Jesus.

People were tossing buckets of water out the windows and spraying foam in each other's faces. There were marching bands led by trumpets and costumed men. Young children danced around me, slinging flowers and blowing up balloons. I broke away from the crowds and walked through the rustic areas of the city. I saw iguanas perched on the walls and trees bursting with oddly-shaped fruits along the ditches.

Out of nowhere, a young kid jumped in front of me and sprayed foam in my face. I started laughing, finally feeling like I was in on the cultural jesting. I removed the glasses and used my shirt to get all the residue off when I felt movement in my pocket. Someone was taking my camera out! Before I had a chance to put the glasses back on, the two boys disappeared. I glanced around my person, feeling totally violated. I felt my pocket and the camera was still there. It must have been too shitty to steal.

It had been a gift from the only high school boyfriend I ever had. It was a little scratched up, sure, but it wasn't worthy of being stolen? Even these kids in ratty clothes didn't want it? I'd never been pick-pocketed before, and even though nothing was stolen from me, I understood the feeling of being tricked by malicious strangers.

A bit disoriented, but still confident, I explored outside of the city. I saw a beautiful pyramid-like structure on the outskirts of the city, but it required an expensive entry fee. I walked past the structure and down a gravel road where perhaps I could explore a jungle.

Three young boys came running up to me covered in red mud, holding long sticks. They surrounded me, beating the sticks on their hands and inching toward me, making annoying noises and trying to taunt me. I assumed they wanted money so they wouldn't cover me in mud.

I took a deep breath and straightened my posture. I looked the most confident kid in the eye, the one in the middle who had the sassiest grin on his face.

"NO." I yelled into that grin. I clenched my fists. I was not about to be harassed again by kids. "No me toques!" Don't touch me!

The small warriors froze for a few seconds. Then they laughed, rolling their heads back and skipping away from me. I kept walking and overheard them heckling someone else behind me. I felt proud I'd stood up to them. Both experiences in such a short window of time caught me completely off guard. I didn't want to go explore some jungle anymore, I just wanted to go somewhere to be sure I wouldn't be bothered.

I walked back to the pyramid structure and paid the few dollars to get in. It was so very ancient, with narrow tunnels leading to places hidden under stairways, tiny windows with various views of the city. There weren't many other people within the walls of this castle.

After a day of solo adventuring, I was feeling quite lonely. I checked my email in the hostel later that night, and my farmer sister, Khaiti, had reached out, wanting to know if I'd gotten to Colombia safely. I wrote about my day alone and concluded, "it's not what I was expecting. I haven't met anyone yet. Should I come home for Christmas and forget about this? Was coming here a mistake?" Having no itinerary was feeling quite aimless already.

I had dinner by myself and planned to go to a different city to see what options were there. The next morning, I found a bus departing further east along the northern coast of Colombia. I gathered my things and walked to a building that a local had directed me to. I was an hour early, so I walked across the street to sit on the beach. My lack of direction was beginning to rub me the wrong way. I wasn't here to have a vacation, spend money in the city and sleep in a clean bed. I wanted a rustic experience and things weren't panning out that way.

As I journaled my frustrations, a woman with dark skin, curly hair, and tattered clothes approached me. She was singing to herself and carrying a bucket of water and a rag. She sat next to me in the white sand and asked me about myself. As I spoke back to her in Spanish, she moved behind me and set the bucket next to her, nodding.

She wiped the wet cloth across the skin of my back that wasn't covered by my tank top and started massaging me. I stopped speaking, mesmerized by her touch, until I snapped out of the spell and stood up. I started yelling at her.

What are you doing, who are you? "No me toques!" I concluded, confidently. She stood up and held out her hand, asking for money.

I laughed. Then I grabbed my backpack and walked away. I looked back from a safe distance and saw her approach another person sitting on the beach. Was that her job? Giving back massages for money? I didn't want a massage from a stranger, and I was on a budget.

Riding a small bus to another city, I gazed out the window, enchanted by the crystal-blue ocean. We were dropped off and I found another gated hostel to sleep in, with a pool surrounded by lounge chairs and a bar with cheap drinks. Many travelers were in the pool, splashing around in the water and blasting music, wearing aviator sunglasses and sipping cocktails. I had a Cuba Libre and met a Canadian couple; we had dinner together. Later, a guy approached me and asked if I thought he could send himself cocaine in the mail. "It's so cheap here," he said in a drunken slur. "And it's so amazing. Do you think it would be sniffed out by drug dogs?"

I laughed and said of course not. It was a great idea. I could feel myself exhausted by people. The locals I'd met so far had seemed eager to exploit me, and the travelers I'd met seemed so comfortable with not engaging in the culture. Yes, send yourself cocaine. Great idea.

I got out of that place the next day, standing on the street until a little van pulled up in front of me, the driver pointing up the mountain. I hopped in the bed of the trunk, across from a woman wearing a smudged white dress and propping a huge basket of vegetables on her lap. She smiled at me. I smiled back. The truck bumped along the path for half an hour, and suddenly the road was engulfed by a thick jungle canopy above us. Adrenaline filled my blood.

I found myself in a lovely hotel called El Mirador. The price was the same as in the city, but it was surrounded by dense vegetation, wildlife, and an incredible view of the ocean. The owner of the hotel was a local with a friendly attitude and lots of advice about exploring the surroundings. I told him I wanted to find a coffee farm to work at and he told me about a coffee plantation an hour's walk away. They gave tours and might need some help.

"Do they take volunteers?" I asked in Spanish.

He shrugged and said it was worth a try.

I headed off down a narrow path, entranced by exotic bugs and brightly-colored birds. I saw a hummingbird that was dark blue with a beak that looked to be nearly a foot long. I saw orchids in their natural habitat, hanging from large limbs and taking in the tree's nutrients; they were parasitic plants, I'd heard. Past dense bamboo clusters, I saw small bushes with red berries on them. Was that a coffee tree?

I approached the plantation and waited until a group of people arrived. We were given a tour for about $5. It was an amazing operation to see firsthand. After the tour and the coffee tasting, I approached the young girl who handed me a cup of the steaming brew. In Spanish, I asked if I could help here. I wanted to work for free for a place to sleep.

She smiled politely and declined. No, she said. They weren't accepting volunteers.

Walking back to my hotel, I still felt displaced. I was a young, fit girl with a passion for agriculture, people, and Spanish. Why didn't they want my help?

That morning, the owner of the Mirador served me *arepas* (thick cornmeal pancakes)*, queso fresco (*fresh cheese), fruit, and a cup of hot coffee. His coffee tasted better anyway. I met a few young travelers that night in the hotel who encouraged me not to give up. They were an American guy and two Russian girls. Over mojitos concocted by the hotel owner, we lounged in hammocks, smoked Marlboro Reds and complained lightheartedly about our bulbous legs covered with mosquito bites.

The next day, a young woman and teenage boy arrived at the hotel. They spoke Spanish in a regional Colombian accent (using a *j* sound instead of a *y* sound) and seemed to know the area. We had dinner together and I learned that she, Adriana, was traveling with her son, Santi. She was in her early thirties and wanted Santi to explore the world more, to get him away from technology and video games. She laughed and slapped him on the shoulder affectionately.

He had headphones on. He rolled his eyes at her, shaking his head so that his long, dark hair covered his eyes once again.

The next day she invited me to come traveling with them. What else was I doing? I graciously accepted. Before our scheduled departure, we went for a long morning hike. We discovered a waterfall nestled deep in the jungle. Water cascaded over gigantic, smooth black boulders and the vibrant vegetation along the edges of the water. Vines dangled down from the jungle canopy.

Adriana and I looked at each other for a second, mesmerized by the beauty before us. A smile crept across her face. Just then, we both ripped off our clothes and dove into the water. We swam around in our underwear, under the rushing, clear water. Santi sat on a boulder staring off into the distance.

We made our way back to the hotel and collected our belongings. We caught a small *colectivo* (or shared taxi) down the mountain, and from there we caught a long bus to Bogota, where her family lived.

When we finally arrived, we tossed our things in her house. Adriana asked if I would like to go out dancing? We hopped on a grungy bus.

"Arepas, you like?" Adriana asked me in English. She sat across from me, perched on the edge of the plastic, blue bus seat. She gripped the pole just firmly enough for stability, but casually enough to prove she knew this city.

"Yes! I had some in the hotel." I smiled. "They are so good."

She laughed and looked out the window. The lights from the street illuminated her easy smile. "You need to try here, in Bogota. It's much better here."

We got off the bus and headed toward a smoky street corner. Adriana hopped in line and beckoned for me to join her. I peeked around the people in line ahead and saw a short man slicing and grilling foot-in-diameter yellow pancakes. He worked alone at assembling them, slicing them in half, filling the half-moons with a wide circle of what-looked-like white cheese, tossing them on the grate over a charcoal grill. Once they had beautiful grill marks, he slathered them with salted butter and set them in paper napkins to hand them to the hungry people.

After what felt like hours of waiting in line, but was probably ten minutes, Adriana gave the man a few coins and he handed us each a steaming pancake. It was hot, gooey cheese and the corn pancake had a mashed-potato-like texture. It was one of the best food experiences I've ever had in my life. I licked my fingers clean and joked with Adriana about my desire to eat the greasy napkin.

We met up with a few of her friends at a tiny bar. They were a graffiti artist, a dancer, and some young guy who loved women. We stayed out late, Adriana's friends were sniffing cocaine on the tables in a club and dancing the night away. I smoked weed and that helped me dance. I fell asleep in the street at 5 AM and somehow woke up back at the house.

Adriana invited me to come stay at the hotel where she worked in San Agustin. She and Santi lived there with her boyfriend, Cesar. "It's near to jungle," she said, in her heavily accented English. I agreed and took many more buses with her and Santi to come to the small city.

She became my lifeline for a few more days as I figured out a plan. I used Workaway to find a coffee farm in the area. I was frustrated by all this vacationing. Thankfully there was one here, in San Agustin. The farm was owned by a man named Edimer. I collected my things and said goodbye to Adriana and Santi and thanked them for allowing me to be a part of their vacation.

Adriana's boyfriend, Cesar, took me by motorbike to find the farm. First, we went through the village and asked all the people if they knew Edimer. It took us a few hours to be pointed in the correct direction, and I held tightly onto his back as we made our way up the mountain. The narrow dirt roads were steep and made me nervous. I distracted myself by speaking Spanish with Cesar. He taught me how to say, "it's more beautiful than I had expected," in Spanish. *Es más bonita de lo que pensaba.*

We stopped at a tiny shack located between huge coffee plantations. Cesar stopped driving and called out to the house. We could see no one.

224

An old woman appeared. She was short and covered in clothing, with long hair and dangly, wrinkled skin. Cesar asked if she knew where Edimer's coffee farm was. She nodded her head gently as she looked me up and down. "Aquí," she said. Here. I smiled at her and got off the motorbike, hugged my friend Cesar and thanked him. The old woman took me into the house and introduced herself as Celfa.

She showed me where to put my things and brought me into the kitchen with her where she was making dinner.

Yes, this was weird for me too. All I had was Edimer's email telling me I could come. There was no specification on *when* I was coming, *where* he lived, or *who* he was. All I knew was that he had a coffee farm and wanted help.

There was one bathroom (cold showers only) and many people who lived there. Edimer and a few other siblings had taken over the coffee plantation from his father who had died. The old woman I had first met, Celfa, was their mother. They treated me like family, and I ended up staying a few weeks. I didn't get to help much with the coffee harvesting, although each day I attempted to follow the men out into the jungle. Celfa would stop me and point to the kitchen. "Enjoy," she would say, in gentle Spanish. I was stuck inside helping cook the Colombian meals, mostly arepas and soup. She had an open fireplace bordered by turquoise and beige tiles, at waist height, where we would set the griddle to cook the white corn arepas.

225

The first few meals were awkward. Like everybody else, she served me a bowl of soup. But this bowl of soup had pork in it, as well as chunks of *platano* (or green banana), onions, and pasta in a yellow broth.

Apologizing, I reminded her, "Soy vegetariana."

Looking upset, she took the bowl of soup back into the kitchen, and I sat back down. I heard a sloshing noise. She came back to the table with the same bowl of soup and a few more arepas. This time the side of the bowl was wet. I gathered she had just spooned out the chunks of meat. I smiled pleasantly, trying to disguise my internal struggle. Do I eat this? When Celfa retreated into the kitchen, I poured it into the now-empty bowl of the man next to me, with a wink.

The next meal we had, I sat next to her daughter, Merly. We started speaking about her life and what she was doing with it when Celfa served the meal. She didn't place a bowl of soup in front of me, but a plate of arepas and some fried sausages. I looked down at the plate sadly. I pointed to the sausages when Celfa turned away and whispered to Merly, "Carne, no?" Is it meat?

She looked at them and giggled. She furrowed her brow. "No, no, Melanie. Son *salchichas*!" That was the name given to fried sausages. "No es carne."

My Spanish education had led me to believe *carne* was the word for meat in general, but she was telling me that sausage wasn't meat? I laughed casually at my misunderstanding and slid the sausages onto her arepas. She shrugged her shoulders and continued eating.

The following meal, Celfa placed a bowl of soup in front of me. I saw large chunks swimming in the yellow broth. Oh shit, I thought to myself. I didn't want to be a jerk to this poor woman again. But I really didn't want to eat meat. I carried the bowl of soup back into the kitchen, where she was standing at the open fire, ladling more bowls for the rest of the hungry group. She turned around when I called her name and I handed the soup back to her.

She took the soup and spooned through it for me to watch. Then she looked up at me blankly. "No," she said, definitively. "No es carne. Es vegetariana."

My body tensed as I rubbed my eyes in frustration. If I let this go, any other person who was vegetarian and came here to volunteer would be expected to eat meat, too. I pointed to the chunks. I put my hand over my heart to show apology. I turned around to head back to the table. She came after me and grabbed my arm firmly. She brought me back into the kitchen and pointed to her collection of spices. She held up a box of bouillon, labeled "*vegetal.*" Then she pointed to a small pot behind the large pot of soup, and the rack of plantains. "Platano," she said. "Es vegetariana?"

I felt my body collapse in embarrassment. I should have trusted her. I nodded my head and apologized as she handed me the bowl of soup with a blank expression. I felt like a jerk.

I spent time between meals playing with the children or sorting through the harvested coffee. One of the little boys, Julian, acted like a little prince, confidently walking everywhere he went, tossing his hair and conversing casually with everyone. He was about ten and had a mohawk, listened to *Reggaeton* on his tiny music player and danced around the house. His confidence was refreshing.

I would spend some mornings writing on my computer about my experiences, and Julian would stand in the doorway watching me. "Qué haces, Melanie?" What are you doing?

I would giggle and explain myself. He would sometimes bring me a Spanish book to look at, or a kitten for me to play with. He pointed to the stack of electronic things I had next to my bed and asked what each item was. My alarm clock, which looked like a cellphone, my computer, iPod, camera, and an assortment of chargers for each. His eyes widened when I told him how much the computer cost.

"Y . . Necesitas todo?" He asked me. And you need all of it?

I looked at the pile and looked at him, holding a kitten and wearing ragged clothes, with dirt on his face and genuine curiosity.

"No, no . . No necesito todo." I said, then attempted to explain why I had everything. He just seemed to be in shock that a single person could own so much electronic stuff. I tried to defend myself by saying my computer, camera, and iPod were all out-of-date technology, and I tried to be very clear that I didn't have NEARLY as much technology as most Americans. But I stopped myself. He was right. Why did I have all this stuff? He left my room then, isolating me in my embarrassment.

I remember sitting on a bench with him near the chicken coop, in their small orchid garden, writing in my journal. He was watching me write words in English, but he didn't speak any English. I was writing about him and his little attitude, but he had no idea. I wrote, *and this kid just won't leave me alone!* I looked up at him and smiled. He smiled back.

The coffee workers would pick berries all morning and toss them in the bags tied to their backs. They would return to the house to unload their harvest, have breakfast and drink a cup of coffee with sugar. Then they would go back out and do it all again, three times a day. I was curious to help with the harvesting process, so one day I begged them to allow me to come with them. I hadn't expected it to be difficult for them to allow me to help them!

They suited me up in a rain jacket, rain boots, a hat, and gloves. I couldn't walk very well with all the extra layers, and I didn't understand how they could be necessary. Weren't we just picking berries from trees? How hard could it be?

We were a long assembly of ten workers, and we walked up a very steep hill. It started raining and immediately the hill turned into mud. We had to scramble up and hold trunks of the coffee trees to maintain our balance as we climbed higher and higher.

We walked through banana trees loaded with fruit. Merly pulled a machete from a sling she had on her back, chopped off a giant bundle of bananas, and put the machete back in one fell swoop like a badass. She set the banana bundle down near a fence post and we caught up to our group. The rain stopped and the sun came out. And with it, mosquitos. So far, the rain jacket, the boots, and the hat were explained. But why was I wearing all these layers of clothing? I suddenly got hot as the sun beat down on us.

She held branches away from my face as she pioneered through vegetation. Then a dramatic cloud covered the sun again and it started pouring rain again! We kept walking and I felt a burning sensation on my right foot. It spread across my ankle, it felt like I was stung by electric fencing over and over, in different places on my foot. It was creeping up my calf, and I had to stop walking. Merly turned around when she realized I was no longer behind her.

She ran back to where I was sitting on a log. "Oh, no!" She exclaimed. "*Ormigas!*" Ants, fire ants! Man, picking coffee was tough, and I hadn't even started.

She laughed as she removed my boot for me and wiped the ants off. She pointed to the ground, a reminder that I always have to watch where I'm walking. Finally, we found a place to pick coffee.

She showed me how to pick the berries, and after a few moments, the rain ceased. She grabbed me by the arm and took me into a pasture with a few horses, right on the top of the hill. The sun cast a warm glow across the surrounding fields of coffee and other crops. We stood there together in silence, chewing on some grass and admiring our surroundings.

I had a few small coffee berries in my bag, which she laughed at.

"It's okay," she assured me. "It's hard work!" I felt a twinge of stubbornness creep up in my stomach, wanting to defend my feeble attempts for lack of preparation, but I was in a good place with good people. And maybe picking coffee just wasn't for me.

We did some more picking for an hour or so, and my bag was filled with something like a sack of flour's worth. After, we walked back to Merly's rack of bananas, which she tossed casually over her shoulder.

The workers brought the red coffee berries back the house and dumped them into a shaft inside a small wooden hut. The shaft would slowly separate the two halves of each berry into two separate coffee beans and drop them into a water bath. The gummy, red outer layer had a small amount of sweetness, so when they sat in the water bath, separated from each other and their outer skins, the beans would ferment in the sweet liquid. I would find that each coffee plantation had a different amount of fermenting time, depending on the altitude.

After the fermentation process, the liquid would be drained, and the beans sifted out. They would be dried and become tiny, nearly recognizable coffee beans covered in a thin outer shell. Then that shell had to be cracked off, the beans roasted over a certain temperature, then ground and brewed. At this farm, I learned that longer roasting time for beans means less caffeine, as it gets roasted out. Therefore, darker roast means less caffeine. I *also* learned that coffee production is lots of work.

One afternoon, Merly, Celfa and some other women brought me down to a church festival in the valley. As we walked down the hill, Merly asked if I liked to dance. I laughed and nodded, not wanting to turn down a single opportunity.

We came upon a large group of about 300 people and sat through an hour-long open-air church service. After the service, Merly said she had to go; they had things to do. But she wanted me to stay, she told me, because there was dancing. Disoriented, yet open-minded, I agreed.

All the chairs from the church service were moved out of the way and an older man stood up on a platform and took a microphone. The audio quality was poor and his accent was strong, so I couldn't understand anything he was saying.

Merly raised her hand after the man finished speaking and pointed to me, describing Melanie, *de los Estados Unidos*, who likes to dance!

Everyone laughed and she squeezed my arm and departed. Soon I was surrounded by short men with eager smiles. One of them brought me a cup of coffee and looked at me nervously. I smiled, and some music started playing.

It was the middle of the day. We had just sustained a boring church service and now they were playing some Reggaeton dance music. The shift in the vibe was like night and day. Most of the men around me were wearing sun hats and rustic farm clothes. But when the music started, the man on stage said something as he gestured to me. Before I knew it, he set the microphone down and approached me, holding his hand out. "Dancing?" He asked me in English, with a superhero smile.

I sighed and looked around. Everyone was watching me expectantly. I smiled, nodded my head, and took his hand.

Those around us started clapping and we danced for a few minutes. I didn't know what I was doing. No one had ever taught me how to sway my hips appropriately. I don't even have hips, really, but I had a forgiving skirt that I flounced around my body.

After the dance, men swarmed around me, holding their hands out. The man I danced with thanked me and picked a different partner. I danced a few more times and then departed back up the hill to my host family.

I saw Merly helping her mother with dinner. I slapped her on the arm casually, laughing as I told her that she had abandoned me. She was glad I got to have some dancing practice, as we had a big party to go to that night. We made dinner together and the kids were swarming around us, watching the kittens catch gigantic moths against the wall.

We had some soup for dinner and then Merly told me to get ready to go out dancing. Again? I didn't have any nice clothes, so I wore the same skirt I'd been wearing earlier and put on my nicest blouse. She invited me on her motorbike, and we went off into the sunset.

We must have ridden at least an hour together as the sun disappeared and nighttime crept across the tremendous landscape. Out of nowhere we happened upon a cluster of tents set up along the side of the road and people gathered in the middle. She parked her bike and we met up with a few of her friends. We could hear loud dance music and smell fried food. We got some pizza and got past a bouncer looking to check ID. I handed him my passport and he gave it back to me without a glance.

We walked under a tent canopy where there was a small stage set up and bright electrical cords draped across it. Just a few couples danced on the stage. We sat down at folding tables on plastic kiddie chairs and Merly got us a few beers. I tried to pay her, but she laughed.

We sat for a few minutes watching the stage. I asked Merly if she wanted to dance with me. She shook her head and took a slug of her beer and whispered that we could only dance with men. Soon a few confident guys came up to ask our friends at our table to dance with them.

Merly came back to catch her breath after her last dance and asked how I was doing. Fine, I told her, and looked toward the stage. She asked if I wanted a man to dance with. I looked around awkwardly. She disappeared, only to come back with a one. He smiled without making eye contact, fixing his gaze behind me. He held out his hand. Merly nodded her head enthusiastically in the background, encouraging me.

I put my hand in his and turned around to look at the girls back at the table, guzzling their beers between giggles and breaths of air. They waved and smiled.

My dance partner led me through the mostly empty plastic chair arena and onto the dance floor, where he clutched me tightly. He kept his gaze behind me, and I looked down as he directed my steps. We danced in a circle like that, not making eye-contact, for the length of the song. He didn't spin me; he didn't direct me to move outside of a small radius. It was weird. I was very aware that this wasn't my culture.

After the dance concluded, he finally made eye contact with me and said, quietly, "*Gracias*," and let go of my hand. I walked back to the giggling girls and they reached out to me, handing me a beer. I sat back down as Merly pointed behind me. I flipped my head around to find three men with their hands out.

"Uh . . ." I stuttered. "Okay." I took one of the hands and was guided back up to the dance floor. It went on like this for hours. Strangers confidently approached me to move around together for the length of a song, and then said goodbye forever.

We stayed out late that night, Merly drove us back to the house in the early morning. I was exhausted. All that anti-climactic dancing and the cultural differences were wearing on me. And I missed my language!

When I woke up the next day, I decided to leave and find another adventure. I got my things together and said my goodbyes, but I couldn't find Julian. I hugged Merly and handed my iPod and charger to her, to give to Julian. He was right, I didn't need it. He would probably enjoy it more.

I headed off into the valley on foot. I walked past a huge mining area, past some curious white cattle with pitchfork horns. I climbed a long way up the steep side of a mountain, following the small trail that looked well-worn enough to follow. After a few hours I arrived back into San Agustin and made my way through the small village to the road I remembered would lead me to Adriana's hotel.

As I started up the road, a man stopped on his motorbike and offered a ride. I accepted gratefully.

Adriana was so excited to have me back and asked me about everything that had happened. I felt frustrated wanting to help them, I recounted to her, but they had nothing for me to do, and no expectations of me.

We made dinner together and relished how life had brought us back together. During my few days with her, I tried to help her with her garden. She was headstrong, though, and didn't want any suggestions. Or any help, for that matter. It was okay; we could just be friends.

I used the internet to find another place, this time in Ecuador. I'd wrestled with the idea of returning home for Christmas, after my frustrating attempts at finding a place to live and work. I came up with a resolution to try one more country. If it didn't work out, I would allow myself to return home.

I left the next day, thanked them for their hospitality, and departed from San Agustin by bus to Popayan, where I would find another bus to Pasto, where I had found a hostel in advance.

The bus ride was beautiful but perilous. I clung to the seat in front of me in expectation of immanent death. These crazy buses! They would drive up the mountain side, on the narrow roads only wide enough for one car and blast their horns as they rounded corners. Sometimes they would try and whip around a corner and another car or bus would be there. One of the motorized vehicles would stop in its tracks and the other would pass slowly, never touching the other car. How were they able to maneuver these large vehicles around each other without even a scrape?

Our bus meandered up the switchbacks and came to the top of an impressive mountain, and we would see women and goats gathered on the side of the road, dressed in long skirts and hair in braids, staring at the bus as it drove past. The landscape rippled like sand dunes, without a city in sight. Doubt seeped through me. Where on earth was I? It felt like the moon.

Then the bus broke down suddenly, and I found myself stranded outside with a nice German Baptist and a balding Dutch guy who coughed a lot. I listened to them complain about travelling in this country.

Finally, a replacement bus arrived and we finished our journey to Popayan. The two guys invited me to sleep on the floor of their hotel with them. I thanked them, but knew I had to continue. I went into the bus station and got a bus ticket to Pasto. I had a half hour to spare, so I crossed the street to a grocery store and picked up some grapes and a few plums and walked back to the bus station.

I finished my fruit and smoked a cigarette outside as I waited for the bus to appear. It was late; over an hour after my ticket had promised departure.

237

Finally, it arrived, and it was already after 4 pm. I knew by the time I arrived in Pasto it would be after midnight. I sat down on the bus and waited patiently for it to depart. I had another long journey ahead.

Sure enough, I didn't arrive in Pasto until after midnight. I considered sleeping in the train station, except that the gates were closing and police officers were waiting outside to make sure all the passengers left the station. I found a colectivo with one passenger, who was laughing with the driver when I hopped in. They were either drunk or just really happy. I handed the driver an address I had scribbled down with the internet from Adriana's hotel. They didn't recognize it.

We drove around the city for another hour and finally pulled up in front of a fancy-pants hotel called "the Lofts." I laughed and insisted this address must be wrong, I'm not fancy. Then one of the guys, Jose Luis, pointed out a small sign that read, "Koala Inn."

I thanked the funny guys as I approached the door to the building. The taxi sat there, waiting to be sure I had a room. A tall man answered with a gentle smile. He opened the door for me, and the taxi sped off. I waved to them. The man working in the hotel gave me my own spacious room because they had so few people staying that night.

In the morning I found a coffee from the common room and got my bag together. I walked into the city to get a taxi to Ipiales, the next nearest town to the border with Ecuador. Adriana had insisted I visit a beautiful church there, called *Las Lajas*. A man was sitting next to a taxi and getting his shoes shined. I asked if he could take me to Ipiales.

"Yes, yes!" He exclaimed excitedly in English, and then told me he was from Canada, which I wasn't sure was true.

I found another taxi to take me to the church in Ipiales. I explored for a while, admiring the ornate altar decorations. The outside of the building resembled a frozen waterfall, with cascading white stone surrounding the entrance.

There were tiny, hand-made altars surrounding the church, adorned with multi-colored candles and black-and-white images of those who've passed out of this life. There was a tremendous wall filled with names that had been scratched into the stone, in remembrance.

I found a place to grab a coffee outside. Then I meandered back up the hill, away from the glorious church, to find a taxi to take me to the bridge between Colombia and Ecuador.

They dropped me off in front of a building that reminded me of Jurassic Park, with thick stone walls and a fence around it. The taxi driver pointed at it and muttered something in rapid Spanish before his car sputtered off. I got my Ecuadorian stamp and was granted access into yet another country where I yearned for some purpose, or maybe just someone to help!

Ecuador

The Married Man

After a taxi to Tulcán and another long, perilous bus ride, I finally arrived in Quito. I had the name of a hostel written down to give to my taxi driver, who dropped me off on a dimly lit street and pointed.

I approached a tall red building and heard chatting. Above me I saw a terrace with people conversing and laughing. Was that English?

I found a small door and knocked. A young woman answered and told me that yes, they had a room available. She led me past the common room, which was attached to the terrace I'd noticed from below. A group of people were sitting at a wooden table with pizza, drinking beer and laughing. They waved to me when I walked in and I smiled. After I put my backpack down next to the bunk bed in my room, I got a beer from the reception desk and sat next to the group.

They asked what I was doing there, and I said I was headed to a farm in the area. There was one local man there from Ecuador, who asked me where the farm was. I shrugged. He laughed and invited me to join me on the terrace.

We smoked a cigarette together and he told me that the streets of Quito were dangerous at night. Take a taxi at night, he advised. Then he complimented me on my Spanish. "I've never met an American who speaks with such a comfortable accent. Your efforts are an honor," he told me in Spanish. He took a long drag of his cigarette as I felt my face redden. "Do you want to come out with us?"

I declined. I knew I had to unwind in a bed and get some sleep. I had no commitment the next day, as I'd scheduled meeting my farmer in a few days. I said goodnight to the crowd of people. "Buenas noches," they called back as I closed the door to my room. I brushed my teeth and crawled into bed with a big grin, proud of the last few days. Even if I hadn't really been involved with anything, I'd traveled a long way.

I woke up the next morning and went exploring in the streets of Quito alone. I stumbled upon a music festival with traditional clothing and instruments. I even managed to find myself inside an auditorium where some sort of interpretive dance was being held, where the ancient Quechua language was spoken and translated into Spanish.

When Ecuadorians spoke to each other, they pronounced their words with diligent intention, as if they were speaking to children. I really appreciated their clear dialect after the many other accents I'd heard. It was closest to the Spanish I'd studied in high school.

Quito is an ancient city with cobblestone paths and unique architecture. It's situated at a high altitude, but in a sort of valley, between high mountains. The streets were filled with locals and tourists alike. I didn't expect to see so many people of different races here, and it was strange how many Americans I overheard here. Personally, I didn't know anyone who'd been to Quito.

That night I hung out at the hostel again and met a young German couple. Josh and Marie were traveling in South America together, working at hostels and taking vacations. Josh and I had a long conversation about food in the small kitchen of the hostel, and I started telling him about my sister's farm, how I had helped her make apple vinegar and ferment kimchi. He was astonished. I told him about Sandor Katz's book *Wild Fermentation*, how it was a good start to understanding the fermenting process, and how it applies to so many things we consume—Soy sauce, Sri Racha hot sauce, and the German classic sauerkraut. He was excited and had me write the title down, saying "Marie's birthday is in a few weeks! It's a perfect gift for her."

The next morning, after sending an email to my new farmer with an expected arrival time, I left. I found a bus to take me out to the little town nearest him. I arrived and found a bench to sit on and wait for a light-skinned American to come pick me up.

After an hour or so, a large pick-up parked in front of me, and a little boy with glasses was standing up in the truck bed. He waved excitedly at me, and the driver got out of the cab.

"Hey, Melanie?" He asked as he approached.

I stretched my arms wide and introduced myself.

My new farm host had a thick moustache and a beer belly, a straw hat, and a stride that said he owned the place. He reached his hand out, "I'm Mathieu." He motioned to a kid in the truck who was looking around, avoiding eye contact. "That's my son, Juan Carlos."

Juan Carlos looked up at me with the mention of his name. I nodded at him and he gave me a goofy grin.

"Well, get in, we'll give you the tour," Mathieu said with a thick Southern accent. He walked back to the truck, looking off into the distance, hopping in the cab, and slamming the door behind him.

Juan Carlos reached out to help me into the truck bed. I laughed and accepted. "You can stand here if you want, it's okay . . Well, maybe it's not." He giggled. "But it's fun!"

The truck started and I flopped my backpack off my shoulders and got my footing. I stood up next to Juan Carlos, holding tightly onto the back of the truck cab. He had light skin, freckles across his face, and spoke English with a perfect American accent.

We dodged branches as the road changed from nicely paved to uneven and rocky. Strangers walking on the side of the road waved to us like they knew us. Mathieu navigated the truck off road to a driveway surrounded by brush.

"And now," Juan Carlos said, "you really have to duck down. It's prickly!"

We crouched down together giggling, and the truck stopped after a few minutes. Mathieu got out of the cab and grabbed my backpack.

As Juan Carlos and I hopped out of the back and followed him, Mathieu said, "You're actually our first volunteer. We've never done this before. We have lots of work to do, but we don't know how to do it. We're hoping with your experience it'll be a good fit." He turned around to look me up and down. "Do you have boots?"

"Yeah," I said. "I have hiking boots with me, but I've never really needed them." I looked around as we walked the small path from the driveway to a large shack. There were pink, purple, and white flowers everywhere. The shack was a huge, open-air, kitchen with an expansive linoleum floor and patio.

"We love to cook," Mathieu said. "I'm from Louisiana, and I make a lot of Southern food, like my mammy taught me!" He tossed his head back to laugh at himself. "Your profile said you been a lotta places. Ever been to Louisiana?"

"No," I said shyly, and stood in the middle of the kitchen to admire the view. The property was situated on a hillside. The stone patio below had a few barstools connecting the kitchen to the patio, bordered by an ancient-looking marble wall. Further down you could see a beautiful pathway with flowers planted around it, and a pond at the very base of the hill.

"Wow, this place is gorgeous," I said, the admiration thick in my voice. "I love this kitchen, and the view of the mountains around us is just incredible."

Mathieu chuckled. "You haven't seen the best view yet!"

He carried my backpack to another shack fifty feet away and opened a door. Inside the room were two bunkbeds. He set my backpack down on the floor and turned to me. "This is your room. It's all yours. I got these beds for volunteers, so I hope you're worth it," he said, and again bellowed a large laugh.

I looked around the room and then into his eyes. "Thank you. Looks perfect."

He smiled and looked away quickly to where Juan Carlos was playing in the yard. "Well, get yourself settled in, and maybe you could make dinner for us tonight?"

"Uh, sure," I said, caught off guard and not knowing what else to say.

"Great. See you later." With that, he was gone.

I sat down on one of the bottom bunks and stared out the window. It was truly a beautiful view. Matthieu's request to have me make dinner felt strange.

I put my things away thoughtfully; there was no dresser, so I folded my clothes into neat stacks in the corner of the room. I went to the bathroom and looked at myself in the mirror. I splashed some water on my face and used a hand towel to wipe it dry. I was tan, suddenly. My hair had turned golden from the sun. My skin was clear and my eyes were bright blue. I almost didn't recognize myself after a few days of being on the road and meeting strangers. Nothing had been familiar; even my own face looked foreign.

That night I did make dinner with what they had, and Mathieu offered me a beer. The kitchen, being open-air, was an awesome place to hang out. There was dim lighting and tons of seating, so whoever was cooking could also be a part of the conversation. When I got the onions simmering for a soup, I sat on the patio with Mathieu. He pulled a cigar out of his chest pocket and grabbed another beer.

"Yeah, this is going to be interesting." He said. "So . . What do you know how to do? How can you help us? What's your specialty?"

Feeling a bit on the spot, I began to explain a few of the various experiences I'd had. First, we could start with a compost pile, then make a huge garden terraced down the hill. "I want to learn more about picking coffee, too," I told him. "That's the reason I came to South America."

"Well, I don't really know what I'm doing with my coffee. I've got a whole hill of coffee trees and cacao trees, loaded with fruit. I've got an employee, Ines, who knows how to do a lot of stuff, local techniques and skills, but she doesn't like to do any extra work if she doesn't have to." He slugged some of his beer, set it down and looked up at the sky, puffing his cigar. "I may have allowed her to feel too much like family, so now she acts kind of *entitled*."

I sipped my beer in contemplation as I hopped up to stir the onions on the stove. He was allowing me into his thought process, and I was learning a lot from him already about how much he expected of people he got involved with.

We finished dinner and I was happy to see Mathieu do the dishes. I retired to my room.

I met Ines the next day. Her thick hair was tucked into a neat bun on the back of her head. She was short and had one eye smaller than the other and was very cavalier with Mathieu. It seemed she *was* like family, joking back and forth with him. When he left with Juan Carlos to do their home-schooling lesson, Ines pulled me aside to complain about how Mathieu always called her when he needed anything.

"Water? *Ines*!!" She imitated him calling for her. "Limonada? *Ines*!!!" She seemed light-hearted enough about it, though.

I became something of a housekeeper, like Ines, as well as a farmworker. Mathieu had goals for me, things he wanted to learn from me, but he didn't seem interested in doing the work himself. He would listen diligently when I explained the benefits of composting, and he would buy the materials and help plan the activity with me, but he would stand there to oversee my work, rather than help.

One of my first days working with the coffee on the hillside, I was picking green berries that were infected by a little bug that crawled inside to eat the sugars that developed as each bean ripened. I picked the green ones infected with the bug and dropped them in a plastic bottle. Then we would fill the bottle with water and close the cap to drown the bugs. Mathieu appeared one day out of nowhere, with his straw hat on and his working boots. He grabbed the bottle from my hand and furrowed his brow in disappointment.

"Is that all you got so far?"

I stopped picking coffee for a second and looked him in the eyes. "Uh, yeah. It's not easy to find them."

He walked away as I was talking to him and motioned to a line of coffee trees. "Are these the ones you've already done?"

Stunned, I responded, "Um, no, I started up further," and pointed to a row behind me.

He followed my direction and started inspecting the coffee trees I had already picked through. I decided to ignore him and carry on with my work. I sighed and remembered I was lucky to be in a beautiful environment, eating fresh bananas and pineapple every day, picking coffee and planning a garden. Whatever.

He called to me a few minutes later. "Hey, I'm going back down to get some lunch. You can come when you finish that row."

I felt a bit violated to have my work inspected, so I decided to stay up on the hill. When I ran into Ines, I would tell her about this weird encounter.

One night, Mathieu had a few guy friends come over, Juan and Paul. Juan was balding and short, very shy yet quite knowledgeable about growing and cooking food. Paul was scrawny with dark hair and loved to practice his English. Each time he asked me a question like, "when did you have your first job?" I would be flattered and answer. Then he would take the conversation back over. It seemed he only wanted to talk about himself, asking about me just to share what he thought were interesting details about his own life. I learned he was a violin player, and he fell in love a lot. That's what Matthieu teased him about, anyway.

248

Things with Matthieu felt forced and uncomfortable. It got better when I understood him more. He gave gifts and did things for me, in contrast to the verbal flattery I was accustomed to. However, he did tell me he'd never seen someone work "so diligently." And with that, he added, "You *must* be American!"

One day I made *limonada* for a bunch of construction workers he had hired to do some tiling in the kitchen. I mixed a plethora of fresh lemon juice (from the orchard located further down the hill on Mathieu's property), panela (brown sugar crafted from the local sugar cane), and water to make the sweetest and best lemonade I'd ever had. The men were sweating and wiping their brows. I placed three glasses of lemonade on the counter for them and called out in Spanish, "*Rata!*" Or, break time!

I clinked glasses with them and we all drank the lemonade together. They smiled and thanked me. Mathieu appeared from the path leading to his and Juan Carlos's study space. "What are you doing?"

"I just made some lemonade for the guys; they were sweating and—"

"Never drink with them. You can't do that."

The men went back to work, oblivious to our English. Mathieu motioned to them as he explained. "If you drink with them, they think you're their friend. You can't be a friend if you want to be a boss."

I stared at him. "That seems very unkind," I responded. "They're working for you. They can be your friend, too, right?"

He laughed dismissively. "There has to be a disconnect between you and them. If they think they're on the same level as you, and you hang out with them like buddies, they'll show up to work late and work less because they don't have to impress you as much. Next time, drink *your* lemonade first."

I went back to washing dishes as the words sunk in. Was that why he was evaluating my work so much? So I wouldn't feel like a friend, or family, or a guest? His sentiment stung, as it suddenly felt personal.

One night a neighbor farmer came over for some beers. Bronze skin, muscles bulging from beneath like cats fighting under a blanket. His name was Pedro. He had straight, white teeth and he lived a five-minute walk away. He tended a huge vegetable patch and picked coffee and cacao for the owner of the farm. He was Ecuadorian and spoke beautiful Spanish. He sat down to talk to Mathieu, but he kept glancing at me.

Mathieu left his seat to grab another beer, so I sat down next to Pedro. We spoke a bit about what he did, how he lived, and how much he loved nature. "And natural women, too," he added. Was he flirting with me? Good thing the sun had gone down for the night, or he would have seen my suddenly rosy complexion.

Juan Carlos was singing along to some *Bachata* music from the radio. Mathieu came back to the table, so I gave his seat back and went to help Juan Carlos make his specialty, French fries. Mathieu had bought a 50 lb. sack of potatoes to encourage his son's interest in cooking.

Mathieu was married to an Ecuadorian woman who lived in Quito with their two other children. He told me late one evening about how he came here without speaking any Spanish, having heard only that Quito was a beautiful city with a lot of American expats. He viewed it as a good business opportunity, as he was in real estate and had rental properties back in Louisiana. That provided sufficient income for him to live in Ecuador, eating tropical fruit and relaxing.

He had a funny voice and a large gap between his teeth. He carried himself as if his shoulders were hung from the sky, and the rest of his body just followed. He allowed me to make as many changes to his property as I wanted. I had some local man cut down bamboo for me from the jungle to layer into terracing for the downward-facing slope. I wanted to make a huge vegetable garden space and Mathieu didn't question it. He only seemed to value my integrity and self-direction.

Christmas time came, and Mathieu invited me to celebrate with his family in Quito. I was honored. I hadn't expected to be with a family for Christmas, so I was truly flattered. He said he would ask Ines to watch the farm when he was gone, as he didn't trust any of the other local people. "But, if she can't watch the farm, would you be able to?"

I laughed and said of course.

The day before we were scheduled to leave for the long weekend, I was digging into the hillside with a small shovel. Mathieu appeared in the shack above me, overlooking the garden space I was creating. He called down to me.

251

"Hey, Melanie, Ines can't watch the farm." He sighed loudly and glanced across the landscape. "I don't know what to do."

I stopped my work for a second to catch my breath. I wiped my brow as I looked twenty feet up to where he stood. "I don't either."

He looked aimlessly out into the beautiful mountains as he pondered his next words. "If you can stay here, that would be great."

I ignored him for a minute and went back to digging. He continued. "We don't have any other option. I can get Pedro to come check on you at night, you would like that. Wouldn't you?"

I was confused. Now he was going to abandon me on his farm alone? Shove his responsibility on me? Maybe staying here and being away from Mathieu would be better anyway, I thought. I could get a lot more done, and I wouldn't have anyone constantly evaluating my work.

"Sure, that's fine," I called back.

Mathieu and Juan Carlos left the next day. As I had predicted, work was much easier when I was under no one's supervision.

It was Christmas Eve. I made arepas, seasoned rice, a spicy salad, and crunchy fried potatoes with cumin. I assembled a plate and crumbled some queso fresco across the top and freshly chopped cilantro. As I sat down to eat, I heard the noise of an engine pulling into the driveway. Then I heard it stop. Someone started walking over and I set my plate down.

It was Pedro, nearing the kitchen in the darkness. He approached me with a giant smile and sat down on the steps entering the lower part of the kitchen. I smiled and continued eating.

Matthieu wanted him to check on me, he explained in slow, clear Spanish. Are you okay?

Yes, I responded curtly. It was too late for a visit. Especially a visit with no warning.

Then suddenly he began talking about his wife, who was leaving him, and his bad relationship with the man he worked for. He went on and on, so I grabbed a beer to share and made him a plate of food. I poured the beer into small cups as he spoke. When I got up to put my plate away, he commented on how beautifully I walked. I smiled and sat back down.

"I love women," he said, as he accepted the plate of food. "There is nothing more beautiful to me. I miss women and love and sex. I can't imagine a person who lives without sex."

I raised my hand. Naively. "Uh, me! I haven't had sex!"

He stopped chewing and stared at me in shock. He swallowed slowly. "Really?"

I laughed confidently and finished my beer. "No, I haven't. I don't really want to."

He looked at me with sudden longing. "Your skin is so white and brilliant. You move so confidently. Your lips, wow." He looked at my lips for a minute in silence. "I wish I could be lucky enough to taste them. If you were mine," he said suggestively, and paused to bite his lip, "I would kiss you all the time."

I blushed and we finished eating. Pedro put some music on, and we stood on the patio together, looking at the stars in silence. I leaned over and kissed him. He was gentle and smooth, sweet and sweaty at the same time. He wrapped me in his muscular arms and held me tightly as we kissed under the moonlight.

After a few minutes, he said he had to go. I wanted more of him, and I was left with longing. The same longing I'd seen in his eyes earlier.

The next day I got more work done, picking coffee by myself near to the jungle. I took a break for lunch and Pedro appeared. I loved how confident he was, making himself available without asking. He had a big smile on his face. "*Hola, bonita*," he said smoothly, and he tried to scoop me up in his arms. I giggled and pushed him away, insisting I had work to do.

"I can help you with your work," he said in Spanish, with a suggestive smile. He had a cap on, and his forehead was dripping in sweat.

"Okay, perfect," and I pointed to a few bushes I wanted cut down. He reached into a small sling he had across his back. He maintained eye contact, pulled out a machete, and sliced the base of one of the bushes without looking away from me. He smiled proudly and used the tail of his shirt to wipe his face off. Conveniently revealing his muscular core.

This continued for an hour or so. I would send him to work far away from me, and he would whistle or sing to himself, completely off-pitch, seemingly unaware that I could hear him. I would tease him through the bushes, and he would come over to pretend to inspect my work.

"I think you should go," I said in Spanish.

"Wow, confident woman, you make all the men work for you?"

I laughed and pushed him away. What was happening here? Why did I want to see him? My sister Khaiti had warned me about *suave* Latino men, but this was ridiculous. Why was he so interested? Was I as beautiful as he had suggested?

He left and I thought about what I was doing here. Why had Matthieu left me all alone? Did he give me Pedro as a confidant, someone to trust? He was charming, but *could* I trust him? I didn't have a phone or any method of getting help if anything were to happen. I didn't have a gun or any form of protecting myself. Was Pedro my protector? Was he supposed to take care of me?

We began a sort of routine, where Pedro would come over during the day and again at night. Then one day he invited me to *his* house.

I walked along the road to where he was living, and there were three children running around. They paused their game and looked up at me curiously as a gorgeous woman with curled locks came out of the house, holding a baby.

"Melanie?" She called out to me, appearing from behind a cloth-covered doorway.

She told me that Pedro had told her about what a wonderful hard-working girl I was, and from America! She invited me in for some lunch. I felt sick to my stomach, but I obliged and entered the little house with a dirt floor. She set her baby in front of me as she finished assembling a plate of bread and queso fresco she had made that morning with fresh milk.

Pedro walked in the door just then, as I sat there, eating their food and playing with their baby. Then three adorable kids came running in after him. Pedro smiled at me, a secret smile, and went into the kitchen to greet his wife with a kiss.

Everything he had told me felt like a lie. I thought they were living separately, I thought she was a nasty woman, and I had no idea they had kids. She was clearly here, kind and sweet, and they had four children together?

I was polite and stayed there on the floor as Pedro switched on a tiny, black-and-white television for the kids to watch. When Pedro's wife returned to the kitchen, he reached over and squeezed my left hand.

I stared at my hand after his touch, racking my brain to make sense of this. I needed to leave. I said bye, thank you, the cheese was delicious.

Later that night Pedro came over again. I didn't acknowledge his arrival, I just pretended he wasn't there. I was making dinner for myself.

He stood there watching me for a moment, I could see him in my peripheral vision. "Melanie?" He called to me sweetly. "You look so beautiful. And wow, you would be an amazing mother, so good with children."

I stopped what I was doing to stare back at him. "Are you still married?"

"Yes, it was my wife," he said, "but she leaves in three days. She's going to take the children. I'm so scared, I don't want her to leave me alone, but she is not happy. She says I'm not a good father, and I don't give her enough attention." He sat down on the step and suddenly started crying, his head in his hands.

I sat next to him, and he reached for my hand to hold. "I am happy you're here, Melanie. You are so much comfort for me."

Then we kissed for a long time. I knew it was wrong, but I believed him that his wife was leaving him. And kissing him just felt so good right now. He pushed me against the wall as he caressed my neck passionately with his lips. He whispered gently in my ear, "I love the way you taste. Your lips have an aroma." His Spanish was so delicate and precise and sultry. And he was speaking it to me.

He whispered, "Can we go to your room?"

I stopped kissing him and said I didn't want to go to my room. He giggled as he bit my bottom lip, seducing me. "Please? It's more comfortable. Please? Just for a little while."

I laughed at his attempts and said no. Then he picked me up and carried me into my room, despite my feeble attempts to defend myself. I was kicking my legs in the air, telling him to let me go. Then he laid me in the bed gently.

"Please, no, I don't want to be here," I whined. I felt like a baby asking for mercy. I felt my eyes stinging. I didn't know what was happening and I didn't want to find out. I wasn't ready for this, I didn't want sex ever and not now, and not with this married man. In the moment, my head said no. What was my heart saying? This sexual monster inside me was suddenly introducing itself.

No, I don't want this. Wait. Yes? My body does.

Pedro smiled at me. I could see the moonlight casting shadows across his face. He took his cap off and I could suddenly see he was balding. He kissed me on the lips gently. "I want only to kiss you, Melanie, relax, it's okay."

I refused and refused, and he tried and he tried. I eventually gave in to him and let him stick his tiny penis inside me. Ten seconds later, after my screaming and squirming in pain, he laid there, frozen on top of me. He snapped out of his sex-haze and kissed me on the cheek. He put his clothes on and left me there, lying alone, wondering what the fuck just happened.

I made my way into the bathroom, suddenly struck with the urge to pee. Blood came out. I laid in bed that night staring at the bottom of the bunk bed above me. I had nothing to distract me from what had just happened, except allowing time to pass. I didn't sleep.

The next morning Pedro didn't come to visit me. I wrote in my journal about the experience. I admitted that I wanted it, my body wanted it. For some reason the bad feeling stimulated me, excited me to know I was doing something I shouldn't have been. I made it clear I wanted him to stop, but after a certain point I gave up. So, it *was* my fault.

I was interrupted in my thoughts by Pedro's wife and children. She stopped in to greet me with a warm smile and asked if I would come to the school to play with the kids. It sounded like a good distraction. The children were so excited to see me, hear me speak Spanish, and we walked to the school a few hundred yards away, kicking a ball along the path.

Within minutes I was surrounded by at least twenty kids, teaching them hand games and singing songs for them in English. They giggled as they listened to my speech, unable to understand. We started playing soccer, and all the boys got out into the field. Out of nowhere, Pedro showed up. He looked at me with a huge smile and came up to kiss me on the cheek when his wife wasn't looking. I let him.

He ripped his shirt off and didn't look at me again as he ran out into the field to play with the kids. I had his baby on my hip and his three children looking at me, while their mother was cooking in the kitchen, preparing a special lunch for the school. I handed the baby to a woman standing nearby and ran into the field.

I could play soccer, I could run, I could show these kids what's up.

I was wrong, as was proven to me within the first few minutes, when I realized just how long the field was. I huffed and puffed to keep up with my team (although, I didn't quite know whose team I was on). Within five minutes, after one attempted (and failed) goal, I sat back down on the grass.

The woman brought the baby back to me. I watched Pedro run around, muscular and proud, knowing he had two women there.

The next few days before Mathieu and his family came home, Pedro and I made a routine of having sex at night. It didn't feel right, but it didn't feel wrong. I was conflicted in the simple fact that I wasn't conflicted at all.

My conservative religion had taught me that this was wrong for two reasons, and basically each time we had sex, not only were we having "pre-marital sex" but also "cheating." So, two sins each night. Would God forgive me? I didn't even feel a desire to apologize for it and I didn't feel God looking down at me, disapproving. In fact, was he even watching?

One time I invited Pedro's family over for dinner and they all came, except him. I left them at my place and walked over to Pedro's house to convince him to come over. I found him in his bedroom. He closed the door and started ripping his clothes off.

"No, no," I said, "we have to go for dinner, your family's waiting for us." He pushed me on the bed forcefully, and I pushed him back with all my strength. He held me down firmly, yet I managed to weasel out from beneath him and get away before he penetrated me. I felt we were crossing a line here.

Not only were my emotions about Pedro crazy, but each day I felt more and more angry about Mathieu. He had such a strange way of treating his employees. He acted like he was the one with all the power, like they needed him and not the other way around. Even though if they had left him, he would be completely helpless. He seemed to have no skill, only money. One day while Mathieu was still away, I went up to pick some coffee. I found Ines up there, chopping down weeds around the coffee trees.

We spoke about how he hadn't paid her as much as he'd promised, how he was always ordering her around and showed her no respect. "He came here to use the local people, no consideration other than a small paycheck. He needs the work to get done and he thinks he will always be able to find someone to do it, we are disposable to him," she explained in rapid Spanish. "It's true, we are. . . If I quit, he will find someone else."

I opened up to her about my feelings, too. How I felt Mathieu had manipulated me into working harder and harder each day. She put her hand on mine as we took a break, sitting on the hillside admiring the view.

"I think you should take this coffee." She looked me in the eyes and smiled. "You take it to America with you. He doesn't know the coffee is ready. Actually, he knows nothing without us."

We laughed together on the hill, bonding that day. I fermented and dried it as I had learned in Colombia.

Ines invited me to her family's sugar cane plantation a few minutes away. They were making panela, the sugar sold everywhere in South America. It was brown because it was unfiltered; most of the sugar we buy in the states has the natural caramel color removed.

The panela process began on the top of a hill, where a man would shove stalks of sugar cane into a huge juicer. The stalk fibers would come out into a large pile, while the juice would be diverted over large metal pans to cook over a gigantic fire brewing beneath them.

Once the juice became more like a syrup, it was diverted into a bathtub, where they add a dollop of shortening to begin the thickening process.

As it solidified while cooling, they would pack it into molds. They could sell each ½ lb. chunk for about a quarter. There were at least ten workers, laboring seamlessly. How much could each of them receive for their day's work? Grungy and smelling like sugar and burnt wood when they returned home, physically exhausted and hungry. It was a rustic processing "facility" and was completely open-air. The sugar was aromatic at first, but quickly felt sticky in the air.

That afternoon, Mathieu came back to the farm with his wife and their three children. Like Juan Carlos, they could all speak fluent Spanish and American English. They had fair complexions and dirty blonde hair with brown eyes, yet his wife had dark features.

Mathieu approached me as he got out of the truck. "Did you have fun alone here? Did you have fun with Pedro?" He laughed to himself as I tried to configure a response. I couldn't tell him anything.

"Yeah, we got along fine. I got a bunch done, but I was really lonely."

They stayed for a few days with us, cooking a bunch of food and admiring the garden I'd made. I'd impressed his family, at least.

Their daughter, around 8 years old, asked me one day, in her sweet, innocent, gentle voice, "Do you like Pedro?"

I stopped what I was doing and chuckled nervously. "Um, no. Who told you that?"

She smiled back into my face. "Nobody. I just thought I could see it. Does *he* like *you*?"

I sighed aloud. "I honestly have no idea. Maybe. But I think he's married."

Here, in the middle of the jungle with no one to trust, I had spilled my secret feelings to this tiny, curious girl. I was clearly desperate to find a confidant.

The family left after just a few days, and again it was Mathieu, Juan Carlos, Ines, and I. Pedro stopped coming to visit me. I thought about him all the time, writing in my journal and wishing for his affection once again. Not that his affection was of true love, but it was affection, nonetheless. I craved validation from men. Competitive through my core, I liked the idea that he wanted *me* more than he wanted that beautiful, young, kind wife of his.

I tried to put him out of my mind. Two more volunteers, Ryan and Melody, were coming today from Scotland. I couldn't wait to meet new people. They arrived, tall and heavily accented, exploring South America for months, wanting to be out of the city, wanting to meet real people.

They got into our work groove rather well, although it didn't seem like either of them had a lot of experience working outside. Ryan saw me whacking down a banana tree with a machete and laughed. He complimented me in his Scottish slur. "Wow, that is ser-r-riously impr-r-ressive."

It was New Year's Eve. Mathieu was going back into Quito to spend it with his family and told us about the crazy party in the village.

"There's tons of dancing, you guys will have so much fun," he said, and thought for a minute, chuckling to himself. "They have a bunch of weird cultural things. It's definitely a once-in-a-lifetime experience."

Mathieu disappeared and arranged for some locals to give us a ride into town. They showed up at the farm and we offered them some beer. Ryan and Melody wanted to learn more Spanish, so I was something like a translator. It felt great to be able to share my skills.

We hopped in the back of the truck and drove into town. The sun went down and the truck was soon navigating in the darkness. Headlights surrounded us; it seemed everyone was going to the party. Out of nowhere, we were stopped in something like a traffic jam. Where did all these cars come from, anyway?

We finally pulled up to a ribbon across the road. A man in drag started dancing across the ribbon, dangling him/herself across the hood of the car. Ryan, Melody, and I looked at each other in the truck bed, laughing so hard we had to hold our stomachs. The glamorous lady kept dancing until the driver gave her some money and the ribbon was let loose so we could drive through. We looked back and saw the whole show happen again to the car behind us.

The rest of the road to the city was filled with these men in drag, dancing for money. It took us at least an hour to finally arrive in the city. We were in hysterics. The truck was parked and we all left the vehicle to join the masses and find some beer.

We stood on a huge cement area where a woman stood behind a tiny cart selling *chochos*, a local delicacy that Mathieu had shared with me. I bought some of the white beans for each of us. They were eaten cold, topped with hot peppers, red onion, cilantro, tomato, toasted corn, and lots of lime. They came in a plastic bag with a spoon.

I heard someone calling my name and oriented myself through the crowd to glance around. I saw Ines standing in front of a shop, waving to me excitedly. She introduced me to a few of her friends who owned the shop. I bought some cigarettes and beer and Ines came with me out to the dance floor to watch a few drag queens parade on stage. It was some sort of competition: there was an announcer and each of the queens had a minute to dance to a song.

Ines invited me to see all their local traditions to ring in the new year. We walked down a path to dimly lit, constructed scenarios. There were various tented enclosures, with characters proclaiming their struggles from the year.

There was a straw man with a wooden plaque around his neck, on which was written a Spanish caption. There were animals and miniature houses. A straw policeman held a toy gun up to a straw farmer, protecting his pigs, with a caption that said something like, *Stay away from my farm with your rules! I know what I'm doing!*

At midnight, Ines informed me, all these small scenes would be set on fire. Out with the troubles of last year, on with the new.

She pointed off in the distance to a huge structure that looked like a Ferris-wheel made of dried corn stalks and adorned with firecrackers.

We went back to the dance floor where music blasted from the speakers. The dance floor was lit more-than-sufficiently by arena lights above. Men swarmed around with women who knew how to sway their hips. Here we could all dance together and we didn't need to hold hands or stare off into the distance looking uninterested.

Ines had a son named David, a nice guy who kept trying to dance with me. I was flattered by the attention. Ines looked happy and also perhaps a bit drunk when she introduced me to his wife, who smiled kindly at me. The dancing went on and the countdown began:

Cinco. Quatro. Tres! Dos! Uno!

Everyone yelled and threw confetti. Ines grabbed me and pulled me out to the sidewalk where all the structures and scenarios were lit up in flames. There was fire everywhere, and kids running freely. I couldn't believe how close the sparks were to lighting us up!

After an hour of more dancing, Ryan and Melody somehow met back up with us. Ryan was quite drunk.

"Hey, Melanie . . I got some liquor. So amazing, it's homemade!"

He took a pull from a large, clear bottle he was holding. "They drink it like water or something . . ."

I propped him against my shoulder as we waited for our ride and took off, once again, into the darkness.

Our driver was swerving all over the road, laughing so loudly I could hear him above the groan of the engine. We rounded a corner; a motorcyclist was zipping around it.

There was a *crash* and a *cr-r-r-unch*. Suddenly sober, I heard a shriek.

The truck stopped around the corner and Melody got out of the back of the truck to see what had happened. From the glow of the taillights, I saw a man lying on the ground, holding his leg and yelling in agony.

Our driver approached the afflicted man, saw the damage he had caused, and picked Melody up. He tossed her in the back of the truck as she screamed.

"He's hurt! He's hurt!" She insisted, "we have to go back!" Her English was of no use, and even if she had used Spanish, the driver probably would have ignored her.

We sped off down the road, looking at each other in shock. "What?" Ryan asked, also suddenly sober. "What the *fuck* just happened?"

"We ran somebody over. He got knocked off his bike." Melody ran her hands through her hair. "I can't believe this is happening. We have to go back!"

I looked behind us to the scene we had fled and heard shouting. "I don't think our drivers want to take the blame," I said.

Shhh, the driver hushed me as he brought the truck up to a tiny, dark trail. They got out of the truck silently and sat in the back with us, putting a finger over his mouth. *Shhhh,* he hushed me again. "Silencio."

It must have been three in the morning, and we waited there for another hour as we heard sirens blasting, investigating the crime we had left.

We looked at each other in silence, as we had been instructed, unsure of how to proceed. Ryan started puking over the back of the truck, and someone handed us a light blue, plastic bowl of water. A dog's water bowl? The moon was peeking through the clouds and I could see the vessel just enough to force water into Ryan's mouth.

After the sirens faded, the men told us we could go home.

We walked alone, down the path, for another half hour, afraid of poisonous snakes, afraid of what just happened, afraid of being found. We hadn't a light or even a clear idea of which direction we were headed. Somehow, I was able to navigate us back home. We got into our beds.

After I'd fallen asleep, I heard a car pull into the driveway. I saw headlights through the window. Then they turned off.

"Melanie? Mel-a-nie? Dónde estás?" Where was I, a man's voice inquired.

I ignored him and turned over in my bed, covering my ears with the pillow.

"Melanie? Estás aquí?" He continued to call out, asking for me. Then he found the door and started banging on it. "Mel-a-nieeeee!"

I mustered whatever energy my body had left and opened the door and approached him on the patio. I told him bluntly to leave.

The man gripped my body tightly and asked if he could sleep with me, please? He pushed me up against the wall of the building forcefully. In the darkness I couldn't see his face, but I recognized his voice. David, Ines's son. He was drunk. I pushed him with all my strength and yelled at him loudly until he left.

The next morning, we woke up hungover and laid in our beds discussing the night before. "It was disgusting. But we didn't do anything wrong, right?" Melody asked. Ryan mumbled from beneath the pillow in response and I agreed we weren't at fault.

We finally got up and fried plantains for breakfast. I made coffee and we stood in the kitchen shading our eyes from the sun, which tried its best to brighten our moods.

A truck pulled up in the driveway. It was a man I'd spoken to about coffee a week earlier. I couldn't remember his name, so I just stayed in the kitchen and ignored him. He approached us and called to me. "Melanie?"

I slammed my coffee cup down, spilling some on the counter. I stomped up the stairs to find out what more someone could ask of me.

He smiled sweetly at me, genuinely. Happy New Year, he said. Would I like to come with him to swim in the waterfall today?

He didn't deserve the wrath I felt for men that morning, so I bit my tongue. I told him I couldn't, because I drank too much last night. He gave me a gentle hug and I cringed. I walked back to the kitchen.

"What are all these men coming here for?" Ryan asked, sitting at the bar table and gripping his mug of coffee. "What was that guy doing last night?"

I sighed aloud and rubbed my forehead. I didn't trust anyone anymore. Even Ines didn't feel like a friend, since her son had tried to sleep with me. I told Ryan that I thought the men were all just drunk, looking for a single girl.

Mathieu showed up that afternoon, as we lazily attempted to collect ourselves. He seemed hugely impressed to see us hungover. "Did you have any fun last night, kids?"

"Ah, there's something I have to talk to you about," I said slowly, and pulled him aside to explain the accident. He advised me not to divulge a word about the accident to anyone. We were not to blame, we did what we could, and we should forget it. Easier said than done.

I didn't stay long on the farm after the accident. I decided to return to my travel plans. I could make my own way and make my own mistakes with their own set of consequences.

Speaking to Pedro's wife on the path, she said she'd heard the Mayor's son was nearly killed in an accident on New Year's. I looked away and bit my tongue, as I'd been instructed.

When I told Matthieu about it, he said the driver and his family had gone to Quito for a week to give themselves an alibi.

Ryan and Melody stayed on the farm and we said our goodbyes. I walked to Pedro's house to say goodbye to his wonderful family, who deserved a better man. I bit my tongue about that, too. It wasn't my fault that he used me to cheat on his wife, was it? Whatever.

As I walked back to Mathieu's, I saw Pedro on the hillside, picking coffee.

"Me voy," I called out to him, I'm leaving. I held my arms out, anticipating a hug.

He stopped picking coffee for a second and looked down at me. He waved one hand in the air nonchalantly.

I cried on my walk back to Mathieu's farm, cried for giving this man too much of myself. For opening my heart when I shouldn't have. For having horrible sex for the first time with a man who wanted only to use me. In my journal, I wrote:

> *I thought maybe he really loved me. But he was just horny, lonely, restless, and curious. He just seemed to really appreciate the things about me that no one else ever noticed. That I speak beautifully, that I have delicate hands, that I have a happy smile, I am good with kids, and have "eyes like crystals," he'd said.*

I never saw him again.

Peru

Dr. Dentist

From Mathieu's farm, I took the bus to Quito and from there began a long stint of sweaty bus rides and transfers at small stations. When I finally arrived in Lima, a nice man who had been sitting next to me on the bus offered me a ride with his friend. I accepted, because the city looked huge from the bus windows. Without a map, I was totally overwhelmed and intimidated.

After sharing lunch at the man's house, his friend brought me to a hostel in Lima that cost only about five dollars a night and was near the airport.

While I'd been traveling in Colombia in late November, I received an email from Scott, whom I'd met with his girlfriend on the farm in Ireland.

The email I received from him had a subject of "What the Fuck is Up?"

"Remember me? Scott?" He wrote with eagerness. "I broke up with my girlfriend and am re-evaluating life. I love your passion for travel. Where you at? Any chance I can join you?"

I responded telling him to get his ass down here to join me in Peru the next month!

He bought his ticket. He would arrive the day after I got into Lima. My hostel's proximity to the airport was perfect. I took a hot shower, the first hot water on my body in months, and washed some of my clothes. I sat on the balcony as the sun went down, perched in a comfortable hammock as I journaled in excitement of being in another new country.

I went back to my room. Two girls were packing up their things. They had a small device blasting music of poor quality. They explained to me they had just been in Peru for a few months, teaching English, and in turn, learning Spanish. The song, "Vivir Mi Vida" by Marc Anthony come on, and they danced around the room dramatically, reliving their emotional connection to the song, whatever it was.

I laid on my bed watching them enviously. They had shared an experience together. I wanted to be a part of their dancing somehow. I felt myself missing home and my family, my friends with common interests.

I slept well that night, anticipating seeing my friend again. I had one full day to explore Lima when I woke up and Scott would be arriving around midnight.

I explored the city alone, taking city buses and getting lost, sitting on a beach, eating street food, and exploring a few local markets. A guy I met in a park introduced himself as Rafi, half Peruvian, half Palestinian. He bought me a beer at a bar where he knew the owner. After our beers, we headed out to a park that Rafi told me the locals call *Parque de Los Gatos* or "park of the cats." Apparently, somebody let a few cats loose to scare away all the birds that picked through the garbage cans. Now, nobody controls the cats, and they were breeding like rabbits, Rafi explained to me. The bird problem was gone, though.

We meandered through an artisanal market in the cat park, and he treated me to a local specialty. They were donuts made with sweet potato flour and deep-fried in vats of oil held in mobile carts across the park. It was like New York City hot dogs, but for homemade donuts.

As we crunched into the greasy, sweet delights, I told him about my friend Scott who was coming to visit tonight. Rafi complimented me on my Spanish, saying he had thought, when we first met in another park, that I was Argentinian.

"And your friend coming tonight, he speaks Spanish?" Rafi asked.

I giggled. "I hope so?"

Rafi got me to the right bus to get back to the airport area. The bus was more like a large cargo van, filled with one-too-many passengers. A woman sitting next to me watched me curiously before she asked if I knew where I was going. I laughed and said yes, of course.

The woman got off at the same stop as I did and walked me a few blocks, explaining that this was a bad neighborhood and I should be more careful. We had some vague discussion about religion, and I told her I had faith that God would take care of me. She looked skeptical and questioned my confidence in strangers. I shrugged my shoulders and explained that I had nothing worth being stolen.

Nothing that mattered, anyway.

I thought about losing my virginity to Pedro; I wasn't scared of sex anymore. My purity was gone. I had nothing to lose. I didn't tell her any of that, of course, just thanked her for the company and wished away the memories.

I waited at the airport for an hour or so. I finally saw his brown ponytail, a head above the rest. I shrieked across the crowd. "*Scott!*"

I crusaded through the crowd and engulfed him in my arms.

"You have no idea how excited I am to have a friend here," I said, as we carried his things through the crowd and perched ourselves outside.

"You have no fuckin' clue how happy I am to *be* here," he said, looking at me and the surrounding landscape. "Wow, it's hot out."

I laughed. "Yeah, dude, and it's only nighttime. Just you wait. Are you tired?"

"Not really," he said. We must have just looked at each other for a few solid minutes of silence. He wasn't awkward and neither was I. Somehow, we felt like siblings or best friends, although we'd only spent three days together and almost a full year had passed.

I smoked a cigarette as we stood there outside the airport, approached by a plethora of taxis and people wanting our money. "I hope it's okay with you, I figured we could just stay here so we don't have to spend money on a hotel tonight."

He laughed and nodded his head. "No problem for me. I knew if I came to visit you, I would be in for a rustic experience."

"You speak Spanish?" I asked him as I took a long drag.

"No," he responded, and we laughed at that together. My body was shaking with adrenaline. I just kept staring at him and then I squeezed his arm. He was cool with it.

We went inside and laid down on the floor, our heads perched on our backpacks as pillows. It wasn't comfortable and I didn't sleep well. I was awakened by the hum of a loud machine. I rubbed my eyes and spotted a clanky motorized vehicle-thing approaching us. It looked like a tractor that was cleaning the floor. I shook Scott awake and went downstairs to get some coffee.

"Here it is, your first cup of authentic Peruvian coffee," I said to him, as we clinked together our paper cups of instant espresso from the beverage dispenser.

We stepped out of the airport and I looked at him. "So, where do you want to go?"

"Umm," he glanced around like a kid in a candy store. "Somewhere real."

"With food?"

"You know me so well," he said with a grin.

I walked him to a small market I'd found the day before. Hunks of flesh were being chopped and handed to people, bowls of soup ladled, and piles of fruit sorted. I looked at Scott after we'd walked under a faded tent, down a dirt path, past a few of the gritty vendors. "Is this okay?"

He laughed contentedly and leaned forward against a glass display to order some noodles from a grouchy-looking woman. She asked if he wanted the gray fish, too?

"Uh," he hesitated. "Yeah. Yes. Si." He put his thumbs up to the woman as he stuttered to remember how to say thank you.

We sat down at a plastic table and I glared at the little fish heads poking out of his noodles. I thought he had promised to go vegetarian with me. I pointed that out.

"I don't know, man, this fish just looked so *good*!" He said sarcastically. "I hope I don't get sick from it."

"Yeah, cause then I could really say 'I told you so,'" I said, laughing.

He choked on the mass of noodles in his mouth and looked at me dismally, no room in his mouth to formulate a comeback.

We found a few different markets, and I bought some beautiful earrings made from the shell of a dried gourd and burned in the pattern of a flower. We found corn nuts with a spicy seasoning to snack on, and Scott tried passionfruit for the first time.

"What, you eat these gray pillows?" He asked me, as he ripped the skin off and discovered what looked like shark eggs inside.

"Best decision you'll ever make," I assured him. I laughed as he tried slurping up the juice-filled pouches for the first time.

Scott and I connected easily those first few days, yet we agreed that this city setting wasn't what we were looking for. Lima felt "Americanized" with huge buildings and familiar brand names. In the middle of the downtown area when I walked into a coffee shop and it cost nearly the same as in America, I knew something was wrong.

We were perched on the rooftop patio of our hotel as I googled farms in the area. Scott was lounging in a hammock and watching some traveling hippies give each other tattoos and smoke weed. I found a farm online in Pichanaki, a subtropical jungle area of Peru. I got a response from the farmer almost immediately. It was all in Spanish. I scanned it quickly and read part of it out loud to Scott.

"Hey, it says they actually pay us to work!"

Scott's attention came to me immediately. "Whoa, that's cool, lemme see," he said. He sat next to me as he looked at the message. "Oh fuck, it's all Spanish?"

"Ha! Scott what do you think you have me for anyway?" I pointed to the line where it said they compensated us. I read it out loud. "*Nos da dinero*, that's awesome."

"Well, I hope they don't work us too hard," Scott laughed.

We took off from the hostel together with all our belongings and bought more fruits on the way. I was delighted to see Scott tuck his banana peel into a small patch of dirt.

I commented, "I do the same thing. I hate to imagine those nutrients going to waste."

He laughed heartily and looked up at me, "Really?" He ate his banana as we kept walking, and then added, "Of course. You hippy."

Our backpacks bumped playfully.

After an hour's walk and purchasing our tickets at the bus station, we waited outside. I walked into the bathroom with my toothbrush and came out to see Scott sitting in silence. He smiled as he saw me tuck my wet toothbrush into a pocket of my backpack.

"You're awesome, Mel," he said.

"Thanks. I know."

We arrived into the lush city of Pichanaki in the early morning. The setting was so very unlike Lima's desert, dry climate. We walked into a tiny café, unsure where or when our farm hosts would be expecting us. I ordered us a few coffees. A little boy sat next to me and stared as I sipped my coffee and looked out the open doorway.

A guy driving a motorbike, with a girl wrapped around his waist, pulled up to the curb. She got off the motorbike and approached us. "Melanie? Scott?" Her bones showed through her chest beneath a mass of necklaces. She had curly black hair and her tank top was cut off above her belly button.

We nodded our heads as I set my coffee down to shake her hand. She introduced herself in English as

Vanessa, with a heavy, melodic accent. She pointed to the man sitting on the motorbike.

"That's Juan Carlos," she reported, as he looked stoically at the road ahead of him. He was thin with a pile of dark hair in a spiral on top of his head and dark skin. He had snail shell gauges in his ears. He held up two fingers to say *peace* with the mention of his name.

Vanessa continued in English. "We have a couple things to do, we can meet you back here in fifteen minutes?"

I smiled and agreed, and they sped off together. Scott and I finished our coffees and soon they returned, this time without the bike. They kept their word.

"Vamonos?" Juan Carlos said, "Ustedes tienen hambre?"

I looked to Scott. "Are *you* hungry?" I asked him, nodding my head slowly in anticipation of his response.

He laughed. "Always!"

We walked off with them, speaking in English about Juan Carlos's piece of land; he grew coffee and vegetables. It was deep into the jungle and we would have to walk part of the way. Juan Carlos explained that they had also purchased a small building in the village where they were trying to make a vegetarian café and hostel.

We went to lunch at a restaurant which Vanessa insisted on paying for. "We feed you, no?" She said. "It's part of the exchange."

Scott and I looked at each other and graciously accepted.

After lunch, Vanessa and Juan Carlos gave us some instruction on how to get to the house where we would stay that night. They had to go to the market, but there were other people in the house that we could meet. We would talk about evening plans and activities, things we could do for them. "We have so much work to do now," Vanessa said, "so your timing is perfect. Thank you for coming! You help so much!"

Scott and I separated from them, looking at each other whimsically. "She's awesome, no?" I said to Scott and he skipped as he was walking.

"Yeah, this place is going to be so great."

We arrived at the house. A big blue door and its proximity to a radio tower matched the description we'd been given. Scott knocked. We waited. "Are you sure this is right?" He asked me, as he put his hand over his brow to shield his view from the sun and peek between the cracks. "You guys were speaking Spanish. If you'd been speaking English I would probably know what was going on."

"I don't know . . I think so?"

We stood for a few moments, looking around. Then I succumbed to that familiar I-don't-know-what-I'm-doing feeling. The feeling I get all the time when I'm traveling alone but no one ever sees so it doesn't usually matter. A flush of anxiety overtakes your bloodstream and you wonder if anything is going to be okay.

I leaned against the peeling paint of the blue metal gate and watched people walking by. Scott tossed his backpack on the ground, sat on it, and joined me in my vacant thoughts.

281

Someone came to the door a few minutes later, a beautiful guy with dark, Hispanic features, yet crystal blue eyes. "Hello, welcome," he said as he opened the door for us. He spoke Spanish, with a European accent.

We walked into a big empty space that was under construction. Lofts were being built up to the right. A huge pad of concrete that looked freshly poured. Piles of new 2x4's and tools lying around everywhere. A small open-air kitchen in the back, with a few cats lounging on the counter and in the sun, and an enclosed building behind the kitchen.

A few other people were there, and a girl with a giant afro was seated at the table, rolling a joint. She was covered in jewelry, tapping her foot and nodding her head to music we couldn't hear. We put our bags down and she greeted us without looking at us. "Hey guys, what's up," she said in English. She had an American accent. "Juan Carlos is glad to have any extra help."

Scott and I sat down at the table. We had anticipated arriving at the farm today, being out in nature. This was transitional, though, so we were just planning to wait until Vanessa and Juan Carlos could take us into the jungle.

Finally, the pair showed up with some building materials. Juan Carlos asked to speak with me into one of the back rooms.

"So," he began in Spanish. "You remember online, where you give us money to stay here? It's twenty soles each day for your room and board."

I stared back at him in response. I wracked my brain to remember his farm profile as we stood there staring at each other blankly. "Um, no, I don't remember that."

He smiled gently and put his hand on my shoulder. "I sent to you an email about this money exchange. It's important we have volunteers to help fund our projects."

All the blood rushed out of my face. I had misunderstood the email he had sent me in Spanish? My mind scrambled to understand it, as I pictured the typed words in my head. *"Usted nos da,"* it had read. Oh, I had gotten the verb order wrong. I looked back to his face as it finally clicked. He had asked *us* to give *him* money to stay here. Twenty soles a day was the equivalent of about $10 USD.

I smiled as things started to make sense in my head. He waited patiently for me to take out my wallet. I nodded my head slowly. "Okay, let me just tell Scott."

He held his hand out gently to stop me. "You agreed to this, remember?"

I laughed. "My Spanish is not so good. I didn't make that connection. I misunderstood."

He smiled and lowered his hand. "It's okay. You just each give 280 soles for the two weeks you stay with us."

With that, I exited the room and did some air math as I pulled Scott aside, to where we had placed our backpacks in the entryway. He was asking for the equivalent of $140 USD. From each of us.

In English, I explained to him what Juan Carlos had divulged to me. Scott laughed awkwardly and ran his hand through his hair. "Damn."

"I know," I said, and laughed out loud. "Maybe we should just do it, whatever. We can help them. They seem like good people, right?"

"Yeah. What am I gonna do with this money except spend it? May as well help somebody." He reached into his wallet and pulled out 300 soles.

I brought our money to Juan Carlos. *"Gracias,"* he said, as he put his hands together at his mouth, in silent regard.

He handed some of the cash to Vanessa to go buy some ingredients for dinner. She invited me to come along.

She explained to me the meal she would make. It was hot pasta tossed with fresh garlic, olive oil, dark purple olives, fresh basil and oregano. "Italian classic," she said, as we waded through the market, glancing at carrots and picking out the freshest basil. "You like to cook?"

I nodded my head enthusiastically, and explained that I'm mostly vegan, and that means you have to know how to cook.

We went back to the house and helped to assemble the meal. Later, after cleaning, we were offered our first tea with coca leaves, traditionally consumed to relax locals and given to travelers to ease altitude sickness. It's also exploited across South America to produce cocaine.

"It's a soothing drink, to relax before sleep," Juan Carlos explained. "The effects of the coca leaves are different for everybody, but when it's a tea, it's only for relax."

A mug of the tea was passed around. I declined, but Scott had some. I watched the expressions of all the partakers shift. It was reminiscent of the first time I had seen my sister smoke marijuana. I felt betrayed, almost, and intimidated by their psychological shift. Everyone's eyes glazed over and sunk into this lull of silence. Sober and aware, I sat at the table and stared at my glass of water.

Scott and I were given our own beds that night, with hard, thin mattresses. The next day we helped a bit with constructing the frame for the restaurant on the upper loft. Balancing on the beams was a bit precarious but thrilling to do some actual construction work. Later that afternoon I asked Vanessa if we could go to the farm. She said we could, but we'd have to go by ourselves and they would meet us later.

Scott and I looked at each other excitedly, took directions from Vanessa, and headed up the mountain. We jumped on the back of someone's truck and got off where we'd been instructed to. We walked down a long road until we came to a tiny house with a small dog barking aggressively. We kept walking and it followed us.

Scott tried to keep his voice low. "Should we scare it away?"

"No, it'll probably leave us alone, let's keep walking."

It followed Scott closely. As we turned a corner and stopped looking at it, when we thought it had disappeared, it came out of nowhere and latched onto Scott's ankle.

"WHAT THE HELL??" Scott yelled in frustration.

Immediately I kicked the dog and saw Scott crumble to the ground, wincing in pain. It continued barking insistently, watching us. I reached down to give Scott an arm.

"Come on dude, let's get out of here!"

I helped support him as we continued walking away until we could be within safe distance from the vicious animal and inspect the damage he'd inflicted on my friend. We sat down a few hundred feet away, on some rocks so we didn't get our butts covered in mud.

Scott's entire sock and shoe was covered in blood. He pulled the sock down from his cut, but the fabric was stubbornly clinging onto the cut. We could nearly see through the hole between the tendon and the bone.

"Fuck, man, that's disgusting," I said to him, trying to brush it off.

He picked up my inflection and tried to stay light. He rolled the sock back up and I picked up his backpack. He hobbled along beside me.

It must have been another hour of slow walking until we finally approached the farm that matched Juan Carlos's description. It was a rustic wood frame with a large open loft overlooking the jungle and valley below. As we walked across a tiny piece of wood from the road to the loft, I could hear music playing. Somehow Juan Carlos had beat us here. He was playing guitar. I called out to him for help and the music stopped. He eased Scott into the loft space and Vanessa came up the stairs with some tea.

"Oh no, what happened?" She asked as she set down the tea tray.

I explained how Scott had been bitten by a strange dog.

"Yeah, hope I don't get rabies or something. It just bit me out of nowhere," he said, as he furrowed his brow, slowly wincing in pain from peeling the sock off his wound.

Juan Carlos said he could take Scott to his brother who practiced medicine in the city. Vanessa cleaned the wound with some hot soapy water and an hour later, Scott and Juan Carlos disappeared together on the motorbike. I was left alone with Vanessa and she offered to give me a little tour of the farm. From the loft, we climbed down a ladder and arrived in the kitchen. We walked out into the yard, where there was a large yard space with no garden. "When we don't have volunteers, we don't have time for a garden," she said.

"But on the farm profile it said you eat vegetables from your garden?" I asked her.

"Not now. We haven't had volunteers like you for a long time. Maybe you can make the garden for us."

I smiled as my eyes scanned the horizon, distracted. "I hope Scott's okay."

She showed me the bathroom, a hole in the dirt with some wooden walls, covered with a shower curtain for privacy. She opened the shower curtain and said, "I hope there's some paper here, for the toilet," and then nodded. "Oh, just a little left. We'll have to get some more." Her voice trailed off. She took me on a small walk around the rest of the property.

She brought me to the top of a hill where I saw that the coffee trees were each only a few feet tall. They wouldn't be producing coffee beans anytime soon.

As we walked back to the main farmhouse, I thought about all the claims they'd made on their website. Did they only *buy* food? They didn't grow anything?

Scott and Juan Carlos arrived a few hours later, after Vanessa and I prepared food in the kitchen with a few root vegetables that were past their prime. There was no refrigerator, so keeping store-bought vegetables fresh was not easy, especially in this humid, warm environment.

Scott laughed when he saw me, as he hobbled into the loft space to sit on a mattress on the floor. "How did it go?" I asked.

"Um, I'll tell you later. I'm starving," he responded.

The four of us descended into the kitchen in near darkness, where Vanessa and I had made dinner over candlelight. There seemed to be tension between Scott and Juan Carlos. We hadn't had any space to discuss his trip to the doctor yet.

We went up to the loft space where there were hammocks and mattresses we could sleep on. Scott whispered to me as the two of them retired to a small room.

"Um, so the doctor I went to see? You know, his brother?"

"Yeah?"

"This guy was a dentist. A *dentist!*" He laughed loudly. "I mean, lousy excuse for a doctor!" He said as he tried to pull the covers over his leg slowly. "He didn't know what the fuck to do, he just cleaned it. He gave me some pain pills, but he stared at the bite like he'd never seen blood before."

I laughed out loud. I couldn't help it. What was happening? Who were these people? I hoped they could impress us soon. I told Scott about the coffee "trees" and all the work it looked like we had to do.

"I don't know what they expect of us. There's really nothing to do here. Except maybe buy toilet paper and move some mud around. We'll see tomorrow, I guess." With that, we rolled over and said goodnight. I wrapped the sheet tightly around my body to deter the relentless jungle mosquitoes.

The next morning Juan Carlos took me down to help with the coffee trees and do some weeding around them. We spoke a bit about his intentions with the property. When we walked back to the loft, covered in dirt, he saw a frilly, gummy-looking fungus growing on a log. It was dark purple and had the texture of frog skin. He picked it up proudly. "This is a good one to eat," he said, and stuck it in his pocket.

That night I fried the fungus he found in oil with greens, and we tossed it all with hot pasta. It had a unique flavor, and the texture added to its intrigue. I'd

never eaten a wild mushroom with such strange char-
acteristics. They left that night after dinner, promising
to arrive the next day with antibiotic medication for
Scott's dog-bitten ankle.

When we woke up in the morning, it was pouring
rain. From the loft, I looked out on the landscape,
where the rain made the colors more intense. I saw a
mother opossum with eight or nine babies on her back,
running to her safe, dry home, under the building's
wooden frame.

Scott played music that day, the first time I'd ever
heard him sing. He had a voice that dulled every negative thought in my head. While he caressed the guitar
and cultivated a melody, my eyes drifted into the space
around us. He sang "Colors" by Amos Lee. I hadn't
heard that song in years. He kept playing and singing,
and I joined him when I knew the chorus. We passed
much of that day watching the rain and forgetting
about his wound and our isolated new life.

That night I made dinner, boiled beets with seasoned rice. As I plated a meal for Scott, his foot draped
across the bench, we heard commotion outside. We
heard rapid speaking above the rain pouring down on
the metal roof. We saw flashlights flickering through
the window. Suddenly a tall man with a blue raincoat
walked in and was followed by a young Peruvian.

The tall guy reached his hand out to me with a big,
confident smile. "Hola, soy Nico. Como va?"

I set down the wooden spoon without breaking eye
contact. He was gorgeous.

I gulped and smiled genuinely, then responded in Spanish, telling him my name. He pulled my shoulders towards him as he kissed me on both cheeks. He took his raincoat off and I saw his glossy red hair. "I'm a Frenchie," Nico said in English, as he shook Scott's hand. He ran his hand through his hair and took his backpack off. Then he switched back to Spanish for me. "Smells *good* in here!"

The other guy smiled gently and sat down at the table. He told me in Spanish that he was a friend of Juan Carlos, and they had called him to tell me that they couldn't drive up in the rain. They would come back when the roads weren't so muddy. Instead of rolling my eyes at more frustration for our hosts, I translated for Scott and we shared a moment of pursed-lip recognition. I asked in Spanish if everyone was hungry. Nico responded in Spanish, saying I was an angel.

I was glad the lighting was dim. My face was red as a cherry.

Nico started eating and didn't stop. "Wowwww," he said as he ate. I watched him closely as I picked at my food. I think Scott saw me. "This is really good," Nico said in Spanish, with his mouth full. We didn't exchange many words over dinner. Everyone seemed to be famished.

Scott and I explained what we were doing here, which was a short explanation. We had no idea what we were doing here.

Nico switched to English when I asked what *he* was doing here. "I've been traveling for six months with my friend. He is French, too, so I didn't get very much

291

Spanish practice in the beginning," he laughed to himself. "And now I get to practice my English! Nice!" He looked at me with a big smile. He continued, "My friend had a sailboat in the Caribbean. And then I went alone, I needed to do some soul-searching. And now, I guess, I am supposed to be here. Maybe I was supposed to meet you two."

My face flushed again. Thankfully Scott broke the tension that perhaps only I felt and asked how he'd learned Spanish.

Nico pulled a cigarette out of his pocket and lit it. The small man who had arrived with him took one too. "I didn't study before South America," Nico said. "I thought, Spanish is easy, no? I'm French. I can learn it, no problem. But it took me a long time."

He took a long drag of his cigarette and pointed at me with it. "Your Spanish is good. It's a good accent. You don't sound American." Did he just wink at me? Oh shit. "Did you study somewhere?"

"Yeah. High school." I didn't want to talk, I just wanted to look at him. I pulled a cigarette out.

Nico shared some beautiful Spanish music from his tiny iPod shuffle. "La Vuelta del Mundo" by Calle 13 was my favorite, a song about a man trying to convince a woman to leave her dull life behind and travel around the world with him. The Peruvian guy sat with his legs hanging off the edge of the loft, overlooking the jungle.

Around the light of a single candle, Nico showed us how to make bracelets, a skill he'd picked up while cruising down the Amazon River on a raft with a bunch of locals. The candle just slightly illuminated the tiny brown hairs sprouting around his jaw. His red hair was dirty but flipped out at the ends.

"I think it's awesome you traveled like that for so long," I said.

He paused, mid-braid. "Oh yeah, but you did more than me, no? I mean, your travel was a lot more difficult than mine I think." Now his face was illuminated by a smile, too. Dare I say a twinkle in his eye?

We went to bed that night, and Nico and the Peruvian chose to sleep in hammocks. I admired Nico's confidence and his presence. Somehow, that night, I dreamed of him.

The next day brought more rain, and with it, another day of isolation. Where were Juan Carlos and Vanessa? What were we supposed to be doing here? The Peruvian guy left us that day, so we spent the afternoon drinking coffee and sharing travel stories on empty stomachs. We made bracelets and used our toes to hold the strings intact as we wove them.

"Yeah, I thought maybe this place was too good to be true," Nico said, as he picked some colors for another bracelet. "I don't think I'm going to pay to stay here." At that, Scott and I laughed and explained my poor Spanish understanding of who was getting paid for what. Nico laughed, too.

Again we slept, anticipating arrival of our hosts the following day. The next morning the rain had stopped, and the Peruvian guy came to meet us. He wanted to take us for a walk to see Juan Carlos's mother and show us some tropical fruits in the jungle. Unfortunately, Scott was still in recovery mode and had to be left at home.

We discovered avocados from someone else's land and ate them on a big rock overlooking a wide stream. We took a picture there, together, balancing my camera on a mossy rock. We found some lemons and a rotted papaya. I didn't believe it could be rotten, so I took a bite of the pink mush inside. Nico laughed at me. "It's a wine, now, I think," he said, referring to how long the sugars had ripened inside the skin of the fruit. I looked up at him with a furrowed brow and papaya seeds dripping down my face.

"No, I think it's delicious. You should try."

Nico smiled down at me where I sat crouched, pretending to devour the fruit. He approached me and held his hand out. I scooped out a big pile of the mush and threw it at his face. He yelled in shock and I ran ahead on the path. He chased me holding the papaya high in the air.

We went back to the farm building and were not surprised to see that in fact, Juan Carlos and Vanessa still had not appeared. The Peruvian guy left us and wished us luck. We sat down and Scott picked up the guitar to relax us with some music.

Finally, at 5 PM, I broke the silence. "Why don't we leave? This is dumb. They abandoned us and we have nothing to do. Let's get out of here and do something. Scott, can you walk on your foot okay for a few hours down the mountain?"

Scott laughed. "Yeah. Let's get out of here."

294

Nico seemed a bit hesitant, but agreed he would like to leave and get on with his travels. "I don't have any other plans. And anyway, I'd like to have an adventure with you guys. Escaping the Peruvian jungle farm with two Americans!" He raised his arms in the air in a grand gesture, and I reached forward to high-five him.

We packed up the craft space and suited up in our boots. We went for a long walk down the mountain, telling stories to maintain our morale.

While the sun was setting, we heard a sudden sound of some tree branches rustling. Three or four tiny gray monkeys flew through the air in the space between branches above us. We paused, mesmerized.

We continued down the mountain and before we knew it, darkness was upon us. Trucks passed us going up the mountain. We had hoped to see a truck driver going down the mountain who could offer us a ride, but no such luck.

We took a small break for a cigarette on a cliff over-looking the glimmering city lights below, hoping we didn't have much further to go. We watched the last bits of the sunlight flicker from view and were interrupted by the sound of a motorbike behind us. We turned around.

It was Juan Carlos and Vanessa.

"What are you doing?" She asked, getting off the motorbike. Juan Carlos wasn't looking at us.

Neither Scott nor Nico said anything, so I decided to take a stand.

"We had to leave . ." I let my voice trail off as I gathered my next words. "To be honest, Vanessa, we were really unhappy. We had nothing to do, and no food, and Scott needed medicine. We paid you, but you left us stranded. We were really hungry, so we figured we would see if we could find you guys."

She stared at me blankly for a moment as my blunt words sank in. She walked back to the motorbike and lifted a few bags from where they were tucked behind her seat. I could make out a plastic bag of toilet paper and some food. Juan Carlos held out a tiny paper bag.

"Here is the medication for Scott," he said in English. "Maybe we will see you later in the village. You can stay at the house in the city tonight, I think someone is there to let you in."

I looked at Nico and Scott and decided to speak for us collectively again. "I don't think we want to stay there anymore. We're gonna get some dinner and leave. I would like to get some of our money back. I don't think this has been fair."

Juan Carlos finally made eye contact and looked vaguely insulted. Vanessa settled in behind him, gripping his waist. "Okay, fine," she said. "There's a good Chinese place with a yellow sign. We'll meet you there in a few hours. Look out for snakes," she called over her shoulder, as they sped off.

The three of us picked up our backpacks and continued walking. Nico had a small flashlight and we walked another hour until a truck passed us, going down the mountain. We waved them to stop and jumped in the back, amidst a bunch of motorbikes that were piled on top of each other.

We got to the town and thanked the driver. We found the Chinese restaurant and ordered a bunch of food and a few beers. We took a picture. As we started drinking, Juan Carlos and Vanessa walked in. They stood above our table.

Juan Carlos looked at my face, and down at the beers on the table. "I don't have the money for you, it's already spent," he said sullenly.

Stubborn as my father, I held my ground. "You promised us work, a place to sleep, and that you would provide food for us. I didn't even understand in the initial email. If I would have known I had to *pay* to help someone, I wouldn't have arranged to stay here."

As the words uttered my mouth, I realized how harsh they sounded. Juan Carlos looked like he'd been slapped across the face.

"You know, we don't have jobs," he said slowly, almost embarrassed. "We live only with the money the volunteers provide, and we can provide an experience for them in return."

I laughed as I took a sip of beer. "No, Juan Carlos," I said, as the server placed large servings of steaming food before us. I channeled the energy of an angry monarch in his castle. "You don't understand. If this was some sort of donation, if I had offered you money as a gift, it would be completely different. No. I felt like this was some sort of business transaction, and with that is a give and take. You didn't hold up your side of the deal. You left us stranded! That's not fair." I picked up my fork and knife. Nico and Scott sat in silence and began eating.

"You can borrow money from someone?" I asked.

"It's not that easy. The money is already spent, I told you." He looked meaningfully at Vanessa. "Maybe I can try. Are you taking the bus tonight somewhere?"

He said he'd try his best to meet us there in two hours with whatever money he could find. With that, Vanessa and Juan Carlos walked out the door.

Scott widened his eyes as he looked down at his plate. "Damn, Mel."

I finally put my fork into my food. I saw one of the purple fungi that looked like the one Juan Carlos had found in the jungle and given me to eat. "Well, someone needs to stand for justice here." I brought the purple mushroom into my mouth and chewed it, allowing the flavors to satiate my craving for justice. I was sick of being a pushover.

We finished dinner and walked out to a park. Nico and I left Scott there to relax on a bench while we went hunting for a few more beers. As we walked back, Nico explained he had no idea where his next journey would be. He didn't know what he wanted to do, who he wanted to be with, where to go.

Like clockwork, a man in a car stopped on the side of the road. "English, English?" He called out the window aggressively, as if addressing us by name. Nico and I looked at each other and nodded our heads slowly.

We learned this man was looking for someone to teach English in his community to kids on their break from school. Nico said he loved kids.

"And I pay for your food, your hotel, your time," the stranger said in Spanish as he gave Nico his number. We kept walking.

"Well, that's pretty awesome," I said to him as we followed the cracked sidewalk, carrying the bottles of beer. "Think you'll do it?"

He looked down at the number. "I guess?" He laughed to himself as we rounded a corner and neared the park where we could see Scott lounging. "It was pretty perfect timing, no?"

We sat down next to our crippled friend and told him about Nico's new English job. We drank our beer on the park bench, giggling, excited to be free once again, in the endless world of opportunity that is spontaneous travel. The three of us went walking to the bus stop, sufficiently buzzed from all the beer.

Juan Carlos was there. He had 100 soles in his hand, which I accepted with a large smile. It was about $50. It hardly seemed worth making him work to attain, but it was the principle that impressed me. I thanked him and gave him a hug. I apologized for all the confusion as he hugged me back.

Scott and I bought bus tickets while Nico smoked a cigarette outside. Our bus would leave in about an hour, so we went out to join him. I reached for Nico's cigarette and he gave it to me with a smile. I took a drag and handed it back to him.

"So, you're sure you don't want to come with us?"

Nico looked out into the street as he exhaled a cloud of smoke. He looked back at me with a sideways grin.

"No, I think I stay here. It was really cool to meet you. Maybe it was destiny?"

"Things happen for a reason," I said confidently.

"I think maybe I will try to teach the kids." He shrugged his shoulders and raised his eyebrows. "So, I guess I'll say goodbye, wish you well, etcetera." And rolled his hand out in front of him. He shook Scott's hand and reached forward to give me a big hug.

"Good luck," I whispered in his ear.

He gave me a firm kiss on the cheek and slipped me a piece of paper with his email address on it. "Keep in touch, no?" With that, he walked off into the night, tossing his bit of a cigarette on the ground and glancing both ways over his shoulder before crossing the street.

Scott looked at me as I watched Nico wave to us from across the traffic.

"Ooh, Mel," he said, as he pushed my shoulder gently to break my intense gaze. "You have a man friend."

I laughed at him casually. "Yeah," I looked back to the street where Nico had disappeared. I hoped I'd see him again. "Wait, you really think he liked me?"

Peru
Paranoid Stoner

Our bus to Huancayo appeared. We slept for the five-hour ride through the mountains at night. We didn't have a plan. We only knew that we wanted to get to Cuzco so we had the option of hiking the Inca Trail. We arrived in Huancayo and caught another bus to Ayacucho, arriving in the early AM.

Scott and I split up for the afternoon in Ayacucho. His foot seemed to be healing well and he could almost walk like a normal person now. I found a bunch of strangers to talk to and was invited into someone's house to learn a few words in Quechua and taste some of their homemade *chicha* (a fermented quinoa and corn drink). They walked me back to the bus station and I saw Scott sitting there talking to a stranger.

We bought our next bus ticket to Cuzco that evening. The bus was jam-packed when we boarded, so he sat near the front and I waved goodbye as I walked to the nearest empty spot in the back.

A young, chubby guy was sitting there, looking out the window. We started speaking in Spanish and he told me about his small cell-phone company. He had just spent a few weeks in the jungle. He pulled a little box out of the bag at his feet and opened it. He reached for my wrist and encircled it with an ornate, hand-beaded bracelet of turquoise, bright red, purple, and black beads, clasped together by small seashells. The bus driver turned up the AC for some reason and my new friend offered me some of his large wool blanket.

Our bus stopped the next morning somewhere for a breakfast, and Scott and I reconnected at a table in the restaurant. He told me about a little girl sitting next to him who had a pet hamster. She was playing with it in her arms and handed it to him, "and the little fucker jumped off my lap! It was crawling all over the floor! She got so mad at me, and it wasn't even my fault."

We laughed loudly in the restaurant. Everyone else seemed to be delirious from the long bus ride. I told him about my new friend who had shared his blanket with me and given me a beautiful bracelet. Just then, he appeared with a smile. Scott raised his eyebrows at me as my over-eager seatmate squeezed in the booth next to me.

We finally arrived in Cuzco in the afternoon. We found an internet cafe and did some online farm searching. Nico had given me a list of contacts through his membership to WWOOF Peru. I researched one farm and sent them an email. Michael, an American man living in Peru, sent me a kind, welcoming response within minutes. We didn't even pay for a hotel that night, just followed Michael's directions on how to get there from Cuzco. It wasn't more than an hour bus ride, so off we went.

We arrived in the charming village of Calca and found a tiny motorized vehicle (something between a taxi and a motorcycle) to take us up a gravel path to the gate of the farm.

We paid the driver, thanked him, and knocked on the door. I could see through crack between the gate and the wall that there was a huge garden with flowers, cacti, and neon Swiss chard. My heart started beating rapidly when I saw the garden.

With a large smile, a sixty-something year-old man opened the door. He avoided direct eye contact and wore loose clothing. "Hey guys! I'm Michael. Welcome, Scott and Melanie?"

His white-gray hair was collected into a thin, greasy ponytail at the nape of his neck. He spoke in our familiar American dialect.

Michael opened the gate for us as we were greeted by a small dog. He gave us a brief tour, pointing out the house in which he lived, various gardens designed with Permaculture principles in mind, a tiny greenhouse filled with sprouting wheatgrass and baby plants. He explained he was from Arizona and had moved here over ten years ago to escape American politics. "The people here are nice," he said. "Genuine. I've never looked back."

He explained that his small farm sold the vegetables, herbs, and seeds to local shops in Pisac and Calca.

"There's lots of hippies in Pisac," he said. "They usually buy anything organic they can get their hands on. Ah well, it's good for me!" He pointed up the hill to a white house. "That's the volunteer house. Pico and Ayla are there now. Go on and make yourself at home."

We thanked him and looked at each other as we walked up the steps. "Um. Is this too good to be true?" I asked Scott in a whisper, with my eyebrows raised to the sky. He chuckled in response.

The volunteer house was beautifully beige with tall ceilings, vintage wooden furniture and dark floors. The kitchen was open to the living room, and there was a fragrant pile of weed sitting on the coffee table. A young girl with dark hair and tight pants came out into the living room. She must have heard us walk in.

"Hey guys, I'm Ayla. How's it going?" Her thin, white tank top showed that she wasn't wearing a bar and she had a nice tan. She had huge headphones resting casually around her neck.

We introduced ourselves and put our backpacks down in the room filled with bunk beds. Ayla called to us from the kitchen. "Want some ginger tea?"

"Sure," I called back down the hallway as we returned into the living space. A well-built man walked into the room from outside. He was wearing a khaki sun hat and a goofy smile and held up two fingers in greeting.

Scott just started laughing and shook his hand as if he knew him. "What's up, man?"

His name was Pico, half Mexican, half African American. He was also from Arizona and spoke with many curse words, casually, like Scott did. The two of them started swearing up a storm while Pico rolled a huge joint. He offered it to both of us.

"If I smoke that," I said, shaking my head slowly, "I'll be useless for the next two days."

Pico laughed. "So?" And shoved the joint in my face.

Ayla came over to sit on the couch next to Pico. She laughed as she placed a mug of tea in front of me.

"You came to volunteer *here*, and you don't smoke weed?" She and Pico looked at each other mischievously. She took the joint from him and took a few long drags and lounged against the back of the couch.

"So, who's up to make dinner tonight?" Ayla asked Pico.

He laughed in response; eyes nearly closed completely. "I don't know, man."

Scott sat there, not stoned but seriously entertained. I went out the door to sit on the patio and watch the sun begin its descent. Scott came to sit next to me. We reflected on the last few crazy days of travel. "This place is probably exactly what we need," he said.

That night we went down to Michael's house for dinner, where we met a young couple who were full-time employees. I was delighted to find that the meal was a delicious vegetarian chili with cornbread and fresh cheese. We sat on the couches and talked about each other's lives.

Our days on Michael's farm ended up being as much about vegetable production as about smoking weed. We had a good mixture of working hard during the day and relaxing at night. Ayla left after a few days; another volunteer popped into the farm one day and swept her off her feet. She decided to leave the next day to travel with him. They wanted to hike the Inca Trail, she told me, and he was Swedish. He entranced her, she said as she kissed us goodbye.

Michael taught me his recipe to make perfect rice every time, at varying altitudes and with any variety of white rice. Sauté one-part rice in some oil, stirring over high heat until the majority of the rice looks toasted. Then measure one-and-a-half parts water to pour over the toasted rice. Toss in some salt and a few crushed cloves of garlic. Stir it until the water begins to boil, then drop the temperature to a simmer and close it tightly. Within exactly 20 minutes, it will be fluffy perfection. Guaranteed.

Scott and Pico and I worked hard during the day, Pico smoking about ten whole joints alone by lunchtime. He and Scott did a lot of tasks together during the day; I spent my time weeding, cleaning out the chicken coop and tending the greenhouse.

One night over dinner, Pico told us about the neighbors, how he had stumbled upon them one night and they invited him in for drinks. He said chicha was passed around in a single cup. The last drop of alcohol was dumped onto the floor, and everyone yelled *"Pacha Mama!"* It stood for "Mother Earth," a tradition the people upheld to appreciate the earth for its blessings.

Pico told us about a well the community needed to build. Michael, the owner of the farm, had asked Pico to come to the community meeting before the well was built, so he could translate for him. Michael didn't speak Spanish. After the meeting, Michael asked Pico to go help the community to dig the well on the mountain. Pico was always up for anything, so he had gone off with strangers for a few days to build a well.

"And we were fuckin' starving," Pico recounted.

"You didn't bring any food, man?" Scott asked.

"I didn't think it was gonna take so long. All we had was chicha." We all burst into a chorus of laughter, imagining of our gentle giant getting drunk on the top of a mountain with all these locals, dirty and digging all day.

One day when Pico was gone, Scott was approached by a local woman with two children. She asked him where Pico was, and he didn't know. She handed a foil packet to him and asked him for a certain amount of local currency. He pulled some cash out of his pocket and handed her the requested amount and she and her kids left. He came back up the stairs to the volunteer house where he told the story to me. He opened up the foil package and saw a clump of weed.

I was shocked. "Why did you give her money?"

"I don't know, she was asking for Pico, I just thought maybe this was for him."

As we laughed, Pico showed up in the doorway.

Scott tossed him the foil pouch. "You owe me 40 soles," he said. "I think I just did a drug deal for you."

Pico's jaw dropped. "Serious? You paid 40 soles for this? She played your ass."

Scott furrowed his brow and rubbed his elbow. "She had kids with her! I thought she was good for it."

"She's a *player*." Pico said as he tossed the foil wrapper onto the table. "I need to find a new dealer."

The three of us occasionally spoke about our frustrations. Michael never did any outside work with us, just came out of his house every few days to get fresh air. We worked hard for him and he never offered any appreciation. Pico had been comfortable and happy with his position on the farm, until Scott and I voiced *our* opinions.

"He's an oily, greasy man," Scott said. "He doesn't even speak Spanish. How long has he lived here?"

Pico smiled and looked at the floor. "I don't know, three years? I have no clue."

I interjected. "I don't think he appreciates you enough, Pico. You are the shit."

Pico laughed at that and ran his hands through his short black hair. "Nah, man, I'm just doing my job. I like working hard. Especially blazed."

"I think maybe we should go, Mel," Scott said to me. "I really want to be somewhere I can learn more Spanish."

We resolved to leave soon. The next day, Michael called us over as we began transplanting some succulents. He invited us to take part in the *Ayahausca* ceremony that he conducted once a month with a bunch of hippies in the area. "It's not a typical, jungle ceremony," he explained from his lounge chair on the patio. He was speaking to us, but his eyes were fixed on the computer resting on his lap. "I invite a bunch of people to join us in the instruction room beneath your volunteer house. The ceremony is religious-based. It will show you some clarity." He picked up his coffee and looked away from his laptop screen for a second. "It's not to get high or out of your body, it's a reflection on your life and will most likely lead to revelations." He glanced between our faces. "I think you would all enjoy it. The ceremony begins tonight at midnight. It costs 80 soles, and it usually lasts for the duration of the evening." He went on to explain the repercussions and different physical reactions it could have on your body. "Puking is normal and encouraged. It gets the old toxins out of the body."

Scott and Pico seemed excited about it as we discussed it later. "I think we should wait to leave until after the ceremony. Are you gonna do it with us, dude?" Scott asked me, as I poured myself a cup of coffee.

"Uh, no. I have enough revelations just being in another country and with strangers. I also feel like the world already makes sense to me," I reached over to pat his forearm. "You know, with my belief in conventional religion."

Scott laughed. We'd always disagreed in all matters existential. He believed we didn't have a purpose, and I believed we did. It was that simple.

"Well, I don't want to tell him we're leaving until after the ceremony. He's a slimy motherfucker, I don't trust him," Scott said. "What if he, like, treated me badly because he was angry at me for leaving early? What if he gave me poison instead of the drug?"

That night they donned white robes and each gave me goodbye hugs, "just in case we shit our brains out and never see you again," Pico said.

"Good luck!" I called out, as they walked toward the door. "And have fun?"

Pico put his fingers through the doorway to give me a peace sign before disappearing. I laughed. I made myself dinner and music began to seep from the floor below. I could almost feel the house shaking as the group of people began singing loudly. After I ate my dinner, wondering what in the world was happening below me, I sat on the patio to have a cigarette. I heard puking noises, and I saw somebody dressed all in white run out to the edge of the grass to throw up. I crushed my cigarette and went inside. I fell asleep restless that night, anticipating some weird stories in the morning.

I woke up and made some coffee. Scott and Pico came out an hour later, looking disoriented. I had secretly imagined they would come out of the ceremony as different people. I expected them to lose their familiar slang and crude language, their easy-going attitudes. I expected them to stop smoking weed or have some pivotal experience convincing them to never again utter an offensive, defaming word.

Instead, Scott announced to the room: "I need some fuckin' coffee."

310

Pico chuckled as he fell into the couch. "Yeah. What the fuck happened last night?"

"Somebody was puking on the grass," I called from the stove.

I turned around to look at them. They looked at each other and burst out laughing. "Yeah, that was *you!*" Pico said to Scott, pointing in his face.

"No way, man, that was you," Scott laughed as he rubbed his forehead.

"Well," I said, as I poured a cup of coffee for Scott. "It could have been both of you. There was a lot of puking last night. Do you guys feel okay?"

"Nah," Scott said. "I actually just feel kinda hungover."

They explained how it had felt, likening it to a wild night of drinking. Michael had mixed the Ayahausca potion and administered it to them individually, but the experiences were had collectively. Scott said he'd only wanted to go outside the whole night and look at the stars, but Michael's regimen required him to stay within the group. They had been led through the experience with songs, worship, and intoxication of a different sort. Pico complained about feeling physically heavy but being told to remain standing when he wanted to lie down.

"I think that fucked with my high," he said.

Now that the Ayahuasca ceremony was over, both of them wanted to leave. Pico divulged that he would like to leave in the middle of the night so Michael wouldn't have to see him leave. I told him that seemed wrong.

We decided to tell Michael, to his face, and let him know reasons why we wanted to leave. I made mashed potato and spinach-stuffed raviolis with a sage pumpkin sauce for dinner. After the meal I explained to him that Scott and I were going to leave. He seemed upset but nodded his head in acceptance.

We left that night and said goodbye to Pico. He planned to have some alone time with Michael and, after, promised to meet us in Calca at a hotel. Scott and I adventured down together, taking small motorized cars and walking through the village to finally arrive. In the hotel we ran into a woman, Marine, who had been around the farm a few days a week helping in the gardens. She was French and had told me to pronounce her name like "submarine" without the "sub." She had an expression of sympathy all the time. If you complimented her on her beautiful shirt, she would wince and smile sadly. "Oh, thank you so much. I don't deserve that. But thank you."

Marine had dinner with us and Pico joined us the next morning as we were drinking coffee. He told us he had left in the middle of the night.

"What? You didn't talk to him?"

"No, he would have been so disappointed in me. He liked me a lot," Pico said. He rubbed his hands together and glanced around the room. "I couldn't deal with seeing him angry or sad or something."

"Dude, he can get as many volunteers as he wants," I said, slapping him on the back. "You're just a paranoid stoner!"

We spent the next few days in Calca, reuniting with other volunteers from the farm and exploring some ruins for free. This Sacred Valley area around Machu Picchu was brimming with ruins along the roadside. We got up early one morning under instruction from the owner of the hotel and climbed up some rocky steps towards some ruins.

The summit of the dry mountain allowed us to see for miles in every direction—the surrounding villages, the hippy area of town with brightly colored buildings and mandala flags, and the pools of the rich ex-pat housing area. We discovered terraced walls built many hundreds of years ago. There were no other visitors, and we watched the sunrise with our bums resting on rocks moved by a civilization we will never know.

Scott broke the awed silence. "I really have to take a shit."

"Ha," Pico laughed. "Me too, man."

I shook my head as Scott took his t-shirt off and ripped it into two parts. "Here you go," he said, as he handed half to Pico.

Marine and I wandered away, seeking distraction. Minutes later, Scott called to us, "That was the best shit I ever had, I think."

"Where did you go?" I asked him, as Pico joined us to the next set of ruins.

"Oh, you know," Scott said slyly, as he pointed toward an old fortress. "Somewhere over there. On top of a mountain. No big deal."

I stared at him with my mouth hanging open. "What about the shirt?"

"Don't worry, Mel! I covered it with a rock."

I sat down alone to imagine what these ruins would have looked like a thousand years ago, bursting with vegetation and animals, a community of people laboring collectively to survive the weather conditions, feed themselves throughout the entire year, and protect themselves from external attacks. Our lives are so easy, I thought to myself in a necessary moment of appreciation. The work of our ancestors had led us all together in this moment in space. Now, was *I* stoned, or what?

Peru

Too Much Caca

Exhausted after a morning of exploring ruins, I sat down at an internet café to discover an email from Nico. He said he'd been on local TV doing a commercial. He hadn't been paid yet for his teaching, but the man we'd met on the street had paid for his hotel and food. He was kind of bored, though, he told me. Could he meet up with us later? I responded that yes, absolutely anytime he was welcome. I also told him we had escaped another farm.

Pico, Scott, Marine and I stuck together. We caught a small bus up into the Andes mountains, where the landscape looked like the surface of the moon and alpacas ran along the roadside. We saw asparagus farms and potato plantations, huge boulders, and large, serene ponds reflecting the cloudy sky. When we arrived at the top, we found a hotel and the owner told us to go to some hot springs, where we then spent our afternoon lounging in the bubbling, mineral-rich waters.

We headed back down the mountain the following day and caught a bus to Cuzco. Marine split off from us and our trio ended up at a pizza restaurant where the server spoke to us in Spanish. I ordered for us all, and Pico added a couple of items. We had a delicious, cheesy pizza filled with vegetables. Scott and Pico goofed around, and I excused myself for a cigarette.

The waitress was outside, also smoking. She introduced herself as Aldana and said she was from Argentina. I muttered a response in Spanish as I took a drag of my cigarette.

"Your accent, it's very good. I might think you are from my country. Those guys inside are American?"

"Yeah, but one of them speaks Spanish better than me," I said, referring to Pico.

She smiled and scribbled her email address on a piece of paper and told me if I was ever coming to Argentina, I should let her know. I thanked her as I crushed my cigarette on the ground and held the door for her.

The next day we bummed around Cuzco, navigating so well we felt like locals. We went to a large indoor market where we bought stuff to make a picnic. We split up. Scott and I were together getting some olives while Pico considered buying some candied cashews. A woman was standing next to me, buying a large bag of purple olives. I commented in Spanish on her choice, asking whether those were the best ones?

She looked startled and responded yes, they were her favorite. When she asked what I was doing here in

Peru, I took a moment's pause. Scott would be leaving me in a few days. I have no idea, I told her.

She gave me her address in Quillabamba. I was welcome anytime, she assured me, and added her name. I stuck the note in my wallet and kissed her on the cheek graciously.

Along with a new contact in Peru, we had scored bread, cheese, avocados, grapes, and olives. We laid our stuff out on the grass in a park and ate everything.

Our little clique decided collectively to go to Puno. We took an overnight bus. Pico puked from the altitude. Sometimes I had the feeling I was alone on another planet, with the desolate, empty rolling landscape ahead, shifting quickly from desert plains to rippling, cold altitudes to lush, green mountains.

After walking around and comparison-shopping at a few different places, we arrived in this new city and found a hotel. We were there early enough in the day, fortunately, but we had also been informed that we'd arrived during a huge festival. Prices were high and Pico was still sick from the crazy ride through the mountains.

We settled into our hotel room and Scott and I headed out to find some food for Pico, to settle his stomach. We stumbled into an outdoor market where I bought a small purse handmade by an older lady. She sold it to me for about $3 USD. I also saw a woman selling a bundle of varied clothes that I'd seen the local people use to carry babies or groceries on their backs. I approached her confidently, asking how much they cost. Thirty soles, she said. About $15 USD.

317

I laughed at her and kept walking. Scott was looking at some other handicrafts and I told him about the cloth assortment I'd seen and the ridiculous price she'd given me. He smiled and said, "That's probably the only tourist she'll see all week. Why *wouldn't* she charge that much?"

He had a valid point. I told him how much I wanted it, and he encouraged me to go back and bargain the price down. So, with my friend's confidence boost, I returned to the woman.

I asked her if I could buy it for half the price. She uttered a small chuckle. "No, no, no," she said and pursed her lips. She stepped away from me to straighten some piles of cloth in an act of dismissal.

I pointed to a dirty one sitting behind her. "How about that one?" I asked in Spanish.

She laughed again at me. A man walking by stopped to watch. "But, this one is mine, and it's dirty," she said.

I smiled confidently back as she picked up the object in question and pointed to smudges on the fabric, rips, and what looked like dried, melted hot glue.

"Yours has the flavor of the local people," I told her, with my back straight and my eyebrows raised. "I would be honored to take it back to America with me."

She looked shocked. A few more people gathered behind me, watching and listening to our discussion. Scott appeared, loyally at my side. The sales lady shook her head dismissively. "No, no, no, the new one here, I give you for 25."

Competitive through my core, my fire had been stoked. All I wanted was that used blanket. I proposed another offer. "This old one, yours, for 15 soles. Then you can have a new one for yourself."

She stared back at me in shock, and the few people who had gathered to watch this American make a deal started a chorus of laughter. I couldn't tell if they were laughing at me or laughing at her for not accepting the offer immediately.

She agreed, reluctantly, and handed her faded cloth to me. "Fifteen soles?" She asked, still appearing confounded. I handed her the money and the little audience who had gathered around me started clapping. We both scored big, was how I saw it.

Scott and I laughed our way over to buy some crackers for poor Pico, who had been left in the hotel room and away from the action. We bought some watermelon and a few apples and went back to check on him. He was just waking up from a nap.

We spent the afternoon and evening with him, making sure he had everything he needed to feel better. We also bought him some coca leaves to chew on, which seemed to help. That night we watched a few movies and I pulled out the coffee beans from Ecuador that I had "stolen" from Mathieu's farm. We cracked the coffee beans out of their thin paper shells as we watched movies on my laptop.

The next morning Pico was feeling better, so we wandered the city with him. We went to see Lake Titicaca. We were shocked to see toilet paper in the marshy outskirts of the water. I saw a few pieces of excrement as well. Lake Titicaca had its name for a reason, apparently, as *caca* in Spanish meant feces. We saw a few people peeing in the lake near us as we crouched down between the marshy grasses to smoke weed in privacy. Strangers approached and asked if we wanted a ride out to the lake. I was stoned and couldn't speak for us. Pico deflected the offer and thanked him anyway.

Before we knew it, the sun was setting and we were hungry. We got some dinner and stumbled into a huge festival. I found clove cigarettes, which I remembered having when I had been in Indonesia and bought them out of nostalgia.

We ended up somehow in the middle of the parade, surrounded by trumpets blasting and people singing. We stopped at an enticing little stand that was serving fried food. The cart was decked out with squirt-able tubes of white, yellow, green, and purple sauces.

I looked at what was in the fryer—potatoes and sausages. I asked for my plate with no salchichas, and all the toppings. The lady raised her eyebrows but appeased my request.

The white tasted like mayonnaise, yellow like mustard, the green was spicy hot, and the purple must have been pureed purple olives. It was delicious, although I definitely chewed on some pork crumbles.

"Damn," Pico said as he watched me devour my greasy meal. "That looks so good."

"What did *you* get?"

"Some sandwich from a stand over there," he pointed behind him as he wiped his mouth. "That looks better, though."

"Well, go get some then," I said, mouth full. "It was only 3 soles."

That night, the three of us wandered the streets for hours before we finally made it back to our hotel. A man stood at the entrance, trying to convince us he was Willie Nelson. He was dark-skinned and obviously Peruvian and apparently drunk. We shrugged him off.

"Yessss," he slurred, his arm blocking me from entering the hotel. "Willee, Nel-sonnnn."

He tried to hug me and sing me a ballad. He got down on his knee and held his arm out in front of his torso dramatically. For some reason, I just wasn't in the mood to stand up for myself.

Pico stepped between us. He told him, in those crude Spanish words he'd learned on the streets of his hometown, to leave me alone. I'd never had someone stand up for me like that before, as I was accustomed to traveling alone. My heart swelled in appreciation as Scott held the door for me to walk inside.

"I don't know what you're going to do after we split up," I told Pico, as I plopped onto our large, shared bed, "but I think you should keep traveling on farms and volunteering. You're a good person." He sat down next to me and I wrapped my arm around his stomach.

"Girl, I been takin' notes since I met you," he said, and his face was illuminated just enough that I could see his smile.

It was late in the evening. Our stay in Puno ended the next morning, as we all took a bus back to Cuzco together. We arrived in the early morning and waited in the city for shops to open so we could get coffee and breakfast. Pico lit up a joint on the sidewalk and I smoked a cigarette. "Dude, someone's gonna see that!" I said to him.

He laughed, as he tried to hold in the smoke, and handed me the joint. I took a puff out of obligation.

We started walking and saw a place that looked open for business. The name of the place was "Rico Pollo." Delicious Chicken.

We walked into the restaurant and were beckoned to a table in an outdoor courtyard, filled with flowers and twinkling lights on a strand. I smiled at Scott and raised my eyebrows, confident of my breakfast-restaurant selection.

We were given a few menus, but barely glanced at them. We were on the edge of the city, away from the tourist area. We expected the food to be cheap no matter what we ordered.

I asked for a papaya juice and a bunch of sides: corn, rice, and French fries. The waitress wrote down my request without a smile or nod of recognition. The two boys ordered the daily special, a picture of it gleaming from a banner behind them: *caldo de gallina*, or chicken stew.

My papaya juice was brought out and the boys looked at it enviously. It didn't have any flavor. I think it was just milk with some pink coloring added. We looked at each other silently and eased back into our seats. We were exhausted and hadn't eaten for a while.

After what seemed like hours later, our plates were set in front of us. Mine was simple as could be: white rice, fries, and unseasoned, cooked white *choclo* (corn native to the area). I had eaten it off the cob on some long bus rides when women would walk down the aisle of the bus calling out to any empty stomachs, "Choc-lo, choc-lo-o-o." It retained its bulbous exterior, while the insides tasted something like mashed potatoes.

The boys were presented with huge bowls of steaming soup consisting of a hard-boiled egg tossed on top of the mixture of broth, chunks of potatoes, and large chunks of chicken.

I cleaned my plate within a matter of minutes. The boys stared at their bowls, unsure how to begin eating. As I wiped my mouth and finished my milk-juice, I watched Pico hesitantly scoop a spoonful of broth, blow on it, and bring it to his mouth. His brow furrowed and he looked at Scott.

"Dude, there's no flavor," Pico said, as he swallowed the broth and looked at Scott.

Scott started laughing and nodding his head. "I'm just excited for this chicken, man," and he grabbed the bone of the drumstick that was resting on the side of his bowl. He picked it up and tried to chew on it carefully over the bowl, without dripping any broth on his lap, proving to be unsuccessful. He had a bite of meat in his mouth and chewed it. Pico followed his lead.

They looked at each other. They spooned around in their bowls, eager to eat anything to give them sustenance. Pico spooned up a chunk of white potato, and slipped it into his mouth. His face contorted.

"This tastes like how a barn yard smells," Pico said aloud, and we all started laughing. "It's not even cooked all the way!"

Scott looked at me and muttered under his breath as if he might offend someone. "That is the toughest motherfuckin' chicken I ever tried to eat."

Pico burst out laughing and blew broth all over the table. They pushed the bowls of soup away from themselves simultaneously.

Although neither Scott nor Pico had come close to finishing their meal, Pico stood up from the table. "I'll get the bill," he said, as he walked off toward the register in the front of the restaurant.

Scott and I gathered our belongings and asked the waitress for a plastic bag. He tossed the chunks of chicken into it. "Maybe we can give this to the dogs in the street," he said to me, with a wink. We met Pico at the counter, where he was staring at the slip of paper.

He turned to me, his face devoid of color. "Um, yeah, that soup." He looked down at the slip. "It was 18 soles."

I laughed out loud and slapped him on the back. "Shut the fuck up, Pico," I said, chuckling and looking at Scott to join me. "How much was it really?"

He looked at me sullenly. "No, it was seriously 18 soles."

"What?" I ripped the piece of paper from his hand in denial. My eyes scanned the list of food frantically. The items were listed in a neat line and the total was something like 60 soles.

The waitress appeared behind the counter, waiting eagerly at the register. I could feel the anger rising within me. My plate alone was 10 soles? My plate of corn, rice, and French fries? 10 soles amounted to about $4 USD. And the disgusting milk-juice was listed at 8 soles.

I slapped our order list on the counter firmly. I looked the woman in the eyes as I contested each price listed. I concluded the reading in laughter. Then she shook her head. Scott and Pico went outside, eager to move on.

After about five minutes of contesting the price, she finally lowered the total bill by one-third. I paid and went outside to Pico and Scott.

Pico looked up at me from where I was standing on the stoop, a foot above him. "You okay, Mel?"

I sighed dramatically and pulled a cigarette out of my pocket. I lit it and laughed. "No. She was a bitch."

We saw a pack of dogs sniffling around in the street, as was common in South America. Scott took the bag of tough chicken and set it on the ground some distance from the dogs. He rolled down the top of the bag so the dogs could find it. We stopped on a street corner where we waited for the dogs to discover the chicken. I leaned against a building, fuming.

"I cannot believe that restaurant. What makes them think they can charge that? We speak Spanish. So *what* if we have light skin." I paced around awkwardly and looked at Pico, with his dark complexion. "How do they know? You could be Peruvian. You speak enough Spanish to be Peruvian." I took a long drag of my cigarette and put my hand on my hip.

Scott and Pico looked at each other and back to me. "It's okay," Scott consoled me. "It's over. It doesn't matter."

Some dogs approached the bag laying on the ground. They sniffed it and walked away.

I tossed my cigarette on the ground and crushed it with my shoe. "No. You know what? It does matter. I don't want them overcharging us just because we're tourists. It's not fucking fair!"

Retracing our steps, I raced back to the restaurant.

Scott yelled after me, but I ignored him. Instead, I yelled back and asked Pico how to say *ass* in Spanish.

I marched back into the restaurant, where two girls—one of them had been our waitress—were sitting down with a meal. Not *caldo de gallina*, I noted.

"Excuse me," I said in the loudest, most obtrusive, aggressive Spanish I could muster. "My friends and I, exhausted and starving, came to you for food."

They put their silverware down, astonished, and stared blankly back at me.

"We ordered food from you, a papaya juice that was only milk, rice and corn that tasted like nothing," I held my fingers out for dramatic effect, counting their faults. "Soup with potatoes that 'tasted like how a barnyard smells' and chicken too tough to eat. We paid, like good people, and brought the leftover chicken from the soup to the dogs in the street. They sniffed it and walked away." I paused, relishing my power. I gathered up all my courage and stared up at the ceiling for strength.

I looked back down to their blank faces. "*Rico Pollo, mi culo!*" I slapped my ass before stomping out the door.

I found Scott and Pico there, waiting eagerly for me leaning against the outside wall of the building. Pico was laughing so hard. He high fived me as I passed.

"Dude, that was amazing," Pico called after me, as I surged ahead on the sidewalk.

"Let's go get some real breakfast," I said as I scanned the horizon for another option. Scott came up and put his arm across my shoulders.

"Do you feel better now?" He asked in my ear.

I nodded my head eagerly and spewed out all the curse words I had learned from them in the past few weeks.

We headed back into Cuzco. Scott and I, wanting a permanent reminder of each other, decided to get piercings together. We found a narrow shop with dark typography and graffiti-covered merchandise. Inside, a man pierced my bottom lip.

"That looks pretty badass," Scott said, slapping me on the back. He had always wanted to get his septum pierced, so why not now, with me, in Peru? The man spoke to me in Spanish, which I translated for Scott. He asked where Scott wanted the piercing and Scott showed him. He lounged back on the chair, with his head tilted back, looking at me.

The first piercing was quick. Scott looked upside-down at me, wincing in the aftermath of the pain. "Does it look okay?"

"Uh . . . Look for yourself," I said.

He got up and inspected himself in the mirror. I stood behind him. The piercing itself was a C shape, with two little balls hanging on the cartilage between his nostrils. It looked uneven. Scott and I noticed at the same time.

"I think maybe you should get that redone," I said, as I giggled to myself quietly, trying to disguise my disapproval from the artist as he shrugged his shoulders. I asked him to redo it.

Scott laid back. "I don't know if this is a good idea," he said, looking at me upside-down again.

I laughed. "You'll be fine."

The artist removed the old piercing from Scott's nose. He cleaned the hole again and got the needle out. Scott closed his eyes tightly in anticipation. I squeezed his pale bicep.

The artist pierced his septum for the second time. A tear tumbled from the corner of Scott's eye onto his forehead. I'd never seen him cry before. My instinct was to hug him, but I had to wait for the artist to finish his work.

Finally, this time, when Scott looked at his reflection in the mirror, he was satisfied. "But I'm never doing that again," he said, laughing, as he handed the cash over and we headed out the door to meet back up with Pico.

328

We had one full day together. Scott and Pico bought some weed off the street and we went for a long walk through the city, up a small mountain to some old ruins. We sat together, smoked some more, and watched the sun go down. In the last efforts of the sun, the roofs of all the adobe buildings were just barely visible.

The three of us got in a taxi, heading to the bus station. Tonight, they would both depart in their own directions. I made sure they had their transportation plans established.

I hugged Pico tightly, excited to have a new close friend. I held Scott for a long time, thanking him for joining me. Then we all had a group hug. Pico waved casually, offering a peace sign. Scott's voice got low as he watched me walk out the door. "See ya, Mel."

I kept it together until I got away from the train station. I walked down a gently lit path, within safe distance from where I'd left the boys at the station. Sadness bubbled up from beneath me, and I suddenly crumbled on to the pavement, alone, mourning the departure of my dear friends. Pico, who taught me to take everything lightly and keep a thick skin, live for the present and the future and never look back in regret. Scott, who taught me to trust my intuition and the passion within me. It felt as if I'd lost them forever.

I picked myself up off the ground and tried to keep walking. Through the glimmer of a lone streetlamp, I saw a small yellow cart. I wiped my eyes with dirty hands and glanced around to see empty streets.

I stumbled to the cart, where a tall glass container was filled with popped corn kernels. A man was standing behind it, with a slight smile on his face.

"Quieres algo?" He asked. Did I want anything?

I nodded my head slowly. He scooped into the container and handed me a paper boat of white popcorn. I reached into my pocket and placed a few coins in his outstretched hand. I walked away, holding the popcorn precariously in front of me. I placed a kernel on my tongue and felt it soften as I closed my mouth.

The emotions came back, this time in a flood. I kept eating the popcorn, now soggy and salty with my tears. The darkness faded as I neared the city lights.

*   *   *

The next morning, I found a small colectivo and headed to Quillabamba. The woman I'd met in the market in Cuzco, a time that felt like months ago, had given me her address. Aimless, I decided to track her down. She'd also told me there were many, many coffee and cacao farms in Quillabamba.

I arrived in this new village, a jungle town with no tourists in sight. It was in a valley bordered by lush green mountains. After giving the driver the piece of paper with the address, I took a small taxi up the side of the mountain. He dropped me off and I walked door to door, knocking and asking if each person I met was Profesora Ibis Salas, or knew of her. The sky was gray, and I was growing tired of receiving blank stares in response. Finally, I had a lead, a glint of recognition in someone's eyes. "Si, la Profesora?" A man with a brown cap asked me.

I nodded my head eagerly. He pointed me to a wooden door that I hadn't approached yet on the other side of the road. I walked over to it and knocked. The professor answered the door, with her eyes wide and a smile across her face. She invited me inside and offered me a coffee.

The house was like a grandmother's—pastel walls and doilies in the windowsills. I painted my fingernails with her older sister, helped them pick plums from their tree in the backyard, and tried some chocolate from their own cacao trees. My Spanish was still subpar, yet I understood that my new friend Ibis had some sort of illness and had given her cacao plantation to her nephews, yet she still got the beans from them and made them into chocolate. She regretted to inform me that she didn't have any work for me to do, yet she advised me to go to the market and ask around. I'm sure you can find someone who needs help, she said as she kissed me goodbye the next morning.

I thanked her for her kindness and headed back to the village below us.

I found a hotel and dropped my stuff off, then asked strangers in the street to guide me to the market. I was pointed to a huge indoor arena. Packaged snacks glistened in the light of the day, and people were selling vegetables, potions, and tonics. There was even a juice bar and what appeared to be a deli. I approached a young woman selling potatoes and asked her, in Spanish, if I could help her with her potato farm.

She smiled at me awkwardly and looked me up and down. I was wearing a skirt and my hair was short and glossy; I'd just taken a shower that morning.

I caught her judgmental inflection and held my hands out to her. "I'm a hard worker," I said, the frustration creeping up in my voice. "Look at my hands, I am calloused!"

She glanced at my hands and shook her head slowly. Potato season is over, she said.

I walked away, my gait a bit less confident than seconds before my rejection. I approached a few more vendors. Can I help you grow these tomatoes? The people all gave me the same look of dismissal, as if I had just asked if I could have some cash for the bus. Yet as I walked away from yet another rejection, a lady came up behind me, grabbing my arm firmly. In a whisper, she asked if I knew how to take care of a baby.

I assumed she was joking and kept walking. She pulled me close to her and looked at me somberly. She explained that her daughter had a baby but couldn't care for it. She was too young. Did I want it? It would only be temporary, she said, for six months.

My smile dripped off my face like melted ice cream when I realized she was serious.

"No, no, no," I insisted, explaining I was looking to take care of vegetables, not a child. She looked offended.

I left the market and wandered back to my hotel in defeat. I pulled my journal out of my backpack and sat on the patio to reflect on my frustrations. A group of young girls approached me, speaking Spanish and twirling around the metal fence of the patio as they watched me curiously.

I went to bed that night, hoping tomorrow would be a better day.

The next morning, I got some coffee and walked to the park. I strolled around the town, looking for a new adventure. No one approached me; nothing was falling into place. A surge of homesickness washed over me. Why was I here? I didn't belong here.

Frustrated, clueless, aimless, I decided to go for a hike. When I'd arrived in the village, I'd noted a white cross on the large hill in the center of the city. I stopped at a small shop to buy some chocolate, necessary energy before some physical exertion. After giving the smiling woman a coin, I turned toward the door. Another woman walked in and eyed my chocolate as she walked past me.

"What are you going to do with that?" She asked in Spanish, as she paid for a bag of chips.

I stared at her as she sat down on a plastic chair in the middle of the shop and opened the chips.

"Nothing," I said. "I just needed something sweet."

She chomped away and I stared at her for a few moments. Then I broke the silence and shared my morning. Here I was, looking for a place just to help, I explained, and nobody wanted me. She had been the first person interested in me in Quillabamba, my captive audience. So, I told her, I was going to eat this chocolate and walk up the to cross.

She rolled her eyes at me dramatically. "You can't go up there alone," she said. "It's dangerous. There are kids doing drugs."

Immediately I thought of Scott and Pico and the weed we had smoked together. Would I be likened to one of those kids doing drugs now? I shrugged off the idea and smiled genuinely at her. She offered me a ride up the hill on her motorbike. "If you really have to go up there," she said, crumpling up the empty bag, "I won't let you go alone."

"Fine," I said with a slight smile.

She walked me to her motorbike and told me to hop on behind her. As we made our way up the muddy road, she turned her head back and told me that her name was Maru, but everyone called her Marujita. She had a friend, Ana. Would I like to meet her now?

We diverted from the road up the mountain to a little shack surrounded by a chunk of jungle. There was a petite woman, Ana, with silky, dark skin and moles on her arms. She showed me some huge cacao trees on the property that her parents had planted. Then she invited us to join her for lunch.

"First, we go up the mountain," Maru said with a grin, as she looked at me.

The three of us piled onto the motorbike and headed up the mountain. *Phew, phew,* the little engine choked as it struggled to accommodate such a load. I opened my bar of chocolate and shared it with them as we rode up the winding path.

We arrived at the top, parked the bike, and started off on foot, as the cross was only a few hundred feet away. I saw a cluster of young boys. Maru pointed at them and raised her eyebrows. "See?" She said, in Spanish. "It would be dangerous for you to be here alone. You're lucky you have Ana and I to protect you," she laughed as she patted Ana firmly on the back. Ana rolled her eyes and pushed Maru as we continued walking up the hill.

When we got to the top, we shared a moment of silence. Maru broke it and said, "Let's go, that's enough." As she hustled past me down the hill, she called back sarcastically, "Worth it, Melanie?"

I laughed and ran down after her. When we got back on the motorbike, Ana asked if I needed a place to stay. I explained I had a hotel room for the night, but maybe tomorrow? Maru piped up, saying I was welcome to come anytime. She would show me her house and I could come tomorrow with my things.

That I did. I found she lived in a house with her many middle-aged siblings, their various children, and her mother, who was ancient and very large. I was given a big bed next to Maru and treated like family.

One morning I went out to buy bread, eggs, and avocados to make breakfast for the family. When I returned with my arms full of food, Maru seemed distraught. She patted me on the back, explaining that I wasn't supposed to do that, I was the guest.

Maru invited me to join her friends for a funeral. We walked through Quillabamba to a lush cemetery. Many of the grave sites had gardens planted around them, and some of them were so old that trees had emerged and the trunks had realigned the funeral plaques. It was like a jungle that just happened to have bodies buried in it.

There were also tall buildings split up into tiny sections where bodies were put in, like dresser drawers. In front of each of the drawers were tiny little shrines, honoring the peoples' lives. You could see old photographs and plastic flowers shoved into them, some filled with incense or even a burnt-out cigarette, in remembrance.

After the funeral procession and the mourning ballads, we walked across the street to a tiny bar. A busty woman, the owner, stood there and welcomed us boisterously, already drunk. Ana, Maru, and I sat down at a table and were presented with beer after beer after beer. We must have sat there for hours, drinking and laughing in Spanish.

"Ana will teach you how to dance," Maru said, as she played some traditional music from Quillabamba. The music was blasting so loudly that I couldn't hear anything else. The singer, Princesita de Quillabamba, had a high-pitched, childish voice. Ana explained to me that the singer came from the high mountains and was very well known.

She pulled my arms out from my sides as we stood in the middle of the bar, and showed me how to hold them out, like a bird soaring through the sky. *Oooooh,* the Princesita cooed. Then Ana showed me to tilt my whole body to the left and run in a circle, tilt my body to the right and do the same thing. Everyone in the bar watched us and giggled. I sat down, dizzy and exhausted, and reached for another beer.

Then someone put on Shakira, hoping I would know the song. I did, in fact, and got to practice shaking my hips for a whole room of Peruvians.

Each day I didn't do much, just accompanied Maru around in her truck. She did some sort of construction work making cement blocks and selling them to construction companies. She liked her work, she told me on our long days together, and assured me she enjoyed having my company.

I checked my email in the internet café daily. Nico was still bored, he said. The English lessons hadn't worked out quite like he had hoped. He was teaching only two children for three hours a day. He was never paid and the man who had recruited him didn't want him exploring by himself. Could he come join me?

I wrote back a short email. "Yeah, meet me in Quillabamba! I'm staying with a lovely family. We can meet you tonight in the park in the center of the city." I didn't wait for a response, as Maru wanted to take me to see some waterfall today. Ana was coming, too. When I met up with them, I shared the news that a friend was coming to visit me. Maru was excited.

We returned home and I walked out the door to look for Nico. Maru and Ana stopped me and insisted on joining. She paid for a taxi ride and we sat in the park to wait for him. Ana bought some popcorn in a paper boat and we surveyed every stranger who walked past us. After about an hour of waiting, I told them I was ready to give up.

"Segura, Melanie?" Ana asked as she crumpled up the paper boat. Are you sure?

I shrugged my shoulders and we all stood up and began exiting the park. Then, by the water fountain, I saw a tall guy with red hair and a blue jacket. I stopped walking and squinted my eyes as I tried to make out his face in the dim lighting. Maru and Ana stopped walking. "Is that him?" Ana asked me.

I nodded my head slowly as I watched him walk around the park. I waited a minute, relishing him the idea of him wanting to find me.

"NICO?"

He stopped walking and turned his face in our direction. He waved one hand in the air and his face lit up with a huge smile. I ran over to him and hugged him tightly. "Bienvenido a Quillabamba," I said, welcoming him to this wonderful city. Ana and Maru came up behind me and introduced themselves. I watched Nico as he spoke confidently, in perfect Spanish. When he looked away, Maru raised her eyebrows at me.

Maru then insisted on taking us out to dinner, and as the four of us walked, she punched me in the shoulder and whispered in my eye that Nico spoke much better Spanish than me. "Thank you, I am aware," I told her, glaring and nodding my head. Then I punched her back. She was a tough lady.

Nico fell easily into our rhythm. We had some wild nights drinking with the family, including visiting a club on Valentine's Day. He and I went off alone to go dance all night at a club with some strong alcohol and ended up falling asleep in the street. He and I shared a bed next to Maru, talking late into the evenings, my head on his chest.

Sometimes, at night, after we brushed our teeth, he would kiss me. Just a brief peck on the lips. I looked forward to it from the moment I woke up.

One morning, Nico made banana pancakes for the family, and we drank Pisco Sours to get over our hangovers. The family had guinea pigs, called *cuy* in Peru, running around on the ground. Sometimes, for dinner, one or two would be picked up, killed, and roasted in the oven. Everyone said they tasted like chicken.

One afternoon, Nico and I went to Ana's house and started picking up garbage that someone had tossed into the patch of jungle, under the citrus and cacao trees. We spoke about our views on trash. The people here had no dumpster, and they didn't realize that tossing garbage where they couldn't see it didn't make it go away. Someone eventually had to deal with it. I told Nico I wanted to save my garbage and have to look at it all the time. He laughed and said I was ridiculous, yet here we were both picking up soggy t-shirts and broken glass on a property that didn't belong to us.

Ana told me to climb a tree and pick a large brown fruit that was hanging. I reached up to get it and she instructed me to drop it on the ground to crack it open.

It was covered in brown bumps and inside were a bunch of white pillows, filled with a small black seed. "Guanabana," Ana said, identifying the fruit. She told me to eat the white part and spit out the seed. It tasted something like pineapple mixed with bubble gum. I saved some of the seeds and stuck them in my pocket. Maybe I would plant them someday.

Maru and Ana pushed us to visit Machu Picchu, as it was only a few hours away from Quillabamba. They explained to us which colectivo to take, where to go once we got there, and the cheapest hotel for the night before making the long hike up the mountain.

We departed one morning and headed out to Aguas Calientes, the small city nestled into the mountain beneath the beautiful ruins. It was a three-hour walk along the train tracks, and we decided to walk instead of pay. The small city was quite glamorous, Machu Picchu being a well-known wonder of the world. We found a place to get French fries and beer and found a hostel to stay at for $5 and shared a bed, snuggling together and exchanging sweet kisses in the darkness.

We got up the next morning around 5 AM and began our long hike up the steep mountain. Nico bought a paper cup of coca tea from a man at the base of the mountain. The path was all stone steps. We raced ahead past all the other travelers, who were stopping to take pictures every hundred feet or so. We got to the top, breathless, and entered the ruins. The fog was thick and we couldn't see anything yet.

We walked towards a lookout point, *Puerta del Sol* or Door of the Sun. As we approached it, the fog began to clear. The sun shone through a rock door frame that was constructed thousands of years ago, perhaps solely for this purpose. The light of the morning refreshed us, and we sat there eating snacks and chewing coca leaves for the altitude.

We explored the ruins together until early afternoon. It was beautiful, but though people had said Machu Picchu was the place to visit, I preferred the free ruins that Scott, Pico, Marine and I had found.

Nico and I headed down the mountain, practically running, and walked back along the train tracks to a small city where we could catch a colectivo to return to our family in Quillabamba.

We held hands in the car as it drove through the winding roads surrounding the mountains. A man spoke Spanish with Nico for a while, before he fell asleep, leaning his head on my shoulder. I couldn't imagine more beautiful scenery. Each time we approached the armpits between the impressive mountains, the roads were flooded by rivers pouring down rainwater. The car drove through them effortlessly. Yet, every time we approached them, I held my breath, imagining the car being pushed too heavily by the force of the water and just rolling down the mountain.

After Nico had fallen asleep and I was clinging to his hand, wishing it back to life, the man who had spoken to him tried to talk to me. He was flirting with me. He asked for my email address and I gave it to him, not sure what else to do.

We finally arrived back in Quillabamba to Maru and her family, who were waiting eagerly to hear how much fun we had. We slept early and well that night. The next morning, I would leave.

Maru arranged a colectivo to Cuzco for me, where I would take an overnight bus back to Lima to catch my flight back home.

My ride pulled up, and I hugged everyone goodbye. I thanked Maru endlessly for her incomparable hospitality. Nico and I hugged for a while.

"Thank you for coming here, to see me," I said as I pulled away from his embrace. "I'm so glad you did."

"It was just meant to be, no?" He responded, with a pained smile.

He kissed me goodbye and I handed him a short letter I'd written for him the night before. My car sped off and I looked through the window to watch the family waving. I waved back eagerly. Nico was just staring with a blank expression on his face. Would I ever see him again?

A few tears slipped down my cheeks as the driver turned the radio on.

I stayed one night in Cuzco by myself and met a man in the street making jewelry. He introduced himself as Rico, and fashioned me a ring. He took me on a small tour of the outdoor market and found a place for me to buy *mapacho*, the local name for the strong unfiltered cigarettes Nico and I had been smoking.

After a few transportation methods, I ended up in Lima where I would catch my flight. I got to the airport in time, said goodbye to South America, and was lifted back into the sky.

I left pieces of my heart behind in many places. Sometimes a chunk of it was torn off unwillingly, sometimes I had thrown pieces of it onto the street.

As the plane rose from the ground, I imagined Maru's family all piled up there, smiling at me. Then Nico standing nearby, waving. I pictured Scott next to him, with a huge smile on his face and his arm around Nico's neck. Pico joined them, pumping his fist in the air and chuckling with Scott. There was that bitch of a waitress, pursing her lips and glaring at me. Juan Carlos and Vanessa stared at me dismally. Matthieu with his hands in his pockets, a cigar hanging out of his mouth and his children at his side. Pedro sat down on the ground, head in his hands. Adriana was illuminated behind them waving her arms in the air, wishing me luck. Santi stood behind her with his headphones on and glanced up at me for a second.

And who was that man in the back, behind everyone else? Willie Nelson?

Epilogue
The Ideal Traveler

Thank you for reading my stories. Here I am now, in a shared, beautiful, dynamic household in Duluth, Minnesota. My travel is in the past, somehow. Leaving the country no longer appeals to me. What does captivate my interest is fostering community and kindness and goodness. Trust. Stretching the boundaries of compassion. Sharing food. Making dreams to spend my life chasing.

Here are updates on the coolest characters I met.

Scott, whom I met in Ireland and who came to visit me in Peru, just concluded some of his own globe-trotting. He might keep going, though. We get together once a year and talk on the phone often. He recently released a beautiful album ("Crookhaven") with a French guy he also met on the farm in Ireland. Buy it, it's freakin' beautiful.

Yola, whom I met in Indonesia, has come to visit me in the US. We bussed and hitch-hiked from the Midwest to the South and the East Coast. More than one time since these travels, I've been back to see her in France.

You remember Gemma. I met her in Turkey. She started her own organic vegetable farm with people in her area. Her goal is "to make good food available to everyone."

In Turkey, I met Romain, who finished his travel-by-bicycle worldwide tour, and now has settled in France with an American girl he met in India. They started a vegetable farm and have a child together.

Nico, coincidentally, lives in the same French city as Yola. He's volunteering his large heart out with every organization he can find to help. I was able to visit them both a few years ago in their shared city and introduce them to each other.

Taylor, my Australian love from the plane ride, is officially a part of my past. We haven't kept in touch. He's probably the reason I love moustaches on a man.

I keep in touch with a few of the farms I was working on, and it's wonderful to think that each time plants are started here in my region, the season begins for all the farms.. Each year bringing new volunteers, new struggles, and new bounties.

*   *   *

Volunteering on farms is a great way to get local flavor and hopefully feel you've left behind a good impression. However, it's not the only option. Workaway connects travelers who want to volunteer with a wide variety of opportunities: horsemanship, wood-crafting, helping in a hostel or a café, teaching English, cooking for a family, etc. If you have the cash to transport your person to a new place and you want to help people,

WWOOF and Workaway are two great platforms that are nearly free.

This book represented nearly three years of on-again-off-again travel. I spent much less than fifteen grand during those three years. I recommend travel as a way to get out of your comfort zone. You meet strangers who change your plans for the afternoon and, if you're open to it, the course of your life. It's easier to care for others in this capacity—almost as if there's nothing at stake. The question I have for you is this: What have you got to lose? Push yourself to connect with others and the future may pepper your life with things you never could have imagined.

The ideal traveler has an obligation to keep their eyes open and their hearts empty, to be filled with the experiences that present themselves. It means you are a blank canvas being painted upon by new people and places and sensory experiences. You, dear reader, are an elemental part of our future. You have a voice and a passion and abilities unique to you. Embrace the things that make you different, shine your light all around, and watch as the world unfolds goodness around you.

Why not always live this way?

Acknowledgments

Who do I have to thank? First of all, YOU, for buying and reading this book! You now know everything about me! Ha! Anyway, thanks to everyone who stood patiently by, supporting my long verbal-expressor one-way word-vomit explanations and complaints and revelations that surface when compiling a book about your experiences. Lots of stuff.

Let's get specific: Elsie Lang (for all the support), Scott Dangerfield (for all the late night phone calls and always believing in me), Ashley Carmichael (for all the love and laughs), Sam Kohlbry (for all our porch watching), Laura Lemieux (for all the real connection), all the friends from high school who still keep me in their lives today! Spencer Carlson (for always showing up), Nikki Reim (for teaching me how to use a box of stale crackers—always so resourceful!), Nico Poirel (for all the inspiration and passion for helping others), Desiree Jenkins (for showing me how to go for it, so gracefully), Yola Corbin and her generous, loving family (for sharing their French world), Gavin St. Clair (all our discussions on how to be better), Mikel Marzofka (for her depth of understanding everything all the time), Suzan Erem (for eradicating the petty like-bug in my speech), Josh Stotts (for providing me with an amazing job while I work this out), my mother Heather (who isn't here anymore but held my hand whenever she could), my father Steve (for all the wild material). Adam {fucking} Herman (for all the fun... and all the help with formatting), Laura Marland (for all her help in professionalism and writing etiquette).

My three beautiful passionate sisters, Khaiti, Liz, and Leah. My niece Mira for always being curious. Prof. Joe Lau who saw something in me and my writing at a young age and encouraged me all the time. All my past lovers for the patience, kindness, and support that filled me up. My coworkers and my roommates for holding me when I cry and listening to me when I chat and enjoying when I laugh.

Thank you to all the strangers who let me into their homes, gave me rides, fed me dinner, introduced me to their friends, shared community with me. You made this book possible. You and your free kindness.

Lest we forget, the people who surround me NOW! I am ever so grateful to be a part of a city that prioritizes music, nature, good food, and protecting our resources. Cheers to the beautiful Northern community of Duluth, Minnesota!

Made in the USA
Monee, IL
19 August 2022